P9-CDB-845

Social Psychology Research

Social Psychology Research: Laboratory-Field Relationships

edited by

Alvin M. Snadowsky

The Free Press, New York
Collier-Macmillan Limited, London

The Free Press
A Division of The Macmillan Company
866 Third Avenue, New York, New York 10022

Collier-Macmillan Canada Ltd., Toronto, Ontario

Library of Congress Catalog Card Number: 70-165101

1 2 3 4 5 6 7 8 9 10

Acknowledgments

I am most grateful to the authors who granted permissions for inclusion of their articles in this volume. Appreciation is expressed to James Cron, Director of The Free Press, for always being available with warm and understanding support. I am particularly grateful to Professors Barry McLaughlin of the University of California, Santa Cruz; Sidney Rosenberg, of York College, CUNY; and Bernard Seidenberg, of Brooklyn College, CUNY, for their many valuable suggestions. Special thanks to Mrs. Janet M. Burns, Miss Robin J. Ginsberg, and Miss Nancy E. Harper for their dedication to the task of preparing this book for publication.

A.S.

Contents

Introduction

During the past two decades social psychologists have shown a decided preference for controlled laboratory experiments while generally neglecting the natural environment as a setting in which to test their hypotheses (Deutsch & Krauss, 1965; McGuire, 1969; McGuire, Chapter 1). This research focus is a function of the efficiency of the laboratory where an investigator tests his hypotheses in contrived situations. On the other hand, circumstances beyond the researcher's control, such as the inability to identify all the forces operating in the situation, often make it difficult for him to test hypotheses rigorously in natural settings. However, as McGuire suggested, improved methodological and statistical techniques, computer simulation, the creation of data archives, and the greater availability of national samples should make basic theory-oriented field research more feasible and more desirable in the near future.

Researchers generally agree that experiments in both laboratory and natural settings are necessary for a balanced social psychology (e.g. Cartwright & Zander, 1968; Deutsch & Krauss, 1965; McGuire, 1969). Findings and hypotheses derived from studies using one method should serve to guide subsequent experiments using the other method. Thus, research in field environments is needed to determine the extent to which generalizations made from studies of artificial situations in the laboratory can be applied to natural settings. Similarly, the laboratory provides more controlled conditions for rigorously testing conclusions derived from research in natural environments. There are some investigators, however, who attempt to strengthen their research designs by combining laboratory methods and field settings in the same experiment. In one procedure, the researcher introduces changes under controlled conditions in a field setting where comparable groups are available or have been created. In another method, subjects move from the laboratory to the field and back to the laboratory in such a way that the effects of controlled variation on natural behavior can be measured effectively.

The articles included in this book reflect a twofold purpose: (1) to sample the use of laboratory and field settings in research strategies, viz., research in which controlled laboratory investigations guided subsequent field research or vice versa, and research in which laboratory methods and field settings were used in the same experiment; and (2) at the same time, to sample some of the salient areas in contemporary social psychology. The articles are presented to the reader for scrutiny and evaluation. Perhaps the strategies which these studies illustrate will stimulate further attacks upon some of the more challenging issues confronting the social psychologist seeking to integrate laboratory-based research and investigations in the natural environment.

REFERENCES

CARTWRIGHT, D., & ZANDER, A. (Eds.) *Group dynamics.* (3rd ed.) New York: Harper and Row, 1968.

DEUTSCH, M., & KRAUSS, R. *Theories in social psychology.* New York: Basic Books, 1965.

MC GUIRE, W. J. Theory-oriented research in natural settings: the best of both worlds for social psychology. In M. Sherif and C. Sherif (Eds.), *Interdisciplinary relationships in the social sciences.* Chicago: Aldine, 1969.

Social Psychology Research

I

Perspective

Social psychologists have expressed concern that basic and applied research have been moving progressively further apart, with an increasing emphasis on the former. McGuire (Chapter 1), however, forecasts a change in this trend. He sees a continuing emphasis on theory development and testing, but predicts an increasing shift from regarding the laboratory as the only *approved* setting in which to test theoretical deductions. The ingenuity now used in creating laboratory conditions will be replaced steadily by equal ingenuity in using the natural environment as a setting in which to test these deductions. Whether social psychology in consequence achieves this "best of both worlds" where theory-oriented research is conducted in natural settings, as McGuire optimistically anticipates, depends on the operation of various technical and social forces which should facilitate basic research in field settings and forces of a negative type that should make artificial laboratory research less attractive.

1

Some Impending Reorientations in Social Psychology

William J. McGuire

The creative tension between basic and applied research gives rise from time to time to feelings of uneasiness such as those recently expressed by Kenneth Ring (1967). Just as anxiety in the individual can have the beneficial function of signaling an imbalance among the contending aspects of his personality, so such expressions of concern about current emphases in our scientific establishment can be a useful warning sign that the dynamic equilibrium between basic and applied research has been disturbed by a temporary perturbation too far in one direction. Ring discerns a current stress in favor of basic, theory-oriented research. It seems undeniable to me that, as Ring contends, the basic and applied streams of research in psychology have been flowing progressively further apart during the past 10 or 15 years, and that the emphasis on basic research has been increasing. I would also agree (though I recognize this point to be more debatable than the foregoing) that these trends have proceeded to an extent that is unfortunate. Indeed, I am in agreement with most of the substance of Ring's paper and differ mainly in that I regard the undesirable trends which he points out as less of a worry than he does.

Where I would disagree with Ring is on his seeming expectation that the separation of the two streams of research and the overemphasis on basic research show signs of being continued and

Excerpted with slight adaptation from "Some impending reorientations in social psychology: some thoughts provoked by Kenneth Ring," *Journal of Experimental Social Psychology*, 1967, *3*, 124–139, with permission of William J. McGuire and the Academic Press.

even accentuated for the foreseeable future in social psychology. I would like to argue here that, on the contrary, we shall in social psychology soon be witnessing a remelding of basic and applied research with increasing attention to the latter. I shall argue that social psychology is moving towards a "best of both worlds" solution in which we shall be doing theory-oriented research in natural settings. The trend which I discern and describe here is, I believe, due to technical and social forces, without conscious intent or even knowledge on the part of the social psychology researchers.

Tension between basic and applied research is no recent development. From a short historical perspective, it might seem that the very notion of basic research has only recently emerged, made possible in an affluent society that can seek knowledge for its own sake as well as knowledge for use (we must recognize, however, that even knowledge for its own sake has a use, an aesthetic use). However, from a longer historical perspective we see that, far from basic research's being an epiphenomenon of applied work which emerged only when the affluence brought about by practical technological advances made such a middle-class luxury possible, there are signs that basic research may have even preceded the applied. Such appears to have been the situation in the Ionian world that was the birthplace of Western scientific civilization. Thales, the first of the Greek thinkers, or at least the first of them who talked, and the other early physicists seem to be strictly speculative theorists whose work promised little practical dividends. Apparently the tension between basic and applied work was felt even in those pre-Socratic days, since legend has it that Thales once responded to the derision of his fellow townsmen by using his astronomical knowledge to corner the olive market and make a small fortune during a bad-weather year, just to show them that his neglect of action-oriented work was by choice and not necessity. Thales was then evidently allowed to go about his basic research until that accursed night when, as the Thracian maidens recited laughingly, "He fell to his death down a well while gazing at the nighttime sky." Perhaps the father of basic research, like many of his followers since, far from taking offense at the maidens' derisive remarks, would settle for them happily as his epitaph.

The anecdote illustrates the two-front war with which even

today we social psychologists are confronted. If our work stays close to the basic, theory-oriented pole, we are liable to laymen's abuse for engaging in a Mandarin activity that is of interest only to our fellow social psychologists and consists in obscuring commonsense truths and fallacies behind professional jargon. If, on the other hand, we go too close to the applied, action-oriented pole, we are exposed to the abuse of the establishment who complain that we have been seeking narrow and possibly incorrect *ad hoc* solutions to specific problems, at a time when more basic, theoretically-oriented research is necessary to allow a broader advance in the near future. The crux of the controversy seems to be whether one should choose his next step in research in order to clarify a theoretical issue or to guide action in the natural environment. It is this formulation of the problem which leads me to the optimistic prediction that we are converging towards a solution that involves testing theoretically-derived hypotheses in natural settings. In such a solution the basic need of theory development would be served, in that problems for testing would be derived with the aim of developing and testing theory; while defining and testing the hypotheses in natural environments would clarify their relevance to the real world and provide directions for social action, either by forethought or at least by what is ludicrously termed "spin-off." Admittedly, this "compromise" admits the priority of theory-oriented research, and shows that my first loyalty lies with this side of the argument; however, it recognizes and provides a partial corrective for the current neglect of applied, action-oriented research in a social psychology in which only laboratory manipulational experimentation has been receiving the imprimatur of the establishment.

In brief, what I see coming for social psychology is a continuing emphasis on theory development and testing, but an increasing shift from regarding laboratory manipulational experiments on college sophomores as the only approved method of testing these theoretical deductions. Rather, I foresee that the ingenuity now exercised in creating laboratory surrogates for the real world will be steadily replaced by equal ingenuity exerted in utilizing the natural environment as a field in which to test these deductions. The solace that I see this prospect offering for those who are concerned with the social uses of science is that a theory tested in the real world is almost certain to prove relevant to the problems existing in the natural environment. Otherwise, the theory will wither away as untestable, or will be revealed as unrealizable under current conditions and hence will force its utilizers to decide whether it is sufficiently attractive to deserve continuing development even though it seems irrelevant to the currently available natural environment. What I will do here is review: first, some of the forces that I see making basic theory-oriented research possible and desirable in natural settings; and secondly, some forces of a more negative type that I see making research under artificial laboratory conditions less attractive to social psychologists in coming years.

ATTRACTIONS OF TESTING HYPOTHESES IN NATURAL ENVIRONMENTS

When I speak of hypothesis testing in natural environments, I have in mind several different types of studies. The least radical departure from the conventional laboratory experiment is carrying out manipulative experiments in natural settings as described some time ago by French (1953) and often carried out by Sherif (Sherif, M., Harvey, White, Hood, & Sherif, C., 1961; Sherif, M., & Sherif, C., 1964). But I include also more radical departures, such as observational work in natural settings where one does not have the possibility of manipulating the independent variable, and I look forward even to work with archival data. I shall review here some of the recent advances that make such an approach to hypothesis testing not only possible, but attractive, though limitations of space will allow me only to indicate in general what I have in mind. We can pass quite briefly over doing manipulatory experiments in natural settings, since this involves only a slight extrapolation beyond our present methodology and allows employment of traditional statistics such as analysis of variance. Even here, however, it is useful and encouraging to note that the availability of sophisticated computer programs is allowing us to employ these traditional analytic techniques even within the limitations of controls that are imposed by having to work in the real world. Thus we can now do analyses of variance relatively conveniently, even when confronted by those onerous problems of unequal *N*'s and contaminated variables that tend to arise in doing research in the "dirty" real world.

Current improvements are more obvious when we turn to more adventurous departures of hypothesis testing in natural environments, in which we can observe, but not manipulate, the independent variables. I have in mind here recent advances in research design and analysis that make possible the detection of causal direction in cases where the several factors in the situation are covarying due to factors beyond our control. Relevant here are such recent advances as the work by Campbell and Stanley (1963) on quasi-experimental designs, and work outside psychology such as cross-lag panel designs and other mathematical techniques proposed by Blalock (1961, 1965, 1966) and Coleman (1964).

Still another line of methodological progress that allows us to do theory-oriented research in natural environments is provided by advances in mathematical modeling and computer simulation, illustrated elegantly in the work by Abelson on the resolution of community controversy over fluoridating water supplies. This work on mathematical modeling and especially on computer simulation in the social psychological area is described in the new edition of the Lindzey and Aronson *Handbook of Social Psychology* (Abelson, 1968), and in Volume III of Berkowitz's *Advances in Experimental Social Psychology* (Abelson, 1967). It is interesting to note in the latter volume (as in the present *Journal*) that the magic word "experimental" is not defined narrowly to exclude hypothesis testing in natural settings, or even testing in natural settings without manipulation by the experimenter of the independent variables. It is a happy portent of the peaceful emergence of the new development that I am predicting here that "experimental" is taken in its etymologically correct meaning of "to test, to try"—rather than in the misuse of it sometimes found in the less perspicacious (or less classically-educated) followers of the establishment, who interpreted it as referring only to manipulational research or, still more erroneously, only to manipulative research in the laboratory.

Still another opening to the real world for social psychological research is allowed by the greater availability of nationwide samples. In the area of survey research this greater availability is provided by at least two recent developments. One is the creation of "caravan"-type nationwide surveys in which a number of researchers, each of whom needs only a few minutes of data, can combine to test their notions at a manageable cost. Some of the better nationwide sampling agencies now conduct such composite nationwide surveys. A second line of progress along these lines, whose full realization is still a few years in the future, is the establishment of a standardized inventory for a continuing nationwide sampling and resampling to collect longitudinal data on some issues of basic social science significance. These developments are all still underdeveloped and so far have been discussed largely in terms of opinion surveys. However, as they become more utilized I believe that the opportunities they offer, not just to ask questions but also to vary experimentally the independent variables presented to the respondents, will become increasingly recognized.

A final technological advance to which I shall call attention in this review of modern developments facilitating hypothesis testing in natural settings is the increasing availability of data archives relevant to the social sciences. An adequate review of this resource would require considerable space. I need mention here only the several forms that these archives take. There is the interuniversity consortion of public opinion survey results from the United States and from several other parts of the world. Testing one's hypothesis against these data which were collected at an earlier time admittedly requires more efficient and sophisticated procedures for retrieval and analysis of the information contained in these massive archives, but work even on this topic is proceeding at a number of institutions (e.g., Stone's work on using the General Inquirer to retrieve data from opinionnaires—Stone, Bales, Namenworth, & Ogilvie, 1962; Stone, Dunphy, Smith, & Ogilvie, 1966). Besides the archives dealing with survey opinion data, other archives (such as ones at Yale and MIT) are collecting background data on national and subnational units that will also inevitably be exploited by social psychology theorists. Consumer panel records and other business data are being put to theory-testing use by Howard (Howard & Sheth, 1969) and others. Some are culling the United States Government's records for archival data that might be of use to social scientists. Except possibly in the latter development, and in some work on compiling county-by-county voting statistics since the beginning of the United States Government, one crying lack in these data archives is the neglect of a long-range historical perspective. Possibly this gap will also be filled in coming years, though providing satisfactory data of this type would require a cooperation by historians which they do not yet seem motivated to make. However, just as the psychologists, sociologists, and political scientists became progressively oriented towards massive data analysis for theory testing, so too, I believe, will the historian recognize as part of his discipline a speciality that tests historical theorizing against massive data as well as by incisive analysis of single cases. Meanwhile, we can make do, as McClelland (1961) has shown, by being our own Sunday historians. The adequate exploitation of these very expensively compiled archives requires that we make knowledge of their existence more widespread and that we develop techniques of analysis more sophisticated than are now available.

Besides these technological factors, which will make hypothesis testing in natural environments more feasible, there are some additional, metapsychological trends which are also making research in the real world somewhat more attractive to sensitive social psychologists. I have in mind here the increasing commitment among the intelligentsia in the United States, which is exhibited in the increased concern about social affairs visible in the current generation of students in contrast to the silent generation of the 1950's. The concern is seen even in their elders who are already part of the academic establishment, as Ring points out. It is not difficult to find a number of reasons for this trend. Certainly the development of nuclear weapons and the nuclear testing issue, and the terrifying war threat that they involve, played a part, as did the unignorable issues of equal rights, the Vietnamese war, etc. The role played by academic circles in our national administration became more visible if not actually greater during the Kennedy Administration than it had previously been. These trends in the United States have simply followed earlier movements in France and elsewhere in Europe, where during the Occupation the intelligentsia achieved an increasing degree of commitment and concern regarding social affairs which has been maintained during the postwar period.

Along this same line is the pressure of self interest in obtaining research funds from the government. Just as, in the words of Francis Bacon, he who has wife and child has given hostages to fortune, so we social psychologists, who like other scientists, have grown accustomed to accepting and depending upon generous research funds from the government, now find ourselves having given hostages to the federal agencies that dole out these resources. Perhaps only a few of us would have the stamina and the ingenuity to continue our research efforts by other means, when pressures are put on us by these agencies to direct our current efforts more towards applied, action-oriented research. It takes no direct access to the inner circle of government to perceive increasing political interest in how and why research funds are being spent. As long as these funds were doled out largely on the advice of the scientific establishment itself, basic research fared very well. Now that the leadership in the Executive and Legislative branches of Government has taken a direct interest in the appropriation of these sizable research funds, there is more interest in the payoff to those outside the separate sciences themselves. While I do not despair of our being able to justify expenditures for basic research even on grounds of public interest, I do suggest as a compromise solution that we continue to do basic, theory-oriented research, as far as hypothesis derivation is concerned, but that we think somewhat more of testing these hypotheses in natural settings rather than in laboratory situations.

A final attraction of doing research in natural settings, with its greater likelihood of applied fallout, is that such applied work offers the possibility of avoiding some of the mass frustrations of scientists. What I have in mind here is my suspicion that as far as basic research is concerned, good work is not enough. It simply clutters our journals and makes it harder to find the only thing that really counts in basic research, which is work of the first order of excellence. Unfortunately, even in social psychology most of the researchers are good rather than truly excellent. The result is that their work does little to advance basic theorizing, thus condemning them to a frustrated or self-deluding existence. It is my intuition that the practical, applied fallout of research in natural settings will have its social uses even if it is only good. This possibility for service gives a greater opportunity for those who cannot attain excellence to yet find satisfaction in social psychological research.

SOME GROWING PROBLEMS REGARDING LABORATORY RESEARCH

Above I have considered the more positive reasons for my prediction that the future would see more social psychological research being carried out in natural settings rather than in the laboratory even when this meant that nature, rather than the experimenter, would manipulate the independent variable. Now, I turn to the other side of the coin and consider the negative reasons for this prediction, reasons which have to do with some growing problems concerning the laboratory manipulational experimentation that constitutes the bulk of current good social psychological research. Probably the most important of the difficulties is the growing realization among laboratory experimenters that our work is troubled by artifacts that make generalization and theoretical interpretation difficult. I merely have to mention such terms as "experimenter effects (Rosenthal, 1966)," "demand character (Orne, 1962)," "evaluation apprehension (Rosenberg, 1965)," etc., to indicate to the reader what I have in mind here. A book by Robert Rosenthal and Ralph Rosnow (1969) is devoted entirely to artifacts in the social psychological laboratory. Usually correlated with laboratory experimentation is the problem of subject representativeness. We have almost grown used to the embarrassment occasioned by the concentration of our research on college students. The proverbial "psychology of the college sophomore" is more worrisome as to generalizability for the social psychologist than for those working in perception, learning, etc.

Secondly, I must also mention, uncomfortable as it is, the ethical concerns that have been increasingly expressed regarding laboratory experimentation in social psychology (Kelman, 1965, 1967). Most serious in my opinion is the use of noxious conditions in our experimental manipulations, including painful or dangerous physiological treatments or anxiety-producing and potentially harmful psychological manipulations. Other complaints, not without some justification, involve our lying to our subjects and the inevitable degrading interpersonal relations that develop in our deception experimentation. Still other criticism is aimed at the invasion of the subject's privacy in our research. The latter problem will by no means be solved and may even be aggravated by our doing our research in natural settings. However, the first two problems can be largely circumvented when the social psychology theorist develops the will and the skill to test his hypotheses in a real world that he never made, and takes experimental advantage of natural manipulations that he can neither produce nor control. It is also possible that the more obvious social relevance allowed by doing work in natural settings will offer more justification for the invasion of privacy that will inevitably occur in the field as well as in the laboratory. Many of us feel that the ethical problems here do not involve absolute answers. By this I mean that we must evaluate the possible benefits as well as the cost of the experimentation. I do not rule out absolutely the possibility that there are times at which our work might be significant enough that we should be allowed to continue it even though some limited harm could possibly result. It is too easy to condemn current laboratory manipulational researchers, as has been done at a recent meeting which I attended, where someone complained that the very expression "we have run some subjects today" reveals an almost Eichmann-like abstraction about one's research and a failure to appreciate that the participants in one's experiment are real people. In response to this position, I feel we must also be concerned about an equally questionable ethical position epitomized by the words, "I have *not* run any subjects today." It seems to me all too simple to decide that it is safer to do no research. We must strictly censor our own work and find ways of maximizing gains and minimizing costs to some point at which we can ethically go ahead, perhaps inevitably with fear and trembling. But go on with our work we must, or else we must change our field. It seems to me that doing theoretically-inspired work in natural settings furnishes some possibility that we can proceed ahead with somewhat less anguish than the more sensitive people in our field are now experiencing regarding our laboratory work.

At the risk of seeming somewhat facetious, I would suggest still a third reason for predicting a shift from the laboratory to the natural environment as the setting for social psychological research in the coming years. Laboratory work has become the "OK" approach in the psychological establishment and new people in the area are flocking to it, as Ring has himself pointed out with some concern regarding its consequents. I would venture the opinion that this concentration of work has reached the point of diminishing returns, and that inevitably the more adventurous people in the field are beginning to deviate into other approaches such as doing research in natural settings. Once these adventurous innovators (who are actually repelled by manipulatory lab work just because it has the establishment's acceptance as the current paradigm) try out the natural environment for their research, I feel that the favorable forces mentioned above will yield them considerably more success than was offered by previous deviations into the natural environment as recently as 10 years ago. As the watchful waiters view the innovators' success from the acceptable premises of the laboratory, the premature elder statesmen and perspicacious Young Turks who are entrenched in the establishment will follow them into the natural environment and these stars will soon be followed by a partial redeployment into this new setting.

Let me stress, though, that the redeployment into the natural environment will be partial. It seems to me that the manipulational laboratory experiment is just too efficient to ever be dropped completely in social psychological research. Indeed, I think the bulk of our research will remain in the laboratory, though I may be prejudiced here by the fact that my own research has in the past involved the laboratory manipulational approach exclusively and I shall probably continue to stress this approach. Still, I am not so wedded to a methodology inspired by physics that I have become too biased to appreciate the methodology suggested by astronomy.

REFERENCES

ABELSON, R. P. Mathematical models in social psychology. In L. Berkowitz (Ed.), *Advances in experimental social psychology.* Vol. 3. New York: Academic Press, 1967.

ABELSON, R. P. Simulation of social behavior. In G. Lindzey and E. Aronson (Eds.), *Handbook of social psychology.* (Rev. ed.) Reading, Mass.: Addison-Wesley, 1968.

BLALOCK, H. M. Evaluating the relative importance of variables, *American Sociological Review,* 1961, *26,* 866-874.

BLALOCK, H. M. Theory building and the statistical concept of interaction. *American Sociological Review,* 1965, *30,* 374-380.

BLALOCK, H. M. The identification problem and theory building: the case of status inconsistency. *American Sociological Review,* 1966, *31,* 52-61.

CAMPBELL, D. T. & STANLEY, J. C. Experimental and quasi-experimental designs for research on teaching. In N. L. Gage (Ed.), *Handbook of research on teaching.* Chicago: Rand McNally, 1963.

COLEMAN, J. *An introduction to mathematical sociology.* New York: Macmillan, 1964.

FRENCH, J. R. P. Experiments in field settings. In L. Festinger and D. Katz (Eds.), *Research methods in the behavioral sciences.* New York: Dryden, 1953.

HOWARD, J. A., & SHETH, J. N. *Theory of buyer behavior.* New York: Wiley, 1969.

KELMAN, H. C. Manipulation of human behavior: an ethical dilemma for the social scientist. *Journal of Social Issues,* 1965, *21,* 31-46.

KELMAN, H. C. Human use of human subjects: the problem of deception in social psychological experiments. *Psychological Bulletin,* 1967, *67,* 1-11.

MC CLELLAND, D. C. *The achieving society.* Princeton, N.J.: Van Nostrand, 1961.

ORNE, M. T. On the social psychology of the psychological experiment: with particular reference to demand characteristics and their implications. *American Psychologist,* 1962, *17,* 776-783.

RING, K. Experimental social psychology: some sober questions about some frivolous values. *Journal of Experimental Social Psychology,* 1967, *3,* 113-123.

ROSENBERG, M. J. When dissonance fails: on eliminating evaluation apprehension from attitude measurement. *Journal of Personality and Social Psychology,* 1965, *1,* 28-42.

ROSENTHAL, R. *Experimenter effects in behavioral research.* New York: Appleton-Century-Crofts, 1966.

ROSENTHAL, R., & ROSNOW, R. *Artifacts in behavior research.* New York: Academic Press, 1969.

SHERIF, M., HARVEY, O. J., WHITE, B. J., HOOD, W. R., & SHERIF, C. W. *Intergroup conflict and cooperation: the Robbers Cave experiment.* Norman: University of Oklahoma Institute of Intergroup Relations, 1961.

SHERIF, M., & SHERIF, C. W. *Reference groups.* New York: Harper, 1964.

STONE, P. J., BALES, R. F., NAMENWORTH, Z., & OGILVIE, D. M. The general inquirer: a computer system for content analysis and retrieval based on sentence as a unit of information. *Behavioral Science,* 1962, *7,* 484-494.

STONE, P. J., DUNPHY, D. C., SMITH, M. S., & OGILVIE, D. M. *The general inquirer: a computer approach to content analysis.* Cambridge: MIT Press, 1966.

II

Motivational And Cognitive Processes

Findings from a series of laboratory studies conducted by Schachter and his colleagues (Chapter 2) suggested that there is not always a direct relationship between the physiological state of "hunger" and eating behavior. Their data showed that the types of stimuli which motivate the individual of normal weight to eat are different from those which motivate the obese person to eat. Subsequent research in a variety of field settings, somewhat free from many of the artifacts found in laboratory experiments, persistently confirmed previous findings that the obese are relatively insensitive to physiological correlates of food deprivation but highly sensitive to environmental, food-associated cues unrelated to nutritional need satisfaction.

2

Obesity and Eating

Stanley Schachter

Current conceptions of hunger control mechanisms indicate that food deprivation leads to various peripheral physiological changes such as modification of blood constituents, increase in gastric motility, changes in body temperature, and the like. By means of some still debated mechanism, these changes are detected by a hypothalamic feeding center. Presumably some or all facets of this activated machinery lead the organism to search out and consume food. There appears to be no doubt that peripheral physiological changes and activation of the hypothalamic feeding center are inevitable consequences of food deprivation. On the basis of current knowledge, however, one may ask, when this biological machinery is activated, do we necessarily describe ourselves as hungry, and eat? For most of us raised on the notion that hunger is the most primitive of motives, wired into the animal and unmistakable in its cues, the question may seem far-fetched, but there is increasing reason to suspect that there are major individual differences in the extent to which these physiological changes are associated with the desire to eat.

On the clinical level, the analyst Hilde Bruch *(1)* has observed that her obese patients literally do not know when they are physiologically hungry. To account for this observation she suggests that, during childhood, these patients were not taught to discriminate between hunger and such states as fear, anger, and anxiety. If this is so, these people may be labeling almost any state of arousal "hunger," or, alternatively, labeling no internal state "hunger."

From *Science,* 1968, *161,* 751–756. [References originally listed as in press were amended to show dates of publication. Ed.]

If Bruch's speculations are correct, it should be anticipated that the set of physiological symptoms which are considered characteristic of food deprivation are not labeled "hunger" by the obese. In other words the obese literally may not know when they are physiologically hungry. For at least one of the presumed physiological correlates of food deprivation, this does appear to be the case. In an absorbing study, Stunkard *(2, 3)* has related gastric motility to self-reports of hunger in 37 obese subjects and 37 subjects of normal size. A subject, who had eaten no breakfast, came to the laboratory at 9 a.m.; he swallowed a gastric balloon, and for 4 hours Stunkard continuously recorded gastric motility. Every 15 minutes the subject was asked if he was hungry. He answered "yes" or "no," and that is all there was to the study. We have, then, a record of the extent to which a subject's self-report of hunger corresponds to his gastric motility. The results show (i) that obese and normal subjects do not differ significantly in degree of gastric motility, and (ii) that, when the stomach is not contracting, the reports of obese and normal subjects are quite similar, both groups reporting hunger roughly 38 percent of the time. When the stomach is contracting, however, the reports of the two groups differ markedly. For normal subjects, self-report of hunger coincides with gastric motility 71 percent of the time. For the obese, the percentage is only 47.6. Stunkard's work seems to indicate that obese and normal subjects do not refer to the same bodily state when they use the term *hunger*.

EFFECTS OF FOOD DEPRIVATION AND FEAR

If this inference is correct, we should anticipate that, if we were to directly manipulate gastric motility and the other symptoms that we associate with hunger, we would, for normal subjects, be directly manipulating feelings of hunger and eating behavior. For the obese there would be no correspondence between manipulated internal state and eating behavior. To test these expectations, Goldman, Gordon, and I *(4)* performed an experiment in which bodily state was manipulated by two means—(i) by the obvious technique of manipulating food deprivation, so that some subjects had empty stomachs and others had full stomachs before eating; (ii) by manipulating fear, so that some subjects were badly frightened and others were quite calm immediately before eating. Carlson *(5)* has indicated that fear inhibits gastric motility; Cannon *(6)* also has demonstrated that fear inhibits motility, and has shown that it leads to the liberation, from the liver, of sugar into the blood. Hypoglycemia and gastric contractions are generally considered the chief peripheral physiological correlates of food deprivation.

Our experiment was conducted under the guise of a study of taste. A subject came to the laboratory in mid-afternoon or evening. He had been called the previous evening and asked not to eat the meal (lunch or dinner) preceding his appointment at the laboratory. The experiment was introduced as a study of "the interdependence of the basic human senses—of the way in which the stimulation of one sense affects another." Specifically, the subject was told that this study would be concerned with "the effects of tactile stimulation on the way things taste."

It was explained that all subjects had been asked not to eat a meal before coming to the laboratory because "in any scientific experiment it is necessary that the subjects be as similar as possible in all relevant ways. As you probably know from your own experience," the experimenter continued, "an important factor in determining how things taste is what you have recently eaten." The introduction over, the experimenter then proceeded as follows.

For the "full stomach" condition he said to the subject, "In order to guarantee that your recent taste experiences are similar to those of other subjects who have taken part in this experiment, we should now like you to eat exactly the same thing they did. Just help yourself to the roast beef sandwiches on the table. Eat as much as you want—till you're full."

For the "empty stomach" condition, the subjects, of course, were not fed.

Next, the subject was seated in front of five bowls of crackers and told, "We want you to taste five different kinds of crackers and tell us how they taste to you." The experimenter then gave the subject a long set of rating scales and said, "We want you to judge each cracker on the dimensions (salty, cheesy, garlicky, and so on) listed on this sheet. Taste as many or as few of the crackers of each type as you want in making your judgments; the important thing is that your ratings be as accurate as possible."

Before permitting the subject to eat, the experimenter continued with the next stage of the experiment—the manipulation of fear.

"As I mentioned," he said, "our primary interest in this experiment is the effect of tactile stimulation on taste. Electric stimulation is the means we use to excite your skin receptors. We use this method in order to carefully control the amount of stimulation you receive."

For the "low fear" condition the subject was told, "For the effects in which we are interested, we need to use only the lowest level of stimulation. At most you will feel a slight tingle. Probably you will feel nothing at all. We are only interested in the effect of very weak stimulation."

For the "high fear" condition the experimenter pointed to a large black console loaded with electrical junk and said, "That machine is the one we will be using. I am afraid that these shocks will be painful. For them to have any effect on your taste sensations, the voltage must be rather high. There will, of course, be no permanent damage. Do you have a heart condition?" A large electrode connected to the console was then attached to each of the subject's ankles, and the experimenter concluded, "The best way for us to test the effect of tactile stimulation is to have you rate the crackers now, before the electric shock, and then rate them again, after the shock, to see what changes in your ratings the shock has made."

The subject then proceeded to taste and rate crackers for 15 minutes, under the impression that this was a taste test; meanwhile we were simply counting the number of crackers he ate *(7)*. We then had measures of the amounts eaten by subjects who initially had either empty or full stomachs and who were initially either frightened or calm. There were of course, two types of subjects: obese subjects (from 14 percent to 75 percent overweight) and normal subjects (from 8 percent underweight to 9 percent overweight).

To review expectations: If we were correct in thinking that

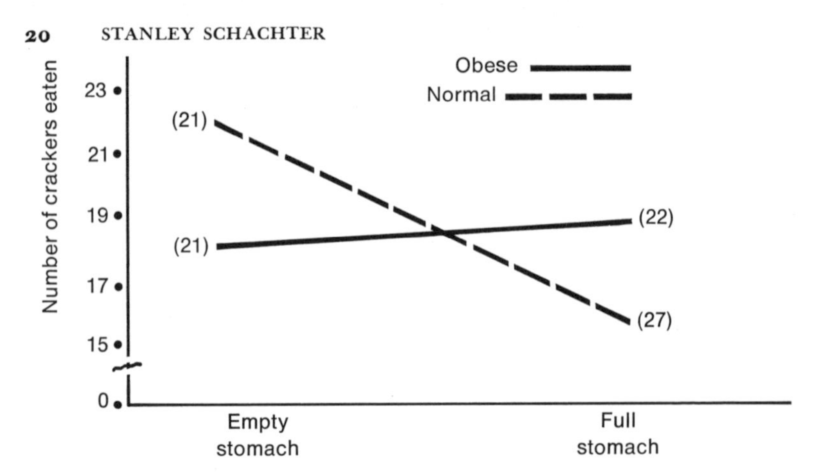

FIG. 2.1. Effects of preliminary eating on the amounts eaten during the experiment by normal and obese subjects. Numbers in parentheses are numbers of subjects.

the obese do not label as hunger the bodily states associated with food deprivation, then our several experimental manipulations should have had no effects on the amount eaten by obese subjects: on the other hand, the eating behavior of normal subjects should have directly paralleled the effects of the manipulations on bodily state.

It will be a surprise to no one to learn, from Fig. 2.1, that the normal subjects ate considerably fewer crackers when their stomachs were full than when their stomachs were empty. The results for obese subjects stand in fascinating contrast. They ate as much —in fact, slightly more—when their stomachs were full as when they were empty (interaction $P < .05$). Obviously the actual state of the stomach has nothing to do with the eating behavior of the obese.

In Fig. 2.2, pertaining to the effect of fear, we note an analogous picture. Fear markedly decreased the number of crackers the normal subjects ate but had no effect on the number eaten by the obese (interaction $P < .01$). Again, there was a small, though nonsignificant, reversal: the fearful obese ate slightly more than the calm obese.

It seems clear that the set of bodily symptoms the subject labels "hunger" differs for obese and normal subjects. Whether one measures gastric motility, as Stunkard did, or manipulates it, as I assume my co-workers and I have done, one finds, for normal subjects, a high degree of correspondence between the state of the gut and eating behavior and, for obese subjects, virtually no correspondence. While all of our manipulations have had a major effect on the amounts eaten by normal subjects, nothing that we have done has had a substantial effect on the amounts eaten by obese subjects.

EFFECTS OF THE CIRCUMSTANCES OF EATING

With these facts in mind, let us turn to the work of Hashim and Van Itallie *(8)* of the Nutrition Clinic, St. Luke's Hospital, New York City. Their findings may be summarized as follows: virtually everything these workers do seems to have a major effect on the eating behavior of the obese and almost no effect on the eating behavior of the normal subject.

These researchers have prepared a bland liquid diet similar to commercial preparations such as vanilla-flavored Nutrament or Metrecal. The subjects are restricted to this monotonous diet for periods ranging from a week to several months. They can eat as much or as little of it as they want. Some of the subjects get a pitcher full and pour themselves a meal any time they wish. Other subjects are fed by a machine which delivers a mouthful every

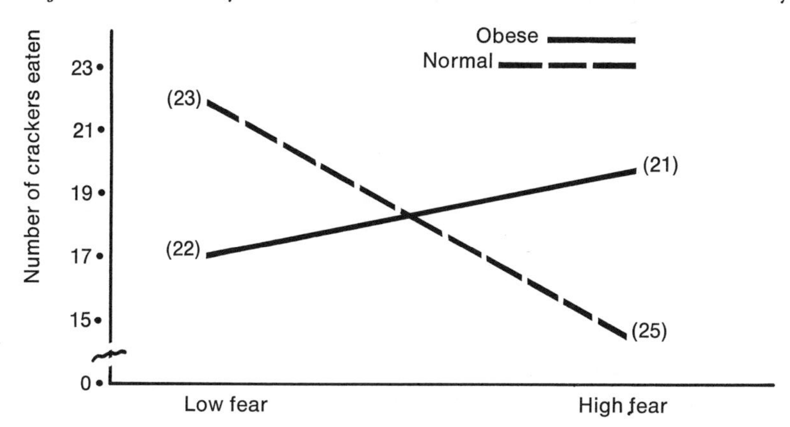

FIG. 2.2. Effects of fear on the amounts eaten by normal and obese subjects. Numbers in parentheses are numbers of subjects.

time the subject presses a button. With either feeding technique, the eating situation has the following characteristics. (i) The food itself is unappealing. (ii) Eating is entirely self-determined: whether or not the subject eats, how much he eats, and when he eats are matters decided by him and no one else. Absolutely no pressure is brought to bear to limit his consumption. (iii) The eating situation is devoid of any social or domestic trappings. It is basic eating; it will keep the subject alive, but it's not much fun.

To date, six grossly obese and five normal individuals have been subjects in these studies. In Fig. 2.3 the eating curves for a typical pair of subjects over a 21-day period are plotted. Both subjects were healthy people who lived in the hospital during the entire study. The obese subject was a 52-year-old woman, 5 feet 3 inches (1.6 meters) tall, who weighed 307 pounds (138 kilograms)

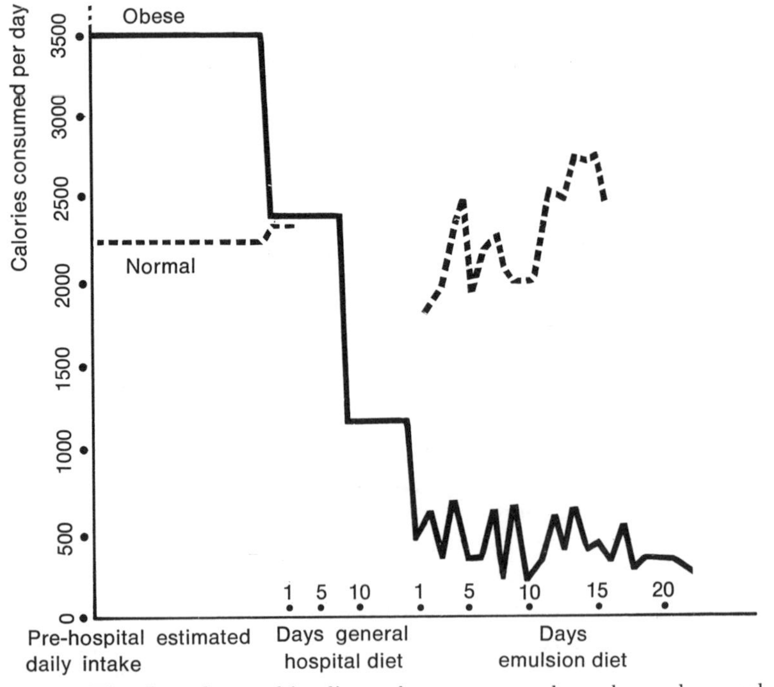

FIG. 2.3. The effects of an emulsion diet on the amounts eaten by an obese and a normal subject.

on admission. The normal subject was a 30-year-old male, 5 feet 7 inches tall, who weighed 132 pounds.

The subject's estimated daily caloric intake before entering the hospital (as determined from a detailed interview) is plotted at the left in Fig. 2.3. Each subject, while in the hospital but before entering upon the experimental regime, was fed a general hospital diet. The obese subject was placed on a 2400-calorie diet for 7 days and a 1200-calorie diet for the next 8 days. As may be seen in Fig. 2.3, she ate everything on her tray throughout this 15-day period. The normal subject was placed on a 2400-calorie diet for 2 days, and he too ate everything.

With the beginning of the experiment proper, the difference in the eating behavior of the two subjects was dramatic and startling. The food consumption of the obese subject dropped precipitately the moment she entered upon the experimental regime, and it remained at an incredibly low level for the duration of the experiment. This effect is so dramatic that the weight of one obese subject who took part in the experiment for 8 months dropped from 410 to 190 pounds. On the other hand, the food consumption of the normal subject of Fig. 2.3 dropped slightly on the first 2 days, then returned to a fairly steady 2300 grams or so of food a day. The curves for these two subjects are typical. Each of the six obese subjects has manifested this marked and persistent decrease in food consumption during the experiment; each of the normal subjects has steadily consumed about his normal amount of food.

Before suggesting possible interpretations, I should note certain marked differences between these two groups of subjects. Most important, the obese subjects had come to the clinic for help in solving their weight problem and were, of course, motivated to lose weight. The normal subjects were simply volunteers. Doubtless this difference could account for the observed difference in eating behavior during the experiment, and until obese volunteers, unconcerned with their weight, are used as subjects in similar studies, we cannot be sure of the interpretation of this phenomenon. However, I think we should not, solely on grounds of methodological fastidiousness, dismiss these findings. It was concern with weight that brought these obese subjects to the clinic. Each of them, before entering the hospital and while in the hospital before being put on the experimental diet, was motivated to lose weight. Yet, despite this motivation, none of these subjects had been capable of restricting his diet at home, and each of them, when fed the general hospital diet, had eaten everything on his tray. Only when the food was dull and the act of eating was self-initiated and devoid of any ritual trappings did the obese subject, motivated or not, severely limit his consumption.

INTERNAL AND EXTERNAL CONTROL

On the one hand, then, our experiments indicate virtually no relationship between internal physiological state and the eating behavior of the obese subject; on the other hand, these case studies seem to indicate a close tie between the eating behavior of the obese and what might be called the circumstances of eating. When the food is dull and the eating situation is uninteresting, the obese subject eats virtually nothing. For the normal subject, the situation is just the reverse: his eating behavior seems directly linked to his physiological state but is relatively unaffected by the external circumstances or the ritual associated with eating.

Given this set of facts it seems clear that eating is triggered by different sets of stimuli in obese and normal subjects. Indeed, there is growing reason to suspect that the eating behavior of the obese is relatively unrelated to any internal state but is, in large part, under external control, being initiated and terminated by stimuli external to the organism. Let me give a few examples. A person whose eating behavior is under external control will stroll by a pastry shop, find the food in the window irresistible, and, even if he has recently eaten, go in and buy something. He will pass by a hamburger stand, smell the broiling meat, and, even though he has just eaten, buy a hamburger. Obviously such external factors—smell, sight, taste, other people's actions—to some extent affect anyone's eating. However, in normal individuals such external factors interact with internal state. They may affect what, where, and how much the normal individual eats, but they do so chiefly when he is in a state of physiological hunger. For the obese, I suggest, internal state is irrelevant and eating is determined largely by external factors.

This hypothesis obviously fits the data presented here, as well it should, since it is an *ad hoc* construction designed specifically to fit these data. Let us see, then, what independent support there is for the hypothesis, and where the hypothesis leads.

EFFECTS OF MANIPULATING TIME

Among the multitude of external food-relevant cues, one of the most intriguing is the passage of time. Everyone "knows" that 4 to 6 hours after eating his last meal he should eat his next one. Everyone "knows" that, within narrow limits, there are set times for eating regular meals. We should, then, expect that if we manipulate time we should be able to manipulate the eating behavior of the obese subjects. In order to do this, Gross and I *(9)* simply gimmicked two clocks so that one ran at half normal speed and the other, at twice normal speed. A subject arrives at 5:00 p.m., ostensibly to take part in an experiment on the relationship of base levels of autonomic reactivity to personality factors. He is ushered into a windowless room containing nothing but electronic equipment and a clock. Electrodes are put on his wrists, his watch is removed "so that it will not get gummed up with electrode jelly," and he is connected to a polygraph. All this takes 5 minutes, and at 5:05 he is left alone, with nothing to do for a true 30 minutes, while ostensibly we are getting a record of galvanic skin response and cardiac rate in a subject at rest. There are two experimental conditions. In one, the experimenter returns after a true 30 minutes and the clock reads 5:20. In the other, the clock reads 6:05, which is normal dinner time for most subjects. In both cases the experimenter is carrying a box of crackers and nibbling a cracker as he comes into the room; he puts the box down, invites the subject to help himself, removes the electrodes from the subject's wrists, and proceeds with personality testing for exactly 5 minutes. This done, he gives the subject a personality inventory which he is to complete and leaves him alone with the box of crackers for another true 10 minutes. There are two groups of subjects—normal and obese—and the only datum we collect is the weight of the box of crackers before and after the subject has had a chance at it.

If these ideas on internal and external controls of eating behavior are correct, normal subjects, whose eating behavior is presumably linked to internal state, should be relatively unaffected by the manipulation and should eat roughly the same number of crackers regardless of whether the clock reads 5:20 or 6:05. The obese, on the other hand, whose eating behavior is presumably under external control, should eat very few crackers when the clock reads 5:20 and a great many crackers when it reads 6:05.

The data of Fig. 2.4 do indeed indicate that the obese subjects eat almost twice as many crackers when they think the time is 6:05 as they do when they believe it to be 5:20. For normal subjects, the trend is just the reverse (interaction $P = .002$)—an unanticipated finding but one which seems embarrassingly simple to explain, as witness the several normal subjects who thought the time was 6:05 and politely refused the crackers, saying, "No thanks, I don't want to spoil my dinner." Obviously cognitive factors affected the eating behavior of both the normal and the obese subjects, but there was a vast difference. While the manipulation of the clock served to trigger or stimulate eating among the obese, it had the opposite effect on normal subjects, most of whom at this hour were, we presume, physiologically hungry, aware that they would eat dinner very shortly, and unwilling to spoil their dinner by filling up on crackers.

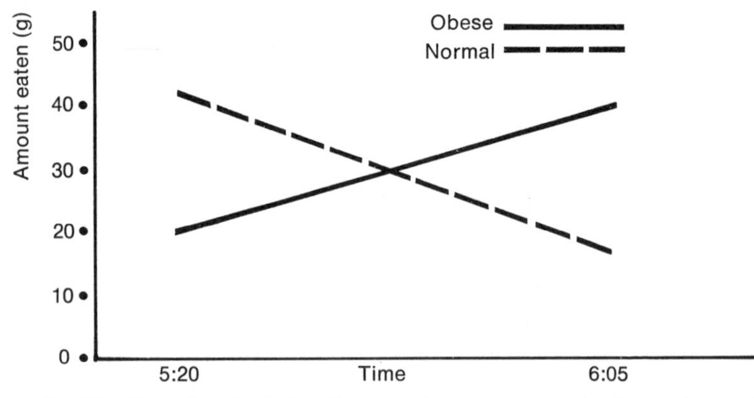

FIG. 2.4. The effects of manipulation of time on the amounts eaten by obese and normal subjects.

EFFECTS OF TASTE

In another study, Nisbett *(10)* examined the effects of taste on eating behavior. Nisbett reasoned that taste, like the sight or smell of food, is essentially an external stimulus to eating. Nisbett, in his experiment, also extended the range of weight deviation by including a group of underweight subjects as well as obese and normal subjects. His purpose in so doing was to examine the hypothesis that the relative potency of external versus internal controls is a dimension directly related to the degree of overweight. If the hypothesis was correct, he reasoned, the taste of food would have the greatest impact on the amounts eaten by obese subjects and the least impact on the amounts eaten by underweight subjects. To test this, Nisbett had his subjects eat as much as they wanted of one of two kinds of vanilla ice cream; one was a delicious and expensive product, the other an acrid concoction of cheap vanilla and quinine which he called "vanilla bitters." The effects of taste are presented in Fig. 2.5, in which the subjects' ratings of how good or bad the ice cream is are plotted against the amount eaten. As may be seen in Fig. 2.5, when the ice cream was rated "fairly good" or better, the obese subjects ate considerably more than the normal subjects did; these, in turn, ate more than the underweight subjects did. When the ice cream was rated "not very good" or worse, the ordering tended to reverse: the underweight subjects ate more than either the normal or the obese subjects. This experiment, then, indicates that the external, or at least nonvisceral, cue *taste* does have differential effects on the eating behavior of underweight, normal, and obese subjects.

The indications, from Nisbett's experiment, that the degree of dependence on external cues relative to internal cues varies with deviation from normal weight are intriguing, for, if further work supports this hypothesis, we may have the beginnings of a plausible explanation of why the thin are thin and the fat are fat. We know from Carlson's work *(5)* that gastric contractions cease after a small amount of food has been introduced into the stomach. To the extent that such contractions are directly related to the hunger "experience"—to the extent that a person's eating is under internal control—he should "eat like a bird," eating only enough to stop the contractions. Eating beyond this point should be a function of external cues—the taste, sight, and smell of food. Individuals whose eating is externally controlled, then, should find it hard to stop eating. This hypothesis may account for the notorious "binge" eating of the obese *(11)* or the monumental meals described in loving detail by students *(12)* of the great, fat gastronomic magnificoes.

This rough attempt to explain why the obese are obese in itself raises intriguing questions. For example, does the external control of eating behavior inevitably lead to obesity? It is evident, I believe, that not only is such a linkage logically not inevitable but that the condition of external control of eating may in rare but specifiable circumstances lead to emaciation. A person whose eating is externally controlled should eat and grow fat when food-related cues are abundant and when he is fully aware of them. However, when such cues are lacking or when for some reason, such as withdrawal or depression, the individual is unaware of the cues, the person under external control would, one would expect,

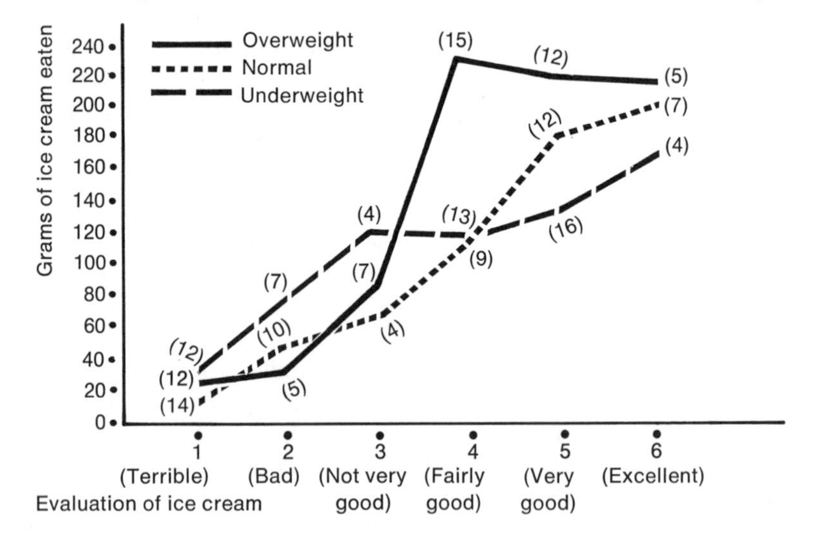

FIG. 2.5. The effects of food quality on the amounts eaten by obese, normal, and underweight subjects. Numbers in parentheses are numbers of subjects.

not eat, and, if the condition persisted, would grow "concentration-camp" thin. From study of the clinical literature one does get the impression that there is an odd but distinct relationship between obesity and extreme emaciation. For example, 11 of 21 subjects of case studies discussed by Bliss and Branch in *Anorexia Nervosa (13)* were, at some time in their lives, obese. In the case of eight of these 11 subjects, anorexia was preceded and accompanied by either marked withdrawal or intense depression. In contrast, intense attacks of anxiety or nervousness [states which our experiment *(4)* suggests would inhibit eating in normal individuals] seem to be associated with the development of anorexia among most of the ten subjects who were originally of normal size.

At this point, these speculations are simply idea-spinning—fun, but ephemeral. Let us return to the results of the studies described so far. These can be quickly summarized as follows.

1) Physiological correlates of food deprivation, such as gastric motility, are directly related to eating behavior and to the reported experience of hunger in normal subjects but unrelated in obese subjects (*3, 4*).

2) External or nonvisceral cues, such as smell, taste, the sight of other people eating, and the passage of time, affect eating behavior to a greater extent in obese subjects than in normal subjects *(8–10)*.

OBESITY AND FASTING

Given these basic facts, their implications have ramifications in almost any area pertaining to food and eating, and some of our studies have been concerned with the implications of these experimental results for eating behavior in a variety of nonlaboratory settings. Thus, Goldman, Jaffa, and I *(14)* have studied fasting on Yom Kippur, the Jewish Day of Atonement, on which the orthodox Jew is supposed to go without food for 24 hours. Reasoning that, on this occasion, food-relevant external cues are particularly scarce, one would expect obese Jews to be more likely to fast than normal Jews. In a study of 296 religious Jewish college students (defined as Jewish college students who had been to a synagogue at least once during the preceding year on occasions other than a wedding or a bar mitzvah), this proves to be the case, for 83.3 percent of obese Jews fasted, as compared with 68.8 percent of normal Jews ($P < .05$).

Further, this external-internal control schema leads to the prediction that fat, fasting Jews who spend a great deal of time in the synagogue on Yom Kippur will suffer less from fasting than fat, fasting Jews who spend little time in the synagogue. There should be no such relationship for normal fasting Jews. Obviously, there will be far fewer food-related cues in the synagogue than on the street or at home. Therefore, for obese Jews, the likelihood that the impulse to eat will be triggered is greater outside of the synagogue than within it. For normal Jews, this distinction is of less importance. In or out of the synagogue, stomach pangs are stomach pangs. Again, the data support the expectation. When the number of hours in the synagogue is correlated with self-ratings of the unpleasantness of fasting, for obese subjects the correlation is $-.50$, whereas for normal subjects the correlation is only $-.18$. In a test of the difference between correlations, $P = .03$. Obviously, for the obese, the more time the individual spends in the synagogue, the less of an ordeal fasting is. For normals, the number of hours in the synagogue has little to do with the difficulty of the fast.

OBESITY AND CHOICE OF EATING PLACE

In another study *(14)* we examined the relationship of obesity to choice of eating places. From Nisbett's findings on taste, it seemed a plausible guess that the obese would be more drawn to good restaurants and more repelled by bad ones than normal subjects would be. At Columbia, students have the option of eating in the university dining halls or in any of the many restaurants that surround the campus. At Columbia, as probably at every similar institution in the United States, students have a low opinion of the institution's food. If a freshman elects to eat in a dormitory dining hall, he may, if he chooses, join a prepayment food plan at the beginning of the school year. Any time after 1 November he may, by paying a penalty of $15, cancel his food contract. If we accept prevailing campus opinion of the institution's food as being at all realistically based, we should anticipate that those for whom taste or food quality is most important will be the most likely to let their food contracts expire. Obese freshmen, then, should be more likely to drop out of the food plan than normal freshmen. Again, the data support the expectation: 86.5 percent of fat freshmen cancel their contracts as compared with 67.1 percent of normal freshmen ($P < .05$). Obesity does to some extent serve as a basis for predicting who will choose to eat institutional food.

OBESITY AND ADJUSTMENT TO NEW EATING SCHEDULES

In the final study in this series (*14*) we examined the relationship of obesity to the difficulty of adjusting to new eating schedules imposed by time-zone changes. This study involved an analysis of data collected by the medical department of Air France in a study of physiological effects of time-zone changes on 236 flight personnel assigned to the Paris–New York and Paris–Montreal flights. Most of these flights leave Paris around noon, French time; fly for approximately 8 hours; and land in North America sometime between 2:00 and 3:00 p.m. Eastern time. Flight-crew members eat lunch shortly after takeoff and, being occupied with landing preparations, are not served another meal during the flight. They land some 7 hours after their last meal, at a time that is later than the local lunch hour and earlier than the local dinner time.

Though this study was not directly concerned with eating behavior, the interviewers systematically noted all individuals who volunteered the information that they "suffered from the discordance between their physiological state and meal time in America" (*15*). One would anticipate that the fatter individuals, being sensitive to external cues (local meal hours) rather than internal ones, would adapt most readily to local eating schedules and be least likely to complain of the discrepancy between American meal times and physiological state.

Given the physical requirements involved in the selection of aircrews, there are, of course, relatively few really obese people in this sample. However, the results of Nisbett's experiment *(10)* indicate that the degree of reliance on external relative to internal cues may well be a dimension which varies with the degree of deviation from normal weight. It seems reasonable, then, to anticipate that, even within a restricted sample, there will be differences in response between the heavier and the lighter members of the sample. This is the case. In comparing the 101 flight personnel who are overweight (0.1 to 29 percent overweight) with the 135 who are not overweight (0 to 25 percent underweight), we find that 11.9 percent of the overweight complain as compared with 25.3 percent of the non-overweight ($P < .01$). It does appear that the fatter were less troubled by the effects of time changes on eating than the thinner flyers *(16)*.

These persistent findings that the obese are relatively insensitive to variations in the physiological correlates of food deprivation but highly sensitive to environmental, food-related cues is, perhaps, one key to understanding the notorious long-run ineffectiveness of virtually all attempts to treat obesity *(17)*. The use of anorexigenic drugs such as amphetamine or of bulk-producing, nonnutritive substances such as methyl cellulose is based on the premise that such agents dampen the intensity of the physiological symptoms of food deprivation. Probably they do, but these symptoms appear to have little to do with whether or not a fat person eats. Restricted, low-calorie diets should be effective just so long as the obese dieter is able to blind himself to food-relevant cues or so long as he exists in a world barren of such cues. In the Hashim and Van Itallie study *(8)*, the subjects did, in fact, live in such a world. Restricted to a Metrecal-like diet and to a small hospital ward, all the obese subjects lost impressive amounts of weight. However, on their return to normal living, to a man they returned to their original weights.

REFERENCES AND NOTES

1. H. BRUCH, *Psychiat. Quart. 35*, 458 (1961).
2. A. STUNKARD, *Psychosomat. Med. 21*, 281 (1959).

3. ——— and C. KOCH, *Arch. Genet. Psychiat. 11,* 74 (1964).
4. S. SCHACHTER, R. GOLDMAN, A. GORDON, *J. Personality Soc. Psychol. 10,* 91 (1968).
5. A. J. CARLSON, *Control of Hunger in Health and Disease* (Univ. of Chicago Press, Chicago, 1916).
6. W. B. CANNON, *Bodily Changes in Pain, Hunger, Fear and Rage* (Appleton, New York, 1915).
7. It is a common belief among researchers in the field of obesity that the sensitivity of their fat subjects makes it impossible to study their eating behavior experimentally—hence this roundabout way of measuring eating; the subjects in this study are taking a "taste test," not "eating."
8. S. A. HASHIM and T. B. VAN ITALLIE, *Ann. N. Y. Acad. Sci. 131,* 654 (1965).
9. S. SCHACHTER and L. GROSS, *J. Personality Soc. Psychol. 10,* 98 (1968).
10. R. E. NISBETT, *J. Personality Soc. Psychol. 10,* 107 (1968).
11. A. STUNKARD, *Amer. J. Psychiat. 118,* 212 (1961).
12. L. BEEBE, *The Big Spenders* (Doubleday, New York, 1966).
13. E. L. BLISS and C. H. BRANCH, *Anorexia Nervosa* (Hoeber, New York, 1960).
14. R. GOLDMAN, M. JAFFA, S. SCHACHTER, *J. Personality Soc. Psychol. 10,* 117 (1968).
15. J. LAVERNHE and E. LAFONTAINE (Air France), personal communication.
16. Obviously, I do not mean to imply that the *only* explanation of the results of these three nonlaboratory studies lies in this formulation of the external-internal control of eating behavior. These studies were deliberately designed to test implications of this general schema in field settings. As with any field research, alternative explanations of the findings are legion, and, within the context of any specific study, impossible to rule out. Alternative formulations of this entire series of studies are considered in the original papers [see Schachter *et al.* (*4* and *9*), Nisbett (*10*), and Goldman *et al.* (*14*)].
17. A. STUNKARD and M. MCLAREN-HUME, *Arch. Internal Med. 103,* 79 (1959); A. R. Feinstein, *J. Chronic Diseases* 11, 349 (1960).

18. Much of the research described in this article was supported by grants G23758 and GS732 from the National Science Foundation.

III

Socialization of Aggression

In a penetrating review of the laboratory studies of aggression, Walters (Chapter 3) cited the extensive research by Bandura and his coworkers as evidence in favor of the view that children should not be exposed to aggressive social models if the aim of our society is to decrease violence. Eron (Chapter 4), testing this assumption in the field, found that for boys there was a positive relationship between aggressive behavior in school and the degree of violence in their favorite TV programs. However, no consistent relationship between TV habits and aggressive behavior was noted for girls. A possible explanation for this sex difference is that in natural settings such children's behavior as the selection of TV programs is mediated by parental values and other cultural factors.

3

Implications of Laboratory Studies of Aggression for the Control and Regulation of Violence

Richard H. Walters

During the present decade there has been considerable interest among child and social psychologists in the problem of the control and regulation of violence. This period, also, has yielded a relatively large number of laboratory studies aimed at determining conditions under which aggressive behavior is learned and at identifying motivational and environmental factors that increase or decrease the probability that aggression will be displayed. Representative samples of these studies, as well as a few earlier studies, are briefly described in this paper, and an attempt is made to assess their implications for the problem of the social control of aggression in real-life situations.[1]

[1] Value judgments are involved in the categorization of an act as aggressive. The concept of aggression is consequently not purely descriptive and thus has limited usefulness in guiding social-psychological research. However, a discussion of possible definitions is beyond the scope of this paper. The problems of defining quasi-objective social-psychological concepts are briefly discussed by Albert Bandura and Richard H. Walters, *Social Learning and Personality Development* (New York: Holt, Rinehart, and Winston, 1963), and by Richard H. Walters and Ross D. Parke, "Social Motivation, Dependency, and Susceptibility to Social Influence," *Advances in Experimental Social Psychology,* Vol. 1, ed. Leonard Berkowitz (New York: Academic Press, 1964), pp. 231–276.

EXPOSURE TO AGGRESSIVE MODELS

Field studies of delinquency[2] and of the effects of parental child-training practices on the behavior of children[3] have yielded findings that strongly suggest that aggressive parents are more likely to have aggressive children than are parents who are relatively nonaggressive. Parents are, of course, not the only transmitters of social-behavior patterns; a child who grows up in an area in which he is surrounded by crime and violence may adopt the prevailing subcultural standards even if his parents are nonviolent and law-abiding.[4] In our "blackboard jungles" children are both provided with ample opportunities to observe successful violence and rewarded for imitative aggressive behavior.

The advent of the motion picture and television permits the exposure of children to a range of models much wider than that which their immediate social environment can supply. Although some major studies of the influence of television on children's behavior do not support the view that the social influence of this medium of communciation is generally deleterious,[5] there seems little doubt that, in some cases, seriously violent episodes might not have occurred if the agent or agents had not been exposed to aggressive movie or television models.

[2] For example: William McCord and Joan McCord, "The Effects of Parental Role Models on Criminality," *Journal of Social Issues,* Vol. 14 (1958), pp. 66–74; Albert Bandura and Richard H. Walters, *Adolescent Aggression* (New York: Ronald Press, 1959).

[3] Albert Bandura, "Relationship of Family Patterns to Child Behavior Disorders, Progress Report (1960)," U.S.P.H.S. Research Grant M-1734, Stanford University; Robert R. Sears, Eleanor E. Maccoby, and Harry Levin, *Patterns of Child-Rearing* (Evanston, Ill.: Row, Peterson, 1957).

[4] Clifford R. Shaw and Henry McKay, "Social Factors in Juvenile Delinquency," *Report on the Causes of Crime,* Vol. II (Washington, D.C.: U.S. Government Printing Office, 1931).

[5] Hilde T. Himmelweit, A. N. Oppenheim, and Pamela Vince, *Television and the Child: An Empirical Study of the Effect of Television on the Young* (New York: Oxford University Press, 1958); Wilbur Schramm, Jack Lyle, and Edwin B. Parker, *Television in the Lives of Our Children* (Stanford, Calif.: Stanford University Press, 1961); J. T. Klapper, *The Effects of Mass Communication* (Glencoe, Ill.: Free Press, 1960).

A series of laboratory studies by Bandura and his coworkers, in which children were exposed to real-life or film-mediated models, provide the strongest evidence in favor of the view that children should not be exposed to aggressive models if the goal of our society is to reduce violence. In the first of these studies,[6] nursery-school children participated in a "game" involving guessing which of two boxes contained a picture sticker. A female experimenter, the other participant, made functionless incidental responses while she took her turn in the game. For children in the experimental condition, the model's incidental responses included aggressive acts directed against dolls; for the control children, the model's behavior was entirely nonaggressive. In executing the discrimination task, aggressive behavior was exhibited by 90 per cent of the children who had been exposed to the aggressive model. In contrast, not one of the control children displayed aggression.

A second study [7] indicated that the model need not be present for imitative aggression to occur. Two groups of nursery-school children spent ten minutes in a room where they could observe the behavior of an adult model. One group saw the model attack an inflated Bobo doll, both physically and verbally; the other group saw the model play with a tinker-toy set in a nonaggressive way. Following exposure to the model, the children were mildly frustrated and then taken to another room containing a variety of toys, some of which could be used as aggressive implements. A control group of children was given a similar experience without prior exposure to a model. Children who had been exposed to an aggressive model showed more imitative physical and verbal aggressive behavior than did children in the other two groups.

Bandura and his associates [8] next compared the influence of an aggressive model presented in person with that of aggressive models

[6] Albert Bandura and Aletha C. Huston, "Identification as a Process of Incidental Learning," *Journal of Abnormal and Social Psychology,* Vol. 63 (1961), pp. 311–318.

[7] Albert Bandura, Dorothea Ross, and Sheila A. Ross, "Transmission of Aggression through Imitation of Aggressive Models," *Journal of Abnormal and Social Psychology,* Vol. 63 (1961), pp. 575–582.

[8] Albert Bandura, Dorothea Ross, and Sheila A. Ross, "Imitation of Film-Mediated Models," *Journal of Abnormal and Social Psychology,* Vol. 66 (1963), pp. 3–11.

presented on film. Four conditions were employed: human adult model, filmed human adult model, filmed cartoon model (an adult dressed up as a cat), and no model. The procedure was otherwise essentially the same as in the study just described. All groups of children exposed to an aggressive model showed more aggression in the test situation than did the control group. The over-all findings, based on a variety of measures of specifically imitative and nonspecifically imitative aggression, indicated that exposure to human subjects portraying aggression in movies was the most effective method of eliciting and shaping aggressive behavior.

Two other studies indicate that observation of filmed aggression increases the probability that children will subsequently display aggressive behavior. In a study by Lövaas,[9] children in a day-care center were provided with the choice of depressing one of two levers, one of which operated a hitting doll, the other a ball in a cage. Half the children were shown an aggressive cartoon film, and the remainder a nonaggressive cartoon. Immediately after watching one of the films, the children were left with the two lever-operated toys for a four-minute period. Children who had seen the aggressive cartoon depressed the lever that operated the hitting doll more frequently than those who had watched the non-aggressive cartoon. Analogous findings are reported by Mussen and Rutherford,[10] who also used cartoon films, but assessed their effects by questioning children concerning their desire to "pop" an inflated balloon held by the experimenter.

The studies so far cited tested child subjects in a play setting and did not use a commercial film sequence typical of those that have been criticized for their possible effects on the viewer. Walters and Llewellyn Thomas [11] studied the effects of presenting the knife-

[9] O. Ivar Lövaas, "Effect of Exposure to Symbolic Aggression on Aggressive Behavior," *Child Development,* Vol. 32 (1961), pp. 37–44.

[10] Paul H. Mussen and Eldred Rutherford, "Effects of Aggressive Cartoons on Children's Aggressive Play," *Journal of Abnormal and Social Psychology,* Vol. 62 (1961), pp. 461–464.

[11] Richard H. Walters and Edward Llewellyn Thomas, "Enhancement of Punitiveness by Visual and Audiovisual Displays," *Canadian Journal of Psychology,* Vol. 16 (1963), pp. 244–255; Richard H. Walters, Edward Llewellyn Thomas, and C. William Acker, "Enhancement of Punitive Behavior by Audiovisual Displays," *Science,* Vol. 136 (1962), pp. 872–873.

fight scene from the movie, "Rebel Without a Cause," to both adolescent boys and male and female adults. Both before and after viewing the movie, the subjects were given the task of inflicting electric shock on a confederate of the experimenter, who was supposedly another subject. In comparison to a control group, who saw a movie sequence depicting adolescents engaged in constructive art-work, the subjects who saw the knife-fight scene exhibited an increased tendency to give more intense shocks in the posttest session.

One recent study [12] examined the influence of both aggressive peer and aggressive adult models, male and female, on the behavior of children in a play situation. The children were tested immediately after seeing the filmed models and again six months later. Children in all four experimental groups, defined in terms of the age and sex of the model, showed more imitative aggression than children who saw no model but were slightly frustrated before being taken into the playroom. The male peer model elicited the most imitative aggression from both male and female subjects. After six months, however, the amount of imitative aggression markedly decreased in all four experimental groups; only exposure to the male adult seemed to have had any lasting effect, and even this was of borderline significance.

The series of studies reported above lend considerable support to the belief that the observation of violence in real life or on film or television can have harmful social consequences. However, it must be remembered that the subjects in the studies were tested in situations in which aggressive behavior was permitted, instigated, or even demanded, and that, with one exception that suggested that modeling effects may be transient, the tests were conducted almost immediately after the subjects had been exposed to the models. In real life, one is rarely provided with an opportunity or with instigation to express aggression immediately after exposure to a film or television sequence depicting violent aggression. Moreover, most acts of aggression incur consequences, both in fiction and in real-life situations; in most movies and television shows, for example, the villain is in some way punished. Studies of the effects of ob-

[12] David J. Hicks, "Imitation and Retention of Film-Mediated Aggressive Peer and Adult Models," *Journal of Personality and Social Psychology,* Vol. 2 (1965), pp. 97–100.

serving rewarding and punishing consequences dispensed to an aggressor are therefore of considerable interest.

EFFECTS OF OBSERVING REWARDS AND PUNISHMENTS DELIVERED TO AN AGGRESSIVE MODEL

Bandura, Ross, and Ross [13] assigned nursery-school children to one of four conditions: aggressive model rewarded; aggressive model punished; no exposure to a model; model expressive, but non-aggressive. Under the first two conditions, the children were shown a film depicting an adult male employing a great deal of physical and verbal aggression to secure the possessions of a second male adult. Under the model-rewarded condition, the aggressor was successful and was shown enjoying the fruits of his victory; under the model-punished condition, the aggressor was severely punished by the intended victim. In a subsequent testing situation, children who witnessed the aggressive model rewarded showed more verbal and physical aggression imitative of the model than did children who saw the model punished or children in the control groups. Aggressive responses that were not precisely imitative were also more frequent among children under the model-rewarded condition than among children under the model-punished and the no-film conditions.

Failure to reproduce a punished model's behavior in a subsequent test situation does not, however, indicate that learning through observation has not taken place. Bandura [14] exposed nursery-school children to one of three conditions: model rewarded for aggressive behavior, model punished for aggressive behavior, and model neither rewarded not punished for such behavior. After exposure to one of these conditions, each child was observed during a ten-

[13] Albert Bandura, Dorothea Ross, and Sheila A. Ross, "Vicarious Reinforcement and Imitation," *Journal of Abnormal and Social Psychology,* Vol. 66 (1963), pp. 3–11.

[14] Albert Bandura, "Influence of Models' Reinforcement Contingencies on the Acquisition of Imitative Responses," *Journal of Personality and Social Psychology,* Vol. 1 (1965), pp. 589–595.

minute free-play situation. During this period, children under the model-rewarded and the no-consequence conditions displayed significantly more imitative aggression than children who saw the model punished. Immediately after the observation period, the children were provided with incentives to reproduce the model's aggressive responses. The introduction of these incentives eliminated differences among the three groups of subjects.

Evidence in support of the above findings has been provided by Walters and his associates [15] in studies of resistance to deviation. Generally speaking, these studies indicate that a model who is rewarded or is not punished for breaking a prohibition is likely to be imitated by children who witness the deviation, whereas imitative prohibition-breaking is unlikely to occur if the model is punished for his behavior. However, if the prohibition is subsequently removed, children who have seen the model punished can reproduce the model's deviant responses almost as precisely as children who have seen the model rewarded or escape without punishment.

Observed consequences to a model probably serve as cues indicating that a particular kind of behavior is permissible or nonpermissible in a given social context. Seeing a model rewarded leads the observer to anticipate that he, too, will be rewarded if he acts similarly to the model; if the model's behavior is deviant, according to prevailing social standards, but nevertheless goes unpunished, the observer anticipates that he, too, under similar circumstances may behave in a deviant manner. On the other hand, the observation of a punished deviant model provides a cue to the observer that he, too, is likely to be punished should he follow the model's example.

The importance of anticipated censure for aggression as an inhibitory mechanism has been demonstrated by Lefcourt and his

[15] Richard H. Walters, Marion Leat, and Louis Mezei, "Inhibition and Disinhibition of Responses through Empathetic Learning," *Canadian Journal of Psychology*, Vol. 17 (1963), pp. 235–243; Richard H. Walters and Ross D. Parke, "Influence of Response Consequences to a Social Model on Resistance to Deviation," *Journal of Experimental Child Psychology*, Vol. 1 (1964), pp. 269–280; Richard H. Walters, Ross D. Parke, and Valerie A. Cane, "Timing of Punishment and the Observation of Consequences to Others as Determinants of Response Inhibition," *Journal of Experimental Child Psychology*, Vol. 2 (1965), pp. 10–30.

associates,[16] who used the same dependent measures as Walters and Llewellyn Thomas together with the "Rebel Without a Cause" excerpt as an aggression-eliciting stimulus. For half the subjects, all of whom were college students, the experimenters' confederate expressed disapproval of the aggressive behavior of the adolescents while the film was being shown; for the remaining subjects, the confederate expressed approval of, and interest in, the aggressive sequence. Subjects under the former condition showed little change in the average level of shock that they administered to the experimenters' confederate, whereas a significant increase in shock intensity occurred among the subjects who heard the confederate condone and approve the aggression depicted in the film. This experimental manipulation may be an analogue of the home situation in which a child observes his father's excitement and involvement in a boxing or wrestling event while the participants inflict pain on one another.

Anticipation of censure or approval may also account for the finding of Berkowitz and his collaborators[17] that filmed violence is less likely to elicit aggressive reactions from recently frustrated observers for whom the violence is presented as unjustified than from those for whom it is presented as justified on account of the fact that the victim is a villain. Justifying filmed violence may provide the observer with a cue that aggression that is expressed against a frustrating agent is likely to be condoned and therefore unlikely to incur punishment. Thus, justification may function in the same way as the observation of reward of, or the omission of punishment for, behavior that ordinarily incurs social disapproval.

An evaluation of the possible influence of film and television productions that depict violence is complicated by the fact that the "hero" often engages in socially sanctioned aggression in order to

[16] Herbert M. Lefcourt, Keith E. Barnes, Ross D. Parke, and Fred S. Schwartz, "Anticipated Social Censure and Aggression-Conflict as Mediators of Response to Aggression Induction," *Journal of Social Psychology*, Vol. 70 (1966), pp. 251–263.

[17] Leonard Berkowitz and Edna Rawlings, "Effects of Film Violence on Inhibitions against Subsequent Aggression," *Journal of Abnormal and Social Psychology*, Vol. 66 (1963), pp. 405–412; Leonard Berkowitz, Ronald Corwin, and Mark Hieronimus, "Film Violence and Subsequent Aggressive Tendencies," *Public Opinion Quarterly*, Vol. 27 (1962), pp. 217–229.

overcome the violent and aggressive villain. In other words, in such productions aggression by some individuals is socially sanctioned and rewarded. While it is true that the hero's violence is usually depicted as counteraggression, these productions reflect an "eye for an eye, tooth for a tooth" philosophy, one danger of which is the perpetuation of violence. Moreover, in most cases the hero ultimately secures unconditional rewards for his counteraggression; consequently, there is an increased likelihood that his aggressive behavior will be imitated. Finally, as Berkowitz's [18] research indicates, the observer who witnesses "justifiable" aggression is inclined to behave violently toward someone who has recently angered him. Since experimental studies have consistently shown that immediately or shortly after exposure to a rewarded model, observers are very likely to imitate his behavior, the "violent-hero" drama may have a very strong potentiality for eliciting violent acts if the observer is already frustrated and has no other readily available means of securing his goals. Thus, the value systems that may be transmitted by such dramas, the models of behavior they present, and their apparent effectiveness as cues for eliciting violence may, in combination, render them a potential social danger.

Laboratory studies thus indicate that the presentation of violent models in real life or in fantasy productions may both provide observers with opportunities to learn new ways of expressing aggression and also provide cues that aggression can be socially acceptable. On the other hand, the pairing of punishment with the socially unacceptable acts of a model undoubtedly has a deterrent effect on the observer. Humanitarians who deny the deterrent effects of the punitive treatment of delinquents and criminals may be commended for their kindheartedness, but not for their objective appraisal of scientific evidence.

EFFECT OF REWARDING AGGRESSION

Walters and his coworkers conducted a series of studies in which children were rewarded with marbles for hitting a specially constructed Bobo clown which permitted the frequency and in-

[18] Berkowitz *et al.*, *op. cit.*

tensity of punches to be automatically recorded. Evidence was first secured that children who have been intermittently rewarded for hitting continue to hit, when rewards are discontinued, for a longer period of time than do children who have been continuously rewarded.[19] Since, in real-life situations, rewards for aggression are inevitably intermittent, conditions are present that facilitate the establishment of habits that are highly resistant to extinction.

In another study,[20] seven-year-old children were assigned to one of four experimental conditions. Under one condition the children were continuously rewarded for hitting the clown with at least moderate intensity during the training session; under a second condition rewards were only intermittently given. A third group of children played with the clown without receiving any rewards, while the fourth group was given no experience with the doll. Under the first three conditions, each child played with the doll in two sessions on different days and was tested on a third day; the remaining children participated only in the testing session.

In advance of the study, each child subject had been randomly paired with another child in his grade who served as a competitor during the testing session. Each subject and his competitor were required to participate in three physical-contact games, and the frequency with which the subject made aggressive responses, both during the games and during a free-play session, was recorded by observers. The intermittently rewarded children made significantly more aggressive responses than those under the other three conditions.

This finding appeared to support the high-magnitude theory of aggression,[21] which states that intense responses are more likely to be regarded as aggressive than are topologically similar responses of lower intensity. It seemed probable that intermittently rewarded subjects had increased the intensity of their punches while reward

[19] Philip A. Cowan and Richard H. Walters, "Studies of Reinforcement of Aggression," Part 1: "Effects of Scheduling," *Child Development*, Vol. 34 (1963), pp. 543–552.

[20] Richard H. Walters and Murray Brown, "Studies of Reinforcement of Aggression," Part III: "Transfer of Responses to an Interpersonal Situation," *Child Development*, Vol. 34 (1963), pp. 563–572.

[21] Albert Bandura and Richard H. Walters, *Social Learning and Personality Development* (New York: Holt, Rinehart, and Winston, 1963).

was delayed and were thus rewarded for relatively intense hits. The reinforced habit of responding intensely to the doll then generalized to the interpersonal situation.

A direct test of the high-magnitude theory followed.[22] In the first part of this study some children were rewarded only when they hit the doll intensely, whereas the remaining children were rewarded only for weak hits. Again, each subject was matched with an untrained competitor in physical-contact games. As anticipated, children who were rewarded for high-intensity responses to the doll were more physically aggressive during physical-contact games than were children who had been rewarded for responding weakly.

The high-magnitude theory leads to the prediction that training a child to respond intensely, though nonaggressively, may result in his responding intensely in other situations, including those in which an intense response would be regarded as an aggressive act. Consequently, in the second part of this study, one group of children was rewarded for depressing a lever with considerable force in order to propel a ball to the top of a cage, while the remaining children were rewarded when they depressed the lever gently. The test for generalization effects, which was the same as in the first part of the study, supported the prediction. Children trained to respond forcefully in the ball-and-cage situation made a reliably greater number of responses that were classified by observers as aggressive than did children who had been trained to depress the lever weakly.

The studies of Walters and Brown indicate that children who are intermittently rewarded for aggressive behavior in play situations in which the target is an inanimate object are likely to behave aggressively in social interactions in which aggressive acts can cause harm and pain to other persons. A father who trains his son to hit a punch-bag and who praises the child when he hits the bag hard is thus providing training that increases the probability of the child's acting aggressively toward other children. Moreover, it seems probable that any treatment of a child that requires him to respond forcefully to gain rewards is liable to establish an habitual

[22] Richard H. Walters and Murray Brown, "A Test of the High-Magnitude Theory of Aggression," *Journal of Experimental Child Psychology*, Vol. 1 (1964), pp. 376–387.

mode of responding that in many situations will be manifested in the form of aggressive behavior directed toward other persons.

INHIBITION OF AGGRESSION

Psychologists have conducted very few experimental studies of the effects of punishment on human social behavior. It has indeed been customary for psychologists to regard punishment as a relatively ineffective means of discipline on account of its potentially undesirable side effects and of the assumed transcience of its effect as a suppressor of undesirable behavior. A change in the climate of opinion is now in evidence,[23] but there has been no recent study of the effects of punishing aggression. On the other hand, evidence is mounting that punishment may, under some circumstances, be a very effective means of preventing a child from breaking a prohibition, with its degree of effectiveness depending on such factors as its nature, intensity, timing, and consistency, and on the relationship between the agent and recipient of punishment.[24]

Nevertheless, when a parent or other socialization agent frequently employs physical or other aggressive forms of punishment as a means of suppressing children's aggressive behavior, he is in danger of defeating his own purpose, since he is serving as an aggressive model.[25] The most likely outcome is that the child will avoid expressing aggression in the presence of his punisher but will behave aggressively in other situations, for example, when interacting with his peers. Much will depend, however, on the context

[23] Russell M. Church, "The Varied Effects of Punishment on Behavior," *Psychological Review,* Vol. 70 (1963), pp. 369–402; O. Hobart Mowrer, *Learning Theory and Behavior* (New York: John Wiley & Sons, 1960); O. Hobart Mowrer, *Learning Theory and the Symbolic Processes* (New York: John Wiley & Sons, 1960); Richard L. Solomon, "Punishment," *American Psychologist,* Vol. 19 (1964), pp. 239–253.

[24] Justin Aronfreed, "Conscience and Conduct: A Natural History of the Internalization Process," *Character Development,* ed. M. Hoffman (New York: Russell Sage Foundation, in press); Bandura and Walters, *op. cit.;* Ross D. Parke and Richard H. Walters, "Some Factors Determining the Efficacy of Punishment for Inducing Response Inhibition," to be published.

[25] Bandura and Walters, *op. cit.*

in which the punishment occurs and especially on the relationship between the disciplinary agent and the child.

One very effective means of inhibiting socially undesirable behavior is to train children to make prosocial responses that are incompatible with aggression, either by exposing them to nonaggressive models or by rewarding them for socially approved behavior. Years ago, Chittenden[26] trained highly aggressive children to make nonaggressive responses to frustration by having them observe a series of "plays" in which dolls exhibited both nonaggressive and aggressive responses in problem situations that generated conflict. The consequences of the alternative aggressive and nonaggressive solutions were discussed with the children after each play in the series. As a consequence of this training, the children subsequently exhibited more co-operative and fewer aggressive responses in interactions with their peers.

In another early study, Davitz[27] praised and approved five groups of four children for making aggressive responses in competitive physical-contact games. Another five groups were praised for constructive and co-operative behavior. After several training sessions, the groups of children were severely frustrated. Films were taken of the groups' free-play behavior before training and again immediately after frustration. Children who had been trained to behave aggressively showed an increase in aggression in the second free-play session, whereas the equally frustrated children who had received training in co-operative behavior showed a decrease in aggression from the first to the second free-play session and an increase in co-operative responses.

Brown and Elliot[28] recently applied techniques derived from social-learning theory to the modification of children's aggressive behavior in a nursery-school setting. Teachers were instructed to ignore aggressive behavior and to reward co-operative and peaceful behavior by means of attention and praise. Observations of the

[26] Gertrude E. Chittenden, "An Experimental Study in Measuring and Modifying Assertive Behavior in Children," *Monographs of the Society for Research in Child Development,* Vol. 7 (1942), No. 1 (Serial No. 31).

[27] Joel R. Davitz, "The Effects of Previous Training on Postfrustrative Behavior," *Journal of Abnormal and Social Psychology,* Vol. 47 (1952), pp. 309–315.

[28] Paul Brown and Rogers Elliot, "Control of Aggression in a Nursery-School Class," *Journal of Experimental Child Psychology,* Vol. 2 (1965), pp. 103–107.

children's behavior before and after each of two two-week treatment periods indicated that the procedure was capable of producing significant decreases in both physical and verbal aggression.

Controlled experimental studies thus provide considerable evidence that inhibition of aggression can be effectively developed through the strengthening of prosocial responses that are incompatible with aggression. The effects of punishing aggression, in the absence of planned reward for incompatible responses, have yet to be satisfactorily determined. It can be safely stated, however, that both direct punishment and the observation of punishment to others can have at least a temporary suppressing effect and can thus provide an opportunity for alternative prosocial responses to be strengthened through reward.

Moreover, studies both of consequences to social models and of punishment training support the view that anticipation of punishment for deviant acts is a potent source of self-control. There is, indeed, some evidence that the level of aggression of some persons may increase, even in the absence of anger, rewards, or the example set by a model, if no untoward social consequences of their previous aggression are apparent.[29] It is probably only the continual expectation that the potential recipients or other members of society will retaliate that prevents many individuals from more freely expressing aggression.

THE CHOICE OF A TARGET FOR AGGRESSION

An individual who has been attacked, thwarted, insulted, or blocked from attaining a goal is likely to direct aggression against the person he considers responsible for his condition unless external circumstances or internal restraints prevent him from doing so. Often, however, such circumstances or restraints exist. The agent may fear counteraggression, either direct or through some agent other than the target of his aggression; the source of his problem may be an impersonal or unidentifiable agency that cannot be directly attacked; it may be a physical or psychological deficit, or

[29] Walters and Llewellyn Thomas, *op. cit.*

an event in his past history that is no longer under his control; he may fear to lose valued rewards as a result of his aggression; or he may respond emotionally to the direct expression of aggression because such behavior violates standards he has adopted. Under such circumstances, the agent may select a target for aggression who is not directly, or not all, responsible for his condition.

The dominant view in psychological theory has been that target choice is a joint function of the strength of the instigation to display aggression and the strength of the inhibition against directing aggression toward the source of frustration. It has been assumed that both the instigatory and the inhibitory tendencies generalize, the strength of the generalized responses being a positive function of the degree of similarity between the agent of frustration and possible object of aggression. If the assumption is made that the strength of the generalized inhibitory response decreases more rapidly than that of the generalized excitatory response, the conclusion is reached that at some point on the assumed dissimilarity continuum aggression will be manifested.[30]

This conceptualization is untenable for a number of reasons.[31] In particular, it ignores the influence of prior social-learning experiences that predispose the agent to direct his aggression toward one class of person rather than another. For example, Southern white children are provided with frequent examples of aggression toward colored people; they see such aggression rewarded, and are rewarded in turn when they emulate the adults in their society. Consequently, when they are prevented from expressing aggression toward a source of frustration, they are especially likely to "displace" the aggression toward the relatively defenseless minority group. Nevertheless, there is no reason to suppose that most aggression that is directed toward minority groups is, in fact, displaced; rather, it reflects the outcome of training deliberately aimed

[30] Neal E. Miller, "Theory and Experiment Relating Psychoanalytic Displacement to Stimulus-Response Generalization," *Journal of Abnormal and Social Psychology,* Vol. 43 (1948), pp. 155–178; John W. M. Whiting and Irvin L. Child, *Child-Training and Personality* (New Haven: Yale University Press, 1953).

[31] Albert Bandura and Richard H. Walters, "Aggression," *Child Psychology: The Sixty-Second Yearbook of the National Society for the Study of Aggression,* Part 1 (Chicago: National Society for the Study of Education, 1963), pp. 364–415.

at teaching children to respond to such groups in an aggressive manner.

The external and cognitive cues that facilitate the learning of aggression directed toward minority groups are relatively easy to identify. The cues involved are much less easily identifiable when the target is a member of the agent's own subcultural group. Berkowitz[32] has tested the hypothesis that a potential target of aggression is capable of evoking aggressive responses only to the extent that it is associated with previous aggression instigators. His experimental procedure consists of introducing male college subjects to a peer, a confederate of the experimenter, who is to judge the subjects' performance on a task. For some subjects, the evaluation takes the form of the delivery of seven electric shocks (an unfavorable judgment), a condition that angers the subjects. The subject and the confederate then witness together either a prizefight scene or an exciting film without aggressive content. Subsequently, the subjects are given an opportunity to administer shocks to the confederate as a judgment of the adequacy of the latter's performance. The degree of association between the confederate and the agent or recipient of aggression in the film is varied by introducing the confederate to the subject by different fictitious names, related in varying degrees to the names given to the movie characters. The more closely the confederate is associated with the *victim* of aggression, the more likely is he to be the target of aggression.

This finding again suggests that anticipations of reward or punishment are crucial factors in determining the agent's selection of a target for aggression. The victim is the person in the film who is rendered incapable of retaliation and of punishing the aggressor for continued attacks. Generalizing Berkowitz's finding, one might say that a person who is associated with defenselessness is most likely to be attacked by others. The available evidence from studies of rewards and punishments received by aggressive models, Berkowitz's studies of the cue values of available targets of aggression, and his studies of justifiable versus nonjustifiable aggression seem

[32] Leonard Berkowitz, "Some Aspects of Observed Aggression," *Journal of Personality and Social Psychology,* Vol. 2 (1965), pp. 359–369; Leonard Berkowitz and Russell G. Geen, "Film Violence and the Cue Properties of Available Targets," *Journal of Personality and Social Psychology,* Vol. 3 (1966), pp. 525–530.

to lead to a similar conclusion: aggression is most likely to be expressed when punishment is not anticipated. Moreover, if displacement occurs, the target selected will most likely be one who cannot easily retaliate and against whom aggression can be displayed with the minimum of social censure.

A COMMENT ON CATHARSIS

In the psychological literature, catharsis has been used in the Aristotelian sense to refer to the reduction of the anger of spectators through their vicarious participation in the aggressive behavior of others and also in the psychoanalytic sense to refer to the liberation of aggressive findings through their expression in fantasy, play, or real-life situations.

The outcome of studies of the influence of aggressive film-mediated models on the behavior of children lends no support whatsoever to the Aristotelian type of catharsis hypothesis.[33] Similarly, studies in which children have been encouraged to participate in aggressive play have not supported the hypothesis that participation has a cathartic effect.[34] While studies with adults have brought less consistent results, those that have demonstrated reduction of aggression among subjects who have observed filmed aggression or have been permitted to express aggression following frustration do not necessarily provide support for the catharsis hypothesis. In practically every case, the aggression reduction can be explained without assuming that catharsis has occurred.[35] The highly consistent evidence from studies of aggressive models by Bandura, Berkowitz, Walters, and others suggests that the catharsis doctrine is not merely mistaken, but that its promulgation can lead to the defense of mass-media content that has socially harmful effects.

[33] Bandura and Walters, "Aggression," *op. cit.*

[34] Douglas T. Kenney, "An Experimental Test of the Catharsis Theory of Aggression," Unpublished doctoral dissertation, University of Washington, 1952; Seymour Feshbach, "The Catharsis Hypothesis and Some Consequences of Interaction with Aggressive and Neutral Play Objects," *Journal of Personality,* Vol. 24 (1956), pp. 449–462.

[35] Leonard Berkowitz, "Aggressive Cues in Aggressive Behavior and Hostility Catharsis," *Psychological Review,* Vol. 71 (1964), pp. 104–122.

THE FRUSTRATION-AGGRESSION HYPOTHESIS

The influential frustration-aggression hypothesis [36] presented aggression as the naturally dominant response to frustration, so that nonaggressive responses to frustration were likely to occur only in situations in which aggressive responses previously had been punished or had brought no reward. This hypothesis has been severely criticized by Buss and by Bandura and Walters and has been defended, with some qualifications, by Berkowitz.[37]

Berkowitz holds that frustration arouses anger and so predisposes a person to respond in an aggressive manner, but that aggression will not occur unless appropriate stimuli are present. In contrast, Bandura and Walters have argued that frustration (defined as delay of reward) has only a general energizing effect and that the behavior manifested by the frustrated person will depend on the relative dominance of the habits that are elicited by internal and external cues. These theories are, nevertheless, essentially in agreement in their emphasis on the importance of social-stimulus variables in determining whether or not aggression will occur on a particular occasion.

At the same time, the theories differ in their answer to the question: "Is aggression an innate, unlearned response to frustration?" Berkowitz [38] has marshaled considerable evidence that, at least in the case of some subhuman species, aggressive responses can be released by appropriate cues even if the organism has neither observed aggressive behavior by another member of its species nor previously been rewarded for aggression in the presence of

[36] John Dollard, Leonard W. Doob, Neal E. Miller, O. Hobart Mowrer, and Robert R. Sears, *Frustration and Aggression* (New Haven: Yale University Press, 1939).

[37] Albert Bandura and Richard H. Walters, *Social Learning and Personality Development* (New York: Holt, Rinehart, and Winston, 1963); Leonard Berkowitz, *Aggression: A Social Psychological Analysis* (New York: McGraw-Hill, 1962); Arnold H. Buss, *The Psychology of Aggression* (New York: John Wiley & Sons, 1961).

[38] Berkowitz, *op. cit.*

these cues. Nevertheless, there are species-specific forms of behavior, and Berkowitz has not proved his case as far as humans are concerned. While it is possible that the emotional behavior exhibited by human infants when frustration occurs may be an unlearned rage response,[39] it seems much more likely that this behavior is an undifferentiated reaction to stress, which, when intense, is interpreted by adults as an instance of rage. Moreover, specific aggressive response patterns probably do not occur at the human level until some social learning has taken place. With the rapidly increasing research on infant behavior, data should soon be available that will bear on the question of the innateness of the frustration-anger or frustration-aggression association. At the present time, the disagreement represents more a conflict of faiths than a conflict based on facts.

SUMMARY

Laboratory studies of imitative behavior indicate that observation of aggressive social models, either in real life or in fantasy productions, increases the probability that the observers will behave in an aggressive manner if the model is rewarded or does not receive punishment for aggressive behavior. On the other hand, punishment administered to an aggressive model decreases the probability that imitation will occur. The permanence of effects of exposure to models is, however, still in doubt. Studies of the effects of rewarding aggression indicate that aggressive habits may be developed and maintained through intermittent rewards and may be generalized to situations other than those in which they are learned. The effects of punishing aggression are complex, since, while punishment may suppress a response, the punitive agent can function as an aggressive model whose behavior may be imitated by the recipient of aggression. Nevertheless, there is good evidence that anticipation of punishment is an important factor in the regulation of aggression. Widely prevalent hypotheses concerning the displacement of aggression, the cathartic effects of vicarious or di-

[39] Sears, Maccoby, and Levin, *op. cit.*

rect participation in aggressive activity, and the association between frustration and aggression are brought into question by the research findings of the past few years.

4

Relationship of TV Viewing Habits and Aggressive Behavior in Children

Leonard D. Eron

Since the advent of television, popular writers and journalists have linked increased rates of crime and delinquency to the increased production of TV sets, much as, in the past, the same effects have been ascribed to radio, movies, dime novels, and comic books. Television executives have stoutly maintained at the same time

From *Journal of Abnormal and Social Psychology*, 1963, *67*, 193–196.

The data on which this article is based derive from a larger study, "The Psychosocial Development of Aggressive Behavior," which has been generously supported by Grant M1726 from the National Institute of Mental Health, United States Public Health Service, and the Columbia County Tuberculosis and Health Association, Incorporated, New York. Thanks are due also to the IBM Watson Scientific Computing Laboratory at Columbia University for making computer time available without charge and to the elementary schools in Columbia County for their continued cooperation in this study.

that, "there is no direct relationship between action or the physical contact that occurs in television and activity of children who are viewing—except in deviant cases, of course" (Aubrey, 1962). However, little convincing research evidence has been amassed either to substantiate or refute the assertion that TV is the cause of an increase in delinquency or is in any way related to overt behavior in real life. An extensive, well designed survey study carried out in England (Himmelweit, Oppenheim, & Vince, 1958) provided no conclusive answer. This study found no more aggressive or delinquent behaviors among children who viewed TV than among their control group who did not watch TV at all. However, these authors, on the basis of their study of the television habits of over 5,000 youngsters in England, did state that they felt the important question was not how long a child watches television but rather what he sees. Schramm, Lyle, and Parker (1961) in a study of American children came to a like conclusion and Newton Minnow, Chairman of the Federal Communications Commission, has made similar statements about the quality of TV programming, especially for children.[1] Although in the laboratory it has been possible to demonstrate that exposure of children to aggressive behavior portrayed in a film increases the probability of aggressive responses to an immediately subsequent frustration (Bandura, Ross, & Ross, 1963); evidence as to the long-term effect of TV programing on real-life behavior has not been forthcoming.

It has been possible, in a larger investigation of the psychosocial antecedents of aggressive behavior in children (Eron, Laulicht, Walder, Farber, & Spiegel, 1961), to accumulate data which indicate that there is a relationship between such TV habits and aggressive behavior in real life.

METHOD

Subjects and Procedure

Two groups of subjects were included. The first consisted of 367 boys and 322 girls who were in the third grade in a semirural

[1] Address to the Radio and Television Executives Society, New York, September 22, 1961.

county of New York's Hudson Valley in the spring of 1960. They comprised all children whose mothers had been interviewed in a study of aggressive behavior of all third graders in the county (875). Also included were 277 boys and 245 girls whose fathers had been interviewed in this same study. There is a large degree of overlap between the two samples and thus separate analyses were done for mother and father.

The measures of aggressive behavior and TV viewing were obtained independently of each other. The former was a peer rating measure (Guess Who?) in which each child rated every other child in his classroom on 10 items having to do with specific aggressive behaviors. A description of the scale and a detailed account of its derivation, scoring, reliability, and validity are contained in a monograph by Walder, Abelson, Eron, Banta, and Laulicht (1961) and in an article by Banta and Walder (1961). Information about TV habits was taken from three questions in a 286-item interview administered individually in the respondent's home. This interview is an extension and refinement of the one described in an article by Eron, Banta, Walder, and Laulicht (1961). The specific questions were:

> How often does [Name] watch TV during the week?
> How often does [Name] watch TV during the weekend?
> What are [Name's] three favorite TV programs?

Two scores were obtained: total number of hours spent in viewing TV; and amount of violence in programs watched. Independent estimates by fathers and mothers of hours watched correlated .54 with each other. While information from father thus cannot be substituted for information from mother and vice versa, this is a sufficiently high relationship to indicate that there is some degree of validity in the reports of viewing hours noted by these independent observers and they were not answering randomly. To obtain the violence score, all TV programs mentioned by the respondents were categorized as to whether or not they emphasized antisocial aggression. No classification was permitted on the basis of the title alone. The raters had to be familiar with the content of the programs mentioned before assigning a rating. This was not difficult since the majority of inhabitants of this area can receive only one channel, and at most three, and the raters were familiar with the programs mentioned. Indication that the raters were not influenced by the program titles, but responded only to the content, is seen in the classification of some westerns as violent and some as nonviolent, of some mysteries as violent and some as nonviolent. For example, the *Lone Ranger* and *Perry Mason* were classified as nonviolent while *Have Gun-Will Travel* and *77 Sunset Strip* were classified as violent.

As one check on the validity of the information itself, i.e., whether the parents were actually giving us the children's three favorite programs or just making it up, we compared the programs mentioned independently by the fathers and mothers for those 509 children both of whose parents were interviewed. Average percentage agreement in naming the child's three favorite programs was 63 which, although again not permitting substitution of father information for mother information, is surprisingly high, considering the number of choices possible. Further evidence of the validity of the violence rating (as well as of the number of hours watched) is seen in the similarity of results whether the mother or father is the informant, which is discussed in the Results section below. Agreement between two independent raters in the categorization of all programs mentioned was 94%.[2] With the remaining 6%, discussion between the raters resolved the differences. On the basis of these ratings each subject was then assigned a score indicating extent of violence observed in TV viewing: 1, no violent programs mentioned; 2, one violent program mentioned; 3, two violent programs mentioned; 4, three violent programs mentioned. For the first measure a threefold classification of hours watched—0–4, 5–9, 10 and over—was used. Since these two variables, hours watched and extent of violence, are not completely independent, two simple randomized analyses of variance (Lindquist, 1953) were then done with aggression score as the dependent variable and, in one case, hours watched and, in the other case, violence ratings of programs as the independent variables. These analyses were done separately for boys and girls, mothers and fathers.

[2] Thanks are due Irene Quinn and Anne Yaeger for their aid in making these ratings.

Table 4.1—Analysis of Variance Relating TV Habits of Boys as Reported by Parents to Aggression as Rated by Peers

Informant	*TV variable*	*Source*	*df*	*MS*	*F*
Mothers	Violence rating	Treatments	3	980.07	
		Within groups	363	233.54	4.196**
Fathers	Violence rating	Treatments	3	550.59	
		Within groups	273	198.22	2.925*
Mothers	Hours watched	Treatments	2	731.57	
		Within groups	364	236.96	3.087*
Fathers	Hours watched	Treatments	2	19.95	
		Within groups	274	203.38	<1.00

* $p < .05$.
** $p < .01$.

RESULTS AND DISCUSSION

The results of the analyses of variance are summarized in Table 4.1. There is a strong positive relationship between the violence rating of favorite programs, whether reported by mothers or fathers, and aggression of boys as rated by their peers in the classroom. There is also a significant negative relationship between amount of time spent in viewing TV as reported by mothers and aggression of boys. Although the results for fathers of boys are in the same direction for number of hours watched, they are not significant. There were no significant relationships when TV habits of girls were reported either by mothers or fathers. The magnitude and direction of the differences for boys can be seen in Tables 4.2 and 4.3. As the amount of violence increases, the aggression rate of the boys also increases; however, as total amount of time watched increases, aggression scores decrease.

Aside from the fact that definite relationships are thus established between TV viewing habits and aggressive behavior in real life, these findings are interesting for a number of other reasons important in child rearing research.

1. They substantiate the assertions of Himmelweit et al.

(1958), Schramm et al. (1961), and Minnow (see Footnote 1) that the relationship of behavior to the quality of programing is of a different order than is relationship of behavior to the sheer amount of time spent in watching TV. In general, boys who watched TV more are not as aggressive as boys who watch it less. Is this because they are by temperament less active; is it because they discharge their aggressive impulses in this fantasylike way and thus do not have to act them out in real life; or is it because their time is taken

Table 4.2—Mean Aggression Scores According to Violence Rating of TV Programs Watched

Informant	*1*	*2*	*3*	*4*
Mother	14.44	14.97	18.32	28.54
Father	12.44	14.23	18.92	20.67

up in watching TV and they have less opportunity to act out aggression? On the other hand, boys who watch more violence on TV are more likely to be aggressive than boys who watch less violence. Is this because aggressive boys prefer violent programs; or is aggressive drive increased by such viewing; or are the subjects modeling their behavior after that of the characters on the TV programs? This survey study of real-life behavior cannot furnish definitive answers as to cause and effect relationships by itself. It can only demonstrate that a relationship exists. However, buttressed by manipulative laboratory studies, such as that of Bandura et al. (1963), we can speculate with some confidence that TV viewing does affect real-life behavior, and that the modeling variable is a crucial one. The drainage hypothesis, as an explanation for the lowered aggression of children who watch TV for longer hours, is unlikely in light of the results of other manipulative studies which show a direct relationship between aggression expressed in fantasy and overt behavior (Buss, 1961).

2. This study contributes further evidence that mothers and fathers are not equally good observers in all areas of child behavior. A previous article demonstrated areas in which fathers gave us better information than mothers (Eron, Banta, Walder, & Lau-

Table 4.3—Mean Aggression Scores According to Number of Hours Watched

Informant	Hours		
	0–4	5–9	10+
Mother	24.26	16.48	15.25
Father	16.00	14.17	14.75

licht, 1961). However, for the present purposes, it seems, fathers do not have as good information as mothers. They very likely do not know about the child's daytime TV behavior and thus cannot give accurate details of total time watched. However, they are usually home in the evening hours and perhaps watch TV along with their children and thus are familiar at least with programs viewed then. Also their children are likely to talk to them about what they see on TV but not give them accurate reports of just how much time is spent in front of the TV. Mother, however, is on hand and can observe for herself; thus her estimates are more relevant. At any rate, when mother and father agree as to what they tell us about their children, we can be more certain we are approximating the truth, especially when the observations of each relate in the same way to an independent criterion.

3. A final observation is the difference in results obtained with boys and girls. This is another indication that it is impossible to generalize from boys to girls in research on socialization, especially as far as the variable of aggression is concerned. This was pointed out by Sears, Whiting, Nowlis, and Sears (1953) a decade ago and is not due merely to the fact that boys score higher on all kinds of measures of aggression than do girls which has been a monotonous finding for even more years (Levin & Wardwell, 1962).

SUMMARY

Information about TV habits, (a) length of time watched and (b) extent of violence in favorite programs, was obtained from 689 mothers and 522 fathers in individual interviews having to do with the psychosocial antecedents of aggressive behavior in their children. This information was related to ratings of aggressive behavior of 3rd-grade children made by their peers. It was found that there was a significant positive relationship between the violence ratings of favorite programs as reported by both mothers and fathers and aggressive behavior of boys as rated in school. Also there was a significant negative relation between total time watched by boys as reported by mothers and aggressive behavior. The results for fathers' reports in this latter case were in the same direction, although not significant. No consistent relationships were noted between girls' TV habits as reported by either mother or father and aggression as rated in school by the peers.

REFERENCES

AUBREY, J. T. Testimony before Federal Communications Commission. *N. Y. Times,* January 26, 1962.

BANDURA, A., ROSS, DOROTHEA, & ROSS, SHEILA A. Imitation of film-mediated aggressive models. *J. abnorm. soc. Psychol.,* 1963, *66,* 3–11.

BANTA, T. J., & WALDER, L. O. Discriminant validity of a peer-rating measure. *Psychol. Rep.,* 1961, *9,* 573–582.

BUSS, A. H. *The psychology of aggression.* New York: Wiley, 1961.

ERON, L. D., BANTA, T. J., WALDER, L. O., & LAULICHT, J. H. Comparison of data obtained from mothers and fathers on childrearing practices and their relation to child aggression. *Child Develpm.,* 1961, *32,* 457–472.

ERON, L. D., LAULICHT, J. H., WALDER, L. O., FARBER, I. E., & SPIEGEL, J. P. Application of role and learning theories to the study of the development of aggression in children. *Psychol. Rep.,* 1961, *9,* 291–334. (Monogr. Suppl. No. 2-V9)

HIMMELWEIT, HILDE T., OPPENHEIM, A. N., & VINCE, PAMELA. *Television and the child: An empirical study of the effect of television on the young.* New York: Oxford Univer. Press, 1958.

LEVIN, H., & WARDWELL, ELINOR. The research uses of doll play. *Psychol. Bull.,* 1962, *59,* 27–56.

LINDQUIST, E. F. *Design and analysis of experiments in psychology and education.* Boston: Houghton Mifflin, 1953.

SCHRAMM, W. A., LYLE, J., & PARKER, E. B. *Television in the lives of our children.* Stanford: Stanford Univer. Press, 1961.

SEARS, R. R., WHITING, J. W. M., NOWLIS, V., & SEARS, PAULINE S. Some child rearing antecedents of aggression and dependency in young children. *Genet. Psychol. Monogr.,* 1953, *47,* 135–234.

WALDER, L. O., ABELSON, R. P., ERON, L. D., BANTA, T. J., & LAULICHT, J. H. Development of a peer-rating measure of aggression. *Psychol. Rep.,* 1961, *9,* 497–556. (Monogr. Suppl. No. 4-V9)

IV

Communication and Persuasion

Attitude or opinion change as a result of attempted persuasion generally has been greater in the laboratory than in the field. Hovland (Chapter 5) offered explanations for the divergencies and suggested ways of using laboratory and field research in a complementary manner so as to provide sufficient information about the influence process.

A persuasive technique that has been used widely in our society is threat or fear arousal. Laboratory studies generally have tested the impact of fear appeals of different intensities on *reported* behavior. Evans, Rozelle, Lasater, Dembroski, and Allen (Chapter 6) used a laboratory-field design to explore the differential effect of various appeals (including fear appeals and a positive motivating appeal) on both *reported* and *actual* behavior. In this experiment, junior high school students were administered, under controlled conditions in the laboratory, persuasive appeals directed at improving toothbrushing behavior. The students carried out their dental hygiene programs in natural situations where the investigators had no control. Post communication measures were taken periodically in the laboratory. A unique behavioral measure, the "disclosing wafer" which reveals the amount of plaque on the teeth, indicated the effectiveness of the dental hygiene program for each subject. The authors concluded that although high fear was effective in changing *reported* behavior, the success of a positive motivating appeal in changing *actual* behavior raised questions concerning the necessity of using fear at all to affect the type of change sought in the present study.

Assuming that an influence process is successful in changing attitudes or opinions, what factors contribute to the persistency over time of the induced change? Newcomb (Chapter 7), in a follow-up of his now classic field study at Bennington College, found that after 25 years the former students who showed the greatest persistence in their liberal attitudes were those with social environments supportive to these attitudes. However, Cook and Insko (Chapter 8) suggested that this supportive environment identified in the field could comprise a number of variables such as reexposure to the conclusion of the original influence appeal (conclusion reexposure), exposure to supportive arguments, and support from like-minded individuals. They designed a laboratory-field experiment to demonstrate the importance of one of these variables, conclusion reexposure, in facilitating the persistence of attitude change. Subjects exposed to a communication in the laboratory were sent postcards advising them of the time and place for the second laboratory session. The reminders also mentioned the communication topic for approximately half of the subjects. The researchers had no control over the extent to which the reexposure subjects consulted the postcards. Conclusion reexposure was shown to yield a greater persistence effect when compared with no reexposure. It is now necessary to determine the significance of conclusion reexposure in relation to the other variables which comprise social environments supportive to attitude change persistence.

5

Reconciling Conflicting Results Derived From Experimental and Survey Studies of Attitude Change

Carl I. Hovland

Two quite different types of research design are characteristically used to study the modification of attitudes through communication. In the first type, the *experiment,* individuals are given a controlled exposure to a communication and the effects evaluated in terms of the amount of change in attitude or opinion produced. A base line is provided by means of a control group not exposed to the communication. The study of Gosnell (1927) on the influence of leaflets designed to get voters to the polls is a classic example of the controlled experiment.

In the alternative research design, the *sample survey,* information is secured through interviews or questionnaires both concerning the respondent's exposure to various communications and his attitudes and opinions on various issues. Generalizations are then derived from the correlations obtained between reports of exposure and measurements of attitude. In a variant of this method, measurements of attitude and of exposure to communication are obtained during repeated interviews with the same individual over a period of weeks or months. This is the "panel method" extensively utilized in studying the impact of various mass media on political attitudes and on voting behavior (cf., e.g., Kendall & Lazarsfeld, 1950).

Generalizations derived from experimental and from correlational studies of communication effects are usually both reported in chapters on the effects of mass media and in other summaries of research on attitude, typically without much stress on the type of study from which the conclusion was derived. Close scrutiny of the results obtained from the two methods, however, suggests a marked difference in the picture of communication effects obtained from each. The object of my paper is to consider the conclusions derived from these two types of design, to suggest some of the factors responsible for the frequent divergence in results, and then to formulate principles aimed at reconciling some of the apparent conflicts.

DIVERGENCE

The picture of mass communication effects which emerges from correlational studies is one in which few individuals are seen as being affected by communications. One of the most thorough correlational studies of the effects of mass media on attitudes is that of Lazarsfeld, Berelson, and Gaudet published in *The People's Choice* (1944). In this report there is an extensive chapter devoted to the effects of various media, particularly radio, newspapers, and magazines. The authors conclude that few changes in attitudes were produced. They estimate that the political positions of only about 5% of their respondents were changed by the election campaign, and they are inclined to attribute even this small amount of change more to personal influence than to the mass media. A similar evaluation of mass media is made in the recent chapter in the *Handbook of Social Psychology* by Lipset and his collaborators (1954).

Research using experimental procedures, on the other hand, indicates the possibility of considerable modifiability of attitudes through exposure to communication. In both Klapper's survey (1949) and in my chapter in the *Handbook of Social Psychology* (Hovland, 1954) a number of experimental studies are discussed in which the opinions of a third to a half or more of the audience are changed.

The discrepancy between the results derived from these two methodologies raises some fascinating problems for analysis. This divergence in outcome appears to me to be largely attributable to two kinds of factors: one, the difference in research design itself; and, two, the historical and traditional differences in general approach to evaluation characteristic of researchers using the experimental as contrasted with the correlational or survey method. I would like to discuss, first, the influence these factors have on the estimation of overall effects of communications and, then, turn to other divergences in outcome characteristically found by the use of the experimental and survey methodology.

Undoubtedly the most critical and interesting variation in the research *design* involved in the two procedures is that resulting from differences in definition of exposure. In an experiment the audience on whom the effects are being evaluated is one which is fully exposed to the communication. On the other hand, in naturalistic situations with which surveys are typically concerned, the outstanding phenomenon is the limitation of the audience to those who *expose themselves* to the communication. Some of the individuals in a captive audience experiment would, of course, expose themselves in the course of natural events to a communication of the type studied; but many others would not. The group which does expose itself is usually a highly biased one, since most individuals "expose themselves most of the time to the kind of material with which they agree to begin with" (Lipset et al., 1954, p. 1158). Thus one reason for the difference in results between experiments and correlational studies is that experiments describe the effects of exposure on the whole range of individuals studied, some of whom are initially in favor of the the position being advocated and some who are opposed, whereas surveys primarily describe the effects produced on those already in favor of the point of view advocated in the communication. The amount of change is thus, of course, much smaller in surveys. Lipset and his collaborators make this same evaluation, stating that:

> As long as we test a program in the laboratory we always find that it has great effect on the attitudes and interests of the experimental subjects. But when we put the program on as a regular broadcast, we then note that the people who are most influenced in the laboratory

tests are those who, in a realistic situation, do not listen to the program. The controlled experiment always greatly overrates effects, as compared with those that really occur, because of the self-selection of audiences (Lipset et al., 1954, p. 1158).

Differences in the second category are not inherent in the design of the two alternatives, but are characteristic of the way researchers using the two methods typically proceed.

The first difference within this class is in the size of the communication unit typically studied. In the majority of survey studies the unit evaluated is an entire program of communication. For example, in studies of political behavior an attempt is made to assess the effects of all newspaper reading and television viewing on attitudes toward the major parties. In the typical experiment, on the other hand, the interest is usually in some particular variation in the content of the communications, and experimental evaluations much more frequently involve single communications. On this point results are thus not directly comparable.

Another characteristic difference between the two methods is in the time interval used in evaluation. In the typical experiment the time at which the effect is observed is usually rather soon after exposure to the communication. In the survey study, on the other hand, the time perspective is such that much more remote effects are usually evaluated. When effects decline with the passage of time, the net outcome will, of course, be that of accentuating the effect obtained in experimental studies as compared with those obtained in survey researches. Again it must be stressed that the difference is not inherent in the designs as such. Several experiments, including our own on the effects of motion pictures (Hovland, Lumsdaine, & Sheffield, 1949) and later studies on the "sleeper effect" (Hovland & Weiss, 1951; Kelman & Hovland, 1953), have studied retention over considerable periods of time.

Some of the difference in outcome may be attributable to the types of communicators characteristically used and to the motive-incentive conditions operative in the two situations. In experimental studies communications are frequently presented in a classroom situation. This may involve quite different types of factors from those operative in the more naturalistic communication situation with which the survey researchers are concerned. In the classroom there may be some implicit sponsorship of the communication by the teacher and the school administration. In the survey studies the communicators may often be remote individuals either unfamiliar to the recipients, or outgroupers clearly known to espouse a point of view opposed to that held by many members of the audience. Thus there may be real differences in communicator credibility in laboratory and survey researches. The net effect of the differences will typically be in the direction of increasing the likelihood of change in the experimental as compared with the survey study.

There is sometimes an additional situational difference. Communications of the type studied by survey researchers usually involve reaching the individual in his natural habitat, with consequent supplementary effects produced by discussion with friends and family. In the laboratory studies a classroom situation with low postcommunication interaction is more typically involved. Several studies, including one by Harold Kelley reported in our volume on *Communication and Persuasion* (Hovland, Janis, & Kelley, 1953), indicate that, when a communication is presented in a situation which makes group membership salient, the individual is typically more resistant to counternorm influence than when the communication is presented under conditions of low salience of group membership (cf. also, Katz & Lazarsfeld, 1955, pp. 48-133).

A difference which is almost wholly adventitious is in the types of populations utilized. In the survey design there is, typically, considerable emphasis on a random sample of the entire population. In the typical experiment, on the other hand, there is a consistent overrepresentation of high school students and college sophomores, primarily on the basis of their greater accessibility. But as Tolman has said: "college sophomores may not be people." Whether differences in the type of audience studied contribute to the differences in effect obtained with the two methods is not known.

Finally, there is an extremely important difference in the studies of the experimental and correlational variety with respect to the type of issue discussed in the communications. In the typical experiment we are interested in studying a set of factors or conditions which are expected on the basis of theory to influence the extent of effect of the communication. We usually deliberately try to find types of issues involving attitudes which are susceptible to modification through communication. Otherwise, we run the risk of no measurable effects, particularly with small-scale experiments. In the survey procedures, on the other hand, socially significant attitudes which are deeply rooted in prior experience and involve much personal commitment are typically involved. This is especially true in voting studies which have provided us with so many of our present results on social influence. I shall have considerably more to say about this problem a little later.

The differences so far discussed have primarily concerned the extent of overall effectiveness indicated by the two methods: why survey results typically show little modification of attitudes by communication while experiments indicate marked changes. Let me now turn to some of the other differences in generalizations derived from the two alternative designs. Let me take as the second main area of disparate results the research on the effect of varying distances between the position taken by the communicator and that held by the recipient of the communication. Here it is a matter of comparing changes for persons who at the outset closely agree with the communicator with those for others who are mildly or strongly in disagreement with him. In the naturalistic situation studied in surveys the typical procedure is to determine changes in opinion following reported exposure to communication for individuals differing from the communicator by varying amounts. This gives rise to two possible artifacts. When the communication is at one end of a continuum, there is little room for improvement for those who differ from the communication by small amounts, but a great deal of room for movement among those with large discrepancies. This gives rise to a spurious degree of positive relationship between the degree of discrepancy and the amount of change. Regression effects will also operate in the direction of increasing the correlation. What is needed is a situation in which the the distance factor can be manipulated independently of the subject's initial position. An attempt to set up these conditions experimentally was made in a study by Pritzker and the writer (1957). The method involved preparing individual communications presented in booklet form so that the position of the com-

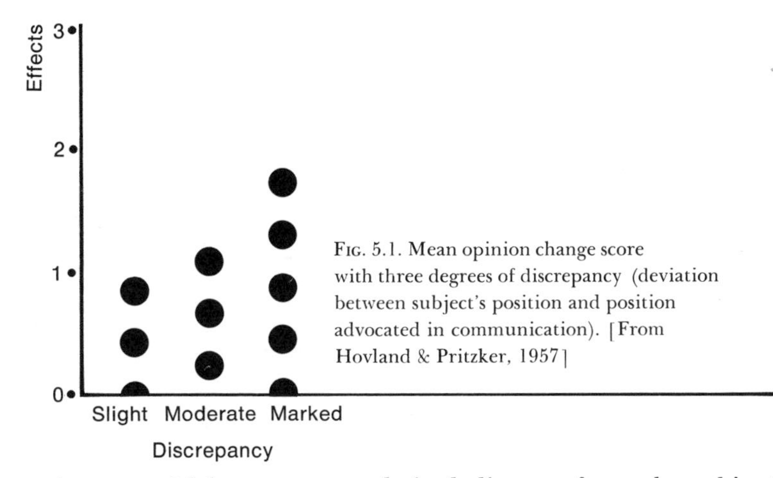

FIG. 5.1. Mean opinion change score with three degrees of discrepancy (deviation between subject's position and position advocated in communication). [From Hovland & Pritzker, 1957]

municator could be set at any desired distance from the subject's initial position. Communicators highly acceptable to the subjects were used. A number of different topics were employed, including the likelihood of a cure for cancer within five years, the desirability of compulsory voting, and the adequacy of five hours of sleep per night.

The amount of change for each degree of advocated change is shown in Fig. 5.1. It will be seen that there is a fairly clear progression, such that the greater the amount of change advocated the greater the average amount of opinion change produced. Similar results have been reported by Goldberg (1954) and by French (1956).

But these results are not in line with our hunches as to what would happen in a naturalistic situation with important social issues. We felt that here other types of response than change in attitude would occur. So Muzafer Sherif, O. J. Harvey, and the writer (1957) set up a situation to simulate as closely as possible the conditions typically involved when individuals are exposed to major social issue communications at differing distances from their own position. The issue used was the desirability of prohibition. The study was done in two states (Oklahoma and Texas) where there is prohibition or local option, so that the wet-dry issues is hotly debated. We concentrated on three aspects of the problem: How favorably

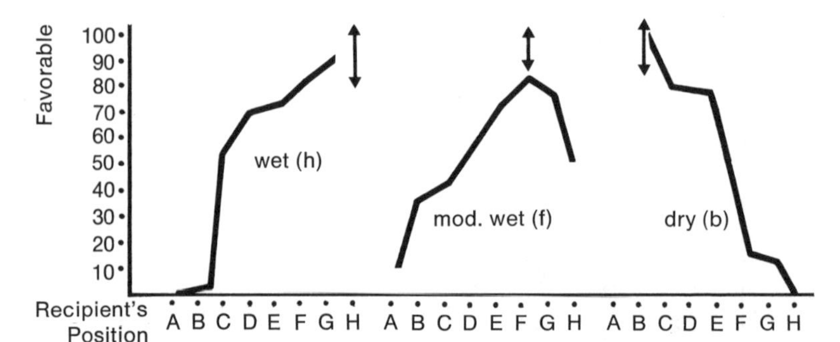

FIG. 5.2. Percentage of favorable evaluations ("fair," "unbiased," etc.) of wet (*H*), moderately wet (*F*), and dry (*B*) communications for subjects holding various positions on prohibition. Recipients position range from *A* (very dry) to *H* (very wet). Position of communications indicated by arrow. [From Hovland, Harvey, & Sherif, 1957]

will the communicator be received when his position is at varying distances from that of the recipient? How will what the communicator says be perceived and interpreted by individuals at varying distances from his position? What will be the amount of opinion change produced when small and large deviations in position of communication and recipient are involved?

Three communications, one strongly wet, one strongly dry, and one moderately wet, were employed. The results bearing on the first problem, of *reception,* are presented in Fig. 5.2. The positions of the subjects are indicated on the abscissa in letters from A (extreme dry) to H (strongly wet). The positions of the communication are also indicated in the same letters, *B* indicating a strongly dry communication, *H* a strongly wet, and *F* a moderately wet. Along the ordinate there is plotted the percentage of subjects with each position on the issue who described the communication as "fair" and "unbiased." It will be seen that the degree of distance between the recipient and the communicator greatly influences the evaluation of the fairness of the communication. When a communication is directed at the pro-dry position, nearly all of the dry subjects consider it fair and impartial, but only a few per cent of the wet subjects consider the identical communication fair. The reverse is true at the other end of the scale. When an intermediate position is adopted, the percentages fall off sharply on each side. Thus under the present conditions with a relatively ambiguous communicator one of the ways of dealing with strongly discrepant positions is to *discredit* the communicator, considering him unfair and biased.

A second way in which an individual can deal with discrepancy is by distortion of what is said by the communicator. This is a phenomenon extensively studied by Cooper and Jahoda (1947). In the present study, subjects were asked to state what position they thought was taken by the communicator on the prohibition question. Their evaluation of his position could then be analyzed in relation to their own position. These results are shown in Fig. 5.3 for the moderately wet communication. It will be observed that there is a tendency for individuals whose position is close to that of the communicator to report on the communicator's position quite accurately, for individuals a little bit removed to report his position to be substantially more like their own (which we call an "assimilation effect"), and for those with more discrepant positions to report the communicator's position as more extreme than it really was. This we refer to as a "contrast effect."

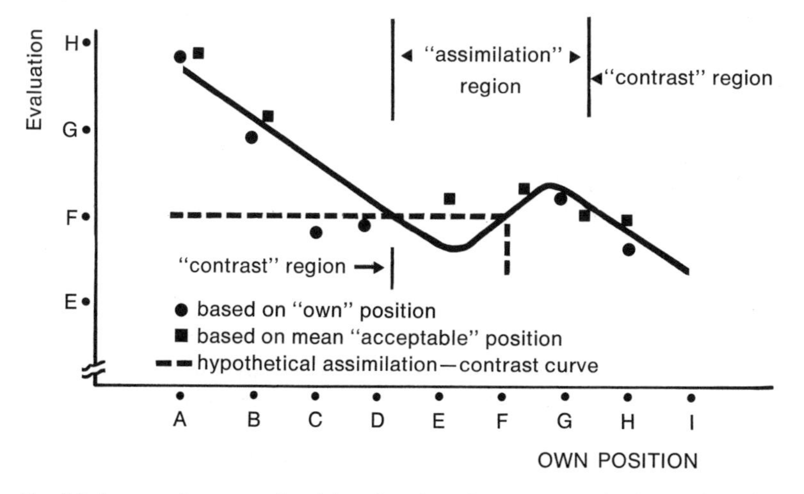

FIG. 5.3. Average placement of position of moderately wet communication (*F*) by subjects holding various positions on the issue, plotted against hypothetical assimilation-contrast curve. [From Hovland, Harvey, & Sherif, 1957]

Now to our primary results on opinion change. It was found that individuals whose position was only slightly discrepant from the communicator's were influenced to a greater extent than those whose positions deviated to a larger extent. When a wet position was espoused, 28% of the middle-of-the-road subjects were changed in the direction of the communicator, as compared with only 4% of the drys. With the dry communication 14% of the middle-of-the-roaders were changed, while only 4% of the wets were changed. Thus, more of the subjects with small discrepancies were changed than were those with large discrepancies.

These results appear to indicate that, under conditions when there is some ambiguity about the credibility of the communicator and when the subject is deeply involved with the issue, the greater attempt at change the higher the resistance. On the other hand, with highly respected communicators, as in the previous study with Pritzker using issues of lower involvement, the greater the discrepancy the greater the effect. A study related to ours has just been completed by Zimbardo (1959) which indicates that, when an influence attempt is made by a strongly positive communicator (i.e., a close personal friend), the greater the discrepancy the greater the opinion change, even when the experimenter made a point of stressing the great importance of the subject's opinion.

The implication of these results for our primary problem of conflicting results is clear. The types of issues with which most experiments deal are relatively uninvolving and are often of the variety where expert opinion is highly relevant, as for example, on topics of health, science, and the like. Here we should expect that opinion would be considerably affected by communications and furthermore that advocacy of positions quite discrepant from the individual's own position would have a marked effect. On the other hand, the types of issues most often utilized in survey studies are ones which are very basic and involve deep commitment. As a consequence small changes in opinion due to communication would be expected. Here communication may have little effect on those who disagree at the outset and function merely to strengthen the position already held, in line with survey findings.

A third area of research in which somewhat discrepant results are obtained by the experimental and survey methods is in the role of order of presentation. From naturalistic studies the generalization has been widely adopted that primacy is an extremely important factor in persuasion. Numerous writers have reported that what we experience first has a critical role in what we believe. This is particularly stressed in studies of propaganda effects in various countries when the nation getting across its message first is alleged to have a great advantage and in commercial advertising where "getting a beat on the field" is stressed. The importance of primacy in political propaganda is indicated in the following quotation from Doob:

> The propagandist scores an initial advantage whenever his propaganda reaches people before that of his rivals. Readers or listeners are then biased to comprehend, forever after, the event as it has been initially portrayed to them. If they are told in a headline or a flash that the battle has been won, the criminal has been caught, or the bill is certain to pass the legislature, they will usually expect subsequent information to substantiate this first impression. When later facts prove otherwise, they may be loath to abandon what they believe to be true until perhaps the evidence becomes overwhelming (Doob, 1948, pp. 421–422).

A recent study by Katz and Lazarsfeld (1955) utilizing the survey method compares the extent to which respondents attribute major impact on their decisions about fashions and movie attendance to the presentations to which they were first exposed. Strong primacy effects are shown in their analyses of the data.

We have ourselves recently completed a series of experiments oriented toward this problem. These are reported in our new monograph on *Order of Presentation in Persuasion* (Hovland, Mandell, Campbell, Brock, Luchins, Cohen, McGuire, Janis, Feierabend, & Anderson, 1957). We find that primacy is often *not* a very significant factor when the relative effectiveness of the first side of an issue is compared experimentally with that of the second. The research suggests that differences in design may account for much of the discrepancy. A key variable is whether there is exposure to both sides or whether only one side is actually received. In naturalistic studies the advantage of the first side is often not only that it is first but that it is often then the only side of the issue to which the individual is exposed. Having once been influenced, many individuals make up their mind and are no longer interested in other communications on the issue. In most experiments on order of presentation, on the other hand, the audience is systematically exposed to both sides. Thus under survey conditions, self-exposure tends to increase the impact of primacy.

Two other factors to which I have already alluded appear significant in determining the amount of primacy effect. One is the nature of the communicator, the other the setting in which the communication is received. In our volume Luchins presents results indicating that, when the same communicator presents contradictory material, the point of view read first has more influence. On the other hand, Mandell and I show that, when two different communicators present opposing views successively, little primacy effect is obtained. The communications setting factor operates similarly. When the issue and the conditions of presentation make clear that the points of view are controversial, little primacy is obtained.

Thus in many of the situations with which there had been great concern as to undesirable effects of primacy, such as in legal trials, election campaigns, and political debate, the role of primacy appears to have been exaggerated, since the conditions there are those least conducive to primacy effects: the issue is clearly defined as controversial, the partisanship of the communicator is usually established, and different communicators present the opposing sides.

Time does not permit me to discuss other divergencies in results obtained in survey and experimental studies, such as those concerned with the effects of repetition of presentation, the relationship between level of intelligence and susceptibility to attitude change, or the relative impact of mass media and personal influence. Again, however, I am sure that detailed analysis will reveal differential factors at work which can account for the apparent disparity in the generalizations derived.

INTEGRATION

On the basis of the foregoing survey of results I reach the conclusion that no contradiction has been established between the data provided by experimental and correlational studies. Instead it appears that the seeming divergence can be satisfactorily accounted for on the basis of a different definition of the communication situation (including the phenomenon of self-selection) and differences in the type of communicator, audience, and kind of issue utilized.

But there remains the task of better integrating the findings associated with the two methodologies. This is a problem closely akin to that considered by the members of the recent Social Science Research Council summer seminar on *Narrowing the Gap Between Field Studies and Laboratory Studies in Social Psychology* (Riecken, 1954). Many of their recommendations are pertinent to our present problem.

What seems to me quite apparent is that a genuine understanding of the effects of communications on attitudes requires both the survey and the experimental methodologies. At the same time there appear to be certain inherent limitations of each method which must be understood by the researcher if he is not to be blinded by his preoccupation with one or the other type of design. Integration of the two methodologies will require on the part of the experimentalist an awareness of the narrowness of the laboratory in interpreting the larger and more comprehensive effects of communication. It will require on the part of the survey researcher a greater awareness of the limitations of the correlational method as a basis for establishing causal relationships.

The framework within which survey research operates is most adequately and explicitly dealt with by Berelson, Lazarsfeld, and McPhee in their book on *Voting* (1954). The model which they use, taken over by them from the economist Tinbergen, is reproduced in the top half of Fig. 5.4. For comparison, the model used by experimentalists is presented in the lower half of the figure. It will be seen that the model used by the survey researcher, particularly when he employs the "panel" method, stresses the large number of simultaneous and interacting influences affecting attitudes and opinions. Even more significant is its provision for a variety of "feedback" phenomena in which consequences wrought by previous influences affect processes normally considered as occurring earlier in the sequence. The various types of interaction are indicated by the placement of arrows showing direction of effect. In

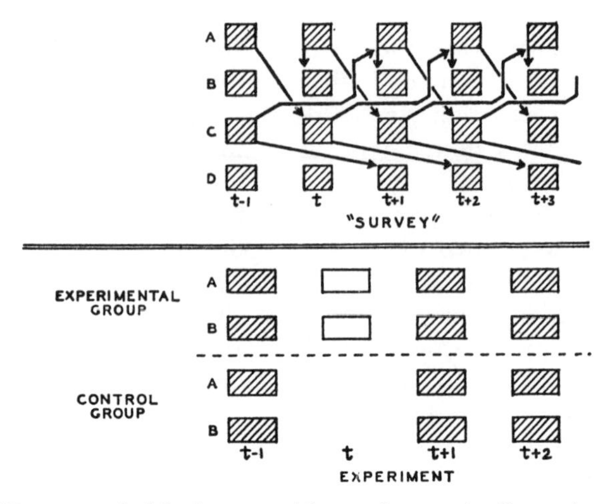

FIG. 5.4. TOP HALF: "Process analysis" schema used in panel research. (Successive time intervals are indicated along abscissa. Letters indicate the variables under observation. Arrows represent relations between the variables.) [From Berelson, Lazarsfeld, & McPhee, 1954] BOTTOM HALF: Design of experimental research. (Letters on vertical axis again indicate variables being measured. Unshaded box indicates experimentally manipulated treatment and blank absence of such treatment. Time periods indicated as in top half of chart.)

contrast the experimentalist frequently tends to view the communication process as one in which some single manipulative variable is the primary determinant of the subsequent attitude change. He is, of course, aware in a general way of the importance of context, and he frequently studies interaction effects as well as main effects; but he still is less attentive than he might be to the complexity of the influence situation and the numerous possibilities for feedback loops. Undoubtedly the real life communication situation is better described in terms of the survey type of model. We are all familiar, for example, with the interactions in which attitudes predispose one to acquire certain types of information, that this often leads to changes in attitude which may result in further acquisition of knowledge, which in turn produces more attitude change, and so on. Certainly the narrow question sometimes posed by experiments as to the effect of knowledge on attitudes greatly underestimates these interactive effects.

But while the conceptualization of the survey researcher is often very valuable, his correlational research design leaves much to be desired. Advocates of correlational analysis often cite the example of a science built on observation exclusively without experiment: astronomy. But here a very limited number of space-time concepts are involved and the number of competing theoretical formulations is relatively small so that it is possible to limit alternative theories rather drastically through correlational evidence. But in the area of communication effects and social psychology generally the variables are so numerous and so intertwined that the correlational methodology is primarily useful to suggest hypotheses and not to establish causal relationships (Hovland et al., 1949, pp. 329–340; Maccoby, 1956). Even with the much simpler relationships involved in biological systems there are grave difficulties of which we are all aware these days when we realize how difficult it is to establish through correlation whether eating of fats is or is not a cause of heart disease or whether or not smoking is a cause of lung cancer. In communications research the complexity of the problem makes it inherently difficult to derive causal relationships from correlational analysis where experimental control of exposure is not possible. And I do not agree with my friends the Lazarsfelds (Kendall & Lazarsfeld, 1950) concerning the effectiveness of the panel method in circumventing this problem since parallel difficulties are raised when the relationships occur over a time span.

These difficulties constitute a challenge to the experimentalist in this area of research to utilize the broad framework for studying communication effects suggested by the survey researcher, but to employ well controlled experimental design to work on those aspects of the field which are amenable to experimental manipulation and control. It is, of course, apparent that there are important communication problems which cannot be attacked directly by experimental methods. It is not, for example, feasible to modify voting behavior by manipulation of the issues discussed by the opposed parties during a particular campaign. It is not feasible to assess the effects of communications over a very long span of time. For example, one cannot visualize experimental procedures for answering the question of what has been the impact of the reading of *Das Kapital* or *Uncle Tom's Cabin.* These are questions which can be illuminated by historical and sociological study but cannot be evaluated in any rigorous experimental fashion.

But the scope of problems which do lend themselves to experimental attack is very broad. Even complex interactions can be fruitfully attacked by experiment. The possibilities are clearly shown in studies like that of Sherif and Sherif (1953) on factors influencing cooperative and competitive behavior in a camp for adolescent boys. They were able to bring under manipulative control many of the types of interpersonal relationships ordinarily considered impossible to modify experimentally, and to develop motivations of an intensity characteristic of real-life situations. It should be possible to do similar studies in the communication area with a number of the variables heretofore only investigated in uncontrolled naturalistic settings by survey procedures.

In any case it appears eminently practical to minimize many of the differences which were discussed above as being not inherent in design but more or less adventitiously linked with one or the other method. Thus there is no reason why more complex and deeply-involving social issues cannot be employed in experiments rather than the more superficial ones more commonly used. The resistance to change of socially important issues may be a handicap in studying certain types of attitude change; but, on the other hand, it is important to understand the lack of modifiability of opinion with highly-involving issues. Greater representation of the diverse types of communicators found in naturalistic situations can also be achieved. In addition, it should be possible to do experiments with a wider range of populations to reduce the possibility that many of our present generalizations from experiments are unduly affected by their heavy weighting of college student characteristics, including high literacy, alertness, and rationality.

A more difficult task is that of experimentally evaluating communications under conditions of self-selection of exposure. But this is not at all impossible in theory. It should be possible to assess what demographic and personality factors predispose one to expose oneself to particular communications and then to utilize experimental and control groups having these characteristics. Under some circumstances the evaluation could be made on only those who select themselves, with both experimental and control groups coming from the self-selected audience.

Undoubtedly many of the types of experiments which could be set up involving or simulating naturalistic conditions will be too ambitious and costly to be feasible even if possible in principle. This suggests the continued use of small-scale experiments which seek to isolate some of the key variables operative in complex situations. From synthesis of component factors, prediction of complex outcomes may be practicable. It is to this analytic procedure for narrowing the gap between laboratory and field research that we have devoted major attention in our research program. I will merely indicate briefly here some of the ties between our past work and the present problem.

We have attempted to assess the influence of the communicator by varying his expertness and attractiveness, as in the studies by Kelman, Weiss, and the writer (Hovland & Weiss, 1951; Kelman & Hovland, 1953). Further data on this topic were presented earlier in this paper.

We have also been concerned with evaluating social interaction effects. Some of the experiments on group affiliation as a factor affecting resistance to counternorm communication and the role of salience of group membership by Hal Kelley and others are reported in *Communication and Persuasion* (Hovland et al., 1953).

Starting with the studies carried out during the war on orientation films by Art Lumsdaine, Fred Sheffield, and the writer (1949), we have had a strong interest in the duration of communication effects. Investigation of effects at various time intervals has helped to bridge the gap between assessment of immediate changes with those of longer duration like those involved in survey studies. More recent extensions of this work have indicated the close relationship between the credibility of the communicator and the extent of postcommunication increments, or "sleeper effects" (Hovland & Weiss, 1951; Kelman & Hovland, 1953).

The nature of individual differences in susceptibility to persuasion via communication has been the subject of a number of our recent studies. The generality of persuasibility has been investigated by Janis and collaborators and the development of persuasibility in children has been studied by Abelson and Lesser. A volume concerned with these audience factors to which Janis, Abelson, Lesser, Field, Rife, King, Cohen, Linton, Graham, and the writer have contributed will appear under the title *Personality and Persuasibility* (1959).

Lastly, there remains the question on how the nature of the issues used in the communication affects the extent of change in attitude. We have only made a small beginning on these problems.

In the research reported in *Experiments on Mass Communication,* we showed that the magnitude of effects was directly related to the type of attitude involved: film communications had a significant effect on opinions related to straight-forward interpretations of policies and events, but had little or no effect on more deeply intrenched attitudes and motivations. Further work on the nature of issues is represented in the study by Sherif, Harvey, and the writer (1957) which was discussed above. There we found a marked contrast between susceptibility to influence and the amount of ego-involvement in the issue. But the whole concept of ego-involvement is a fuzzy one, and here is an excellent area for further work seeking to determine the theoretical factors involved in different types of issues.

With this brief survey of possible ways to bridge the gap between experiment and survey I must close. I should like to stress in summary the mutual importance of the two approaches to the problem of communication effectiveness. Neither is a royal road to wisdom, but each represents an important emphasis. The challenge of future work is one of fruitfully combining their virtues so that we may develop a social psychology of communication with the conceptual breadth provided by correlational study of process and with the rigorous but more delimited methodology of the experiment.

REFERENCES

BERELSON, B. R., LAZARSFELD, P. F., & MCPHEE, W. N. *Voting: A study of opinion formation in a presidential campaign.* Chicago: Univer. Chicago Press, 1954.

COOPER, EUNICE, & JAHODA, MARIE. The evasion of propaganda: How prejudiced people respond to anti-prejudice propaganda. *J. Psychol.,* 1947, *23,* 15–25.

DOOB, L. W. *Public opinion and propaganda.* New York: Holt, 1948.

FRENCH, J. R. P., JR. A formal theory of social power. *Psychol. Rev.,* 1956, *63,* 181–194.

GOLDBERG, S. C. Three situational determinants of conformity to social norms. *J. abnorm. soc. Psychol.,* 1954, *49,* 325–329.

GOSNELL, H. F. *Getting out the vote: An experiment in the stimulation of voting.* Chicago: Univer. Chicago Press, 1927.

HOVLAND, C. I. Effects of the mass media of communication. In G. Lindzey (Ed.), *Handbook of social psychology.* Vol. II. *Special fields and applications.* Cambridge, Mass.: Addison-Wesley, 1954. Pp. 1062–1103.

HOVLAND, C. I., HARVEY, O. J., & SHERIF, M. Assimilation and contrast effects in reactions to communication and attitude change. *J. abnorm. soc. Psychol.,* 1957, *55,* 244–252.

HOVLAND, C. I., JANIS, I. L., & KELLEY, H. H. *Communication and persuasion.* New Haven: Yale Univer. Press, 1953.

HOVLAND, C. I., LUMSDAINE, A. A., & SHEFFIELD, F. D. *Experiments on mass communication.* Princeton: Princeton Univer. Press, 1949.

HOVLAND, C. I., MANDELL, W., CAMPBELL, ENID H., BROCK, T., LUCHINS, A. S., COHEN, A. R.. MCGUIRE, W. J., JANIS, I. L., FEIERABEND, ROSALIND L., & ANDERSON, N. H. *The order of presentation in persuasion.* New Haven: Yale Univer. Press, 1957.

HOVLAND, C. I., & PRITZKER, H. A. Extent of opinion change as a function of amount of change advocated. *J. abnorm. soc. Psychol.,* 1957, *54,* 257–261.

HOVLAND, C. I., & WEISS, W. The influence of source credibility on communication effectiveness. *Publ. opin. Quart.,* 1951, *15,* 635–650.

JANIS, I. L., HOVLAND, C. I., FIELD, P. B., LINTON, HARRIETT, GRAHAM, ELAINE, COHEN, A. R., RIFE, D., ABELSON, R. P., LESSER, G. S., & KING, B. T. *Personality and persuasibility.* New Haven: Yale Univer. Press, 1959.

KATZ, E., & LAZARSFELD, P. F. *Personal influence.* Glencoe, Ill.: Free Press, 1955.

KELMAN, H. C., & HOVLAND, C. I. "Reinstatement" of the communicator in delayed measurement of opinion change. *J. abnorm. soc. Psychol.,* 1953, *48,* 327–335.

KENDALL, PATRICIA L., & LAZARSFELD, P. F. Problems of survey analysis. In R. K. Merton & P. F. Lazarsfeld (Eds.), *Continuities in social research: Studies in the scope and method of "The American Soldier."* Glencoe, Ill.: Free Press, 1950. Pp. 133–196.

KLAPPER, J. T. *The effects of mass media.* New York: Columbia Univer. Bureau of Applied Social Research, 1949. (Mimeo.)

LAZARSFELD, P. F., BERELSON, B., & GAUDET, HAZEL. *The people's choice.* New York: Duell, Sloan, & Pearce, 1944.

LIPSET, S. M., LAZARSFELD, P. F., BARTON, A. H., & LINZ, J. The psychology of voting: An analysis of political behavior. In G. Lindzey (Ed.), *Handbook of social psychology.* Vol. II. *Special fields and applications.* Cambridge, Mass.: Addison-Wesley, 1954. Pp. 1124– 1175.

MACCOBY, ELEANOR E. Pitfalls in the analysis of panel data: A research note on some technical aspects of voting. *Amer. J. Sociol.,* 1956, *59,* 359–362.

RIECKEN, H. W. (Chairman) Narrowing the gap between field studies and laboratory experiments in social psychology: A statement by the summer seminar. *Items Soc. Sci. Res. Council*, 1954, *8*, 37–42.
SHERIF, M., & SHERIF, CAROLYN W. *Groups in harmony and tension: An integration of studies on intergroup relations.* New York: Harper, 1953.
ZIMBARDO, P. G. Involvement and communication discrepancy as determinants of opinion change. Unpublished doctoral dissertation, Yale University, 1959.

6

Fear Arousal, Persuasion, and Actual Versus Implied Behavioral Change:

New Perspective Utilizing A Real-Life Dental Hygiene Program

Richard I. Evans, Richard M. Rozelle, Thomas M. Lasater, Theodore M. Dembroski, and Bem P. Allen

From *Journal of Personality and Social Psychology*, 1970, *16*, 220–227.

This research was supported in the context of Psychology Research Training Grant 5 TI DE 138 from the National Institute of Dental Research under

The present report presents the results of an investigation designed to explore the differential impact of various patterns of appeals on retention, intention to behave, reported behavior, and, most significantly, on actual behavior. The focus on the effects of persuasive communications on actual behavior and the utilization of an innovative behavioral measure (Evans, Rozelle, Lasater, Dembroski, & Allen, 1968) in the present study is responsive in general to the growing need for research in social psychology which examined the effects of persuasion on actual behavior, as well as on attitudes, beliefs, and intended or reported behavior. More specifically, it attempts to utilize as a criterion a specific behavioral measure to further explore the effect of fear arousal in persuasion communications.

In his review of research in the fear arousal area during the past 15 years, Higbee (1969) pointed to inconsistencies in the findings. In spite of such contradictions in the literature, the present authors agree with Higbee and suggest further that there exists at least some evidence for the following generalizations: (*a*) Generally, high fear is more effective than low fear, or there is no difference between the two in changing intentions to behave, self-report of behavior, or actual behavior. (*b*) The effect is usually greatest immediately following the communication and dissipates with time. (*c*) The effects of fear-arousing communications are more clearly demonstrated through changes in reported intentions to behave, attitudes toward the topic of the appeal, or for self-reports of behavior than for changes in actual behavior. (*d*) At least some minimum level of affect arousal coupled with instructions

---

the direction of the first author. Thanks are expressed for the fine cooperation of the Aldine Independent School District, Houston, Texas, and in particular, Superintendent W. W. Thorne and Nurse Barbara Wallace. Special thanks are expressed to Dean Sumter S. Arnim of the University of Texas Graduate School of Biomedical Sciences for his advice from a dental perspective in the adapting of the disclosing tablet (which he developed clinically) to the special requirements of our investigation and contributing the supply of dental kits used in the study through his affiliation with the Proctor and Gamble Company. Thanks are expressed to psychology graduate student and NIDR trainee William Forbes for his able assistance in some additional statistical calculations and preparation of tables and to Mariam Thompson for her fine job in the preparation of the manuscript.

appears to be involved in most of the fear-arousal studies. *(e)* There have been few if any comparisons made between effectiveness of negative (fear) appeals and positive (optimistic) appeals. *(f)* There is a need in fear-arousal studies to not only examine the immediate effects of the communication, but to examine the relative long-term effects as well. *(g)* There may be an overriding need that aside from affect arousal, the instructions in such studies should be quite specific. *(h)* Learning and retention as well as anxiety may be crucial considerations in studies in the effectiveness of communications.

THE PRESENT STUDY

The present study was designed both to further clarify issues suggested in the above eight generalizations and to consider some yet unexplored considerations in the area of affect-arousing communications. It utilizes the pretest-treatment—posttest design found in virtually all the affect-arousing communication studies reported in the literature.

An innovative aspect of the present study is the inclusion of a novel behavioral measure of toothbrushing behavior, which was developed to fill the need for more adequate criteria of behavior in such studies.

Another aspect of the present study rarely found in previous studies is the utilization of three posttreatment periods: immediately following the presentation of the message, 5 days after the presentation, and 6 weeks after the presentation.

Still another aspect of the present study not often found in previous ones is the inclusion of a positive (optimistic) affect appeal. It is possible that fear-arousal appeals may not have the persuasive effectiveness of an appeal emphasizing positive consequences. Because positive consequences are often not visible, examining the effects of positive appeals are difficult in some health communications. However, because of its nature, the dental hygiene situation permits the inclusion of positive affect appeals.

Given a certain amount of motivation, subjects need also to know when and where to behave and have access to the necessary equipment needed to behave if persuasion is to be effective in line with the findings of Leventhal, Singer, and Jones (1965). It was in response to this consideration that the procedure was included of giving each subject a dental care kit, as well as the detailed recommendations for its use. In fact, one plausible explanation for the relative ineffectiveness of high fear as a persuasive condition found in the Janis and Feshbach (1953) study is the possibility that inadequate recommendations were provided with the high-fear message. For example, Janis and Feshbach (1953) reported the following quotes from subjects in the high-fear condition: "Leave out the slides that show the rottiness of the teeth and have more in about how to brush your teeth; I don't think you should have shown so many gory pictures without showing more to prevent it [p. 83]."

So the present investigation is an extension of the basic approach utilized in the earlier study (Evans et al., 1968), more systematically reexamining and extending several facets of the problem of fear-arousal persuasive communications, the background of which were reviewed by Janis (1967) and Higbee (1969). To more completely measure our knowledge of the impact of persuasive communications, measures of information retained and anxiety were also included.

On the basis of the rationale thus presented and generalizations in terms indigenous to the interaction of the independent and dependent variables in the present investigation, the following hypotheses were formulated: *(a)* The high-fear appeal generates a higher degree of anxiety than a low-fear appeal; the least amount of anxiety is generated by the positive appeal. *(b)* No significant differences are obtained in information retention among any of the conditions. *(c)* The high-fear, low-fear, and positive appeals generate a significantly greater intention to behave, in accordance with the recommendations, than the recommendations only and the elaborated recommendations. *(d)* The high-fear, low-fear, and positive appeals generate a significantly greater report of behavior in accordance with the recommendations than the recommendations only and the elaborated recommendations. *(e)* The high-fear, low-fear, and positive appeals generate a significantly greater behavior change in accordance with the recommendations than the recommendations only and the elaborated recommendations.

The present investigation thus explores the relative impact on the anxiety level, information retained, and on intended, reported, and actual toothbrushing behavior (as measured by the "disclosing wafer" technique) of persuasive communications involving high fear arousal low fear arousal, a positive affect message, elaborated dental hygiene instructions presented without affect, and simple dental hygiene instructions presented without affect.

METHOD

The present investigation was conducted in the context of an ostensible program of dental hygiene training. The programs were part of the physical education curricula of the junior high schools in an independent school district near Houston, Texas, thus insuring a natural setting for the study.

Subjects

Students from the independent school district constituted the population from which the present sample was drawn. Subjects were 394 junior high school children from the population. The administration of a questionnaire which yielded demographic data covering the subject population at the various schools indicated that the subjects ranged from 12 to 15 years of age and that all subjects were homogeneous with respect to socioeconomic level, roughly lower middle-class. It was necessary to gain permission from subjects' parents for their participation. Therefore, only subjects who returned a permission slip that indicated parental acceptance were included in the sample. There appeared to be an approximate 70% return rate. However, upon further investigation, it was discovered that some of the teachers had misplaced return slips, so this 70% may be a susbstantial underestimate of the actual return rate.

One junior high school was randomly selected for the presentation of two fear communications. Another was randomly selected for the presentation of the positive communication and the elaborated recommendations communication. A third was randomly selected for presentation of the recommendations only and to provide a control group which received no communications. However, the group intended as a control was not considered in the analysis of the results because the class had been dismissed to attend a track meet on the occasion of the fourth subject contact. Classes selected for the various messages were counterbalanced with respect to time of day (morning verus afternoon).

Persuasive Appeals (Independent Variables)

Five varieties of persuasive appeals were used in all. Three of the persuasive appeals, high fear, low fear, and positive, were each followed by an identical set of specific recommendations. A fourth communication consisted only of a set of these specific recommendations. A fifth communication condition consisted of an elaboration of the specific recommendations utilized in the other four appeals.

The positive communication began with a non-specific reference to the good health and popularity obtainable by those who take proper care of their teeth. This section was followed by the chronicle of a boy and his sister. Events in the lives of these two persons were integrated with their dental history, and several slides of these persons were shown. It was emphasized that both had always taken proper care of their teeth and that both had always been popular and otherwise socially successful. A cause and effect relationship between proper dental care and popularity was thus suggested. The communication ended with the suggestion that anyone can be healthy and popular if he takes proper care of his teeth.

The specific recommendations which were included in all communication conditions (see the discussion of Leventhal & Singer, 1965) began with a suggestion that procedures for the proper care of the teeth do exist and can, in fact, be stated. This suggestion was followed by the presentation of a step-by-step procedure concerning how to care for the teeth. This consisted of four specific recommended steps:

1. Brush your teeth with toothpaste in your usual way, but as thoroughly as you can and remember to brush the back of your teeth. Try to brush all of your teeth and be sure to clean in be-

tween your teeth. After brushing them as clean as you can, rinse your mouth thoroughly with water.

2. Clean more thoroughly in between the teeth. The dental floss is used to help clean the places a toothbrush misses. This is easy to do. Cut off a piece of dental floss about a foot or so long. Wrap the floss around your index finger and grab the loose end with your other hand, so about an inch of floss is left between your hands. Slip the floss between each pair of teeth by moving it gently back and forth. Then scrape the floss against both sides of the teeth until you feel they are clean.

3. Chew the disclosing wafer and swish it around your teeth to see if you have missed any places.

4. Spot brush the few remaining places away and remember these places you've missed the next time you're brushing your teeth.

The "dental care kit" (produced by Proctor and Gamble) was given to all subjects at the conclusion of each message. The kit contained some disclosing wafers, a toothbrush, some toothpaste, and a cylinder of dental floss. Each kit contained a precise set of printed instructions which consisted of a restatement of the step-by-step recommendations presented in the communications presented orally.

The remaining communication condition was included in the light of results reported by Leventhal et al. (1965) which suggest the importance of elaborating instructions. These elaborated recommendations were combined with the set of recommendations which were included in all other communications, but were more detailed in describing proper dental hygiene practices.

An actor was hired and trained to present the various communications. This individual was chosen because he looked mature and had the appearance of a professional person. The actor, although identified as only a member of the research team, was told to speak with authority and confidence.

Dependent Variables

The behavioral measure. Arnim (1963) developed a "disclosing wafer" which, when chewed, stains the plaque on the teeth red and thereby reveals the amount of this plaque. According to Arnim, this has proven to be a reliable indicator of dental hygiene behavior involving toothbrushing and use of dental floss. Using the disclosing wafer and a technique for photographing the teeth and gums, Evans et al. (1968) standardized a 5-point scale for rating plaque concentration which reflects such dental hygiene behavior. This scale was utilized to measure dental hygiene behavior in the present investigation. The ratings ranged from 1 (very clean) to 5 (very dirty).

Reported behavior. Reported behavior was measured by subjects' responses to a question eliciting information concerning the relative frequency of toothbrushing behavior. The alternatives were scored from 1 (never) to 5 (two times a day).

Anxiety. A gross measure of anxiety was used to determine the degree to which affect was aroused by the communications. Using four questions which requested subjects to report their own anxiety level, scores of 4 (high anxiety) to 20 (no anxiety) were recorded.

Intention to behave. Intention to behave was determined from subjects' responses to two questions eliciting estimates of intended frequency of engaging in dental hygiene behavior. Scores ranged from 2 (lowest intention to behave) to 10 (greatest intention to behave).

Information retained. The measure of information retained by the subject was composed of five multiple-choice questions covering only the content of the specific recommendations which were present in all communication conditions. Scores ranged from 4 (lowest retention) to 16 (highest retention).

Also administered in the present investigation were various attitudinal and personality measures including the Locus of Control scale (Rotter, 1966), Dogmatism scale (Rokeach, 1960), the Social Approval Scale (Crowne & Marlowe, 1964), and a measure of attitudes indirectly related to the dependent variables. Results of this aspect of the study and related theoretical and methodological considerations involving instruments with the exception of the Social Approval Scale have been reported elsewhere (Allen, 1969; Dembroski, 1969; Lasater, 1969). Complete results of the findings concerning the Social Approval Scale will be reported elsewhere.

Procedure

The experimental portion of the present investigation consisted of five subject contacts. Each subject contact involved a visit by three experimenters and their assistants to three junior high schools.

First subject contact. The first subject contact took place 6 weeks after the permission slips were distributed to potential subjects to avoid the possibility of subject reactivity to the permission slips.

The experimenters introduced themselves and their assistants. One of the experimenters told the subjects that they were to take part in a dental health program as part of their physical education class requirements. Following this brief introduction, the subjects were told how to complete the questionnaire booklets. Assurances of anonymity were given to the subjects.

After the questionnaire booklets had been administered, the procedure for utilizing the dental wafer and photographing subjects' gums and teeth was implemented.

Second subject contact. The second subject contact took place 1 week after the first and involved the administration of the personality and attitudinal measures.

Third subject contact. The third subject contact occurred 1 week after the second, and the persuasive communications were presented. The anxiety, intention to behave, reported behavior, and retention measures were administered. Since only three schools were made available for the present investigation and five experimental groups were to be formed, a system for combining conditions within schools was developed.

Fourth subject contact. The fourth subject contact occurred 5 days after the third. The procedures were repeated involving the behavior measure, and measures of reported behavior, intention to behave, anxiety, and retention were once again administered.

Fifth subject contact. The fifth subject contact occurred approximately 6 weeks after the presentation of the communications (third subject contact). The same measures which were obtained during the fourth subject contact were again administered.

RESULTS

While all conditions were homogeneous with reference to socioeconomic level, an erratic pattern of differences was obtained among conditions for the preexposure measures of reported behavior and actual behavior. As a result, difference scores [1] were used

[1] In developing an analysis for the present investigation, the writers were immediately confronted with the often-discussed problem of developing a plausible rationale for the use of difference scores when there are initial differences between the comparison conditions. It would seem that the decision whether or not to use difference scores is in the final analysis rather an arbitrary one. In this instance in a complex field setting where it was virtually impossible to insure preexperimental equivalence, the investigators concluded that since the effects of the independent variables were ultimately in terms of merely grossly effecting existing health habits, this use of change scores was at least reasonably justified. An alternative approach, the after-only design, of course, would have automatically assumed preexperimental equivalence which is not by definition taken for granted in the analysis utilizing change scores. In summary, because of the intrinsic nature of quasi-experimental studies such as this, it would appear to justify the use of pre-post test difference scores as at least one plausible solution to this difficult problem.

in the analysis of these measures for the purpose of assessing relative change among treatment conditions. Since there were no precommunication measures obtained for anxiety, retention of information, and intention to behave, means for each of these were obtained on each of the three postcommunication measurement occasions and used for the analyses of these measures. The data were analyzed by means of analysis of variance using the unweighted means formula for unequal *ns* with repeated measures given by Winer (1962, pp. 374–378). The n for each analysis was the number of subjects measured on all pretest and posttest occasions. Differences between the various treatment conditions were assessed by t tests.

Reported anxiety. A main effect was observed for reported anxiety ($F = 14.3$, $df = 4/364$, $p < .001$). In support of the first hypothesis, subjects in the high-fear condition displayed the greatest amount of anxiety immediately following the communication and were significantly higher in anxiety than the low-fear-appeal condition ($t = 2.22$, $p < .05$) and the positive-appeal condition ($t = 6.40$, $p < .001$). In further support of the first hypothesis, the low-fear-appeal condition was higher in anxiety than the positive-appeal condition ($t = 4.4$, $p < .001$). A significant main effect was obtained for time ($F = 6.5$, $df = 2/728$, $p < .001$). The magnitude of the differences between conditions decreased over time, and, although the rank order of the conditions was somewhat altered on the 5-day and 6-week postcommunication measure, no significant reversals for relative amount of anxiety were obtained. Also found was a significant interaction between time and condition ($F = 5.3$, $df = 8/728$, $p < .01$).

Information retained. Contrary to the second hypothesis, a significant main effect was observed for information retention ($F = 4.25$, $df = 4/364$, $p < .005$). The positive-appeal-condition groups retained significantly more information than all the other condition groups (high fear, $t = 4.1$, $p < .001$; low fear, $t = 2.6$, $p < .01$; recommendations only, $t = 2.4$, $p < .05$; elaborated recommendations, $t = 2.2$, $p < .05$). The elaborated recomendation groups in comparison with the other groups retained the second greatest amount of information. They retained significantly more information than the high-fear-condition group ($t = 2.3$, $p < .05$). A significant difference was also obtained between the amount of retention in the recommendations-only-condition groups and the high-fear groups ($t = 2.4$, $p < .05$), with the recommendations-only-condition group retaining the greater amount of information. A main effect was observed for time ($F = 47.0$, $df = 2/728$, $p < .001$). The magnitude of the differences between the information-retention means generally decreased over time with no significant reversals in rank order among the conditions occurring. The differences attenuated to such an extent that there were no significant differences between any of the conditions on the 6-week posttest measure. Also obtained was a significant interaction between time and initial level of cleanliness ($F = 2.5$, $df = 8/728$, $p < .05$).

Intention to behave. A significant main effect was obtained for intention to behave ($F = 4.37$, $df = 4/364$, $p < .005$). Partial support of the hypotheses was obtained as the high- and low-fear conditions reported mutually equal and stronger intentions to behave than were expressed in the positive and elaborated recommendation groups (high fear versus positive, $t = 2.4$, $p < .05$; high fear versus elaborated recommendations, $t = 2.5$, $p < .05$; low fear versus positive, $t = 2.9$, $p < .01$; low fear versus elaborated recommendations, $t = 3.1$, $p < .01$). A significant main effect was obtained for time ($F = 46.5$, $df = 2/728$, $p < .001$). For every condition the intention to behave decreased over time. On the 6-week postcommunication measure, the only significant differences were between the high-fear condition and both the positive ($t = 2.7$, $p < .01$) and the recommendations-only conditions ($t = 2.1$, $p < .05$). Thus, the high-fear appeal seemed to have the greatest effect in sustaining an intention to behave in accordance with the message. Parenthetically, no significant interaction effect was obtained between time and condition.

Reported behavior change. A significant main effect was obtained for reported behavior change ($F = 2.7$, $df = 4/364$, $p <$

.05). Fig. 6.1 presents the mean reported behavior change scores for the five conditions of the experiment (the change scores consist of the difference between the score for the measurement occasion indicated and that of the pre-communication measure). The mean reported behavior score taken immediately after the subject had been exposed to the communication was more similar to the precommunication score than that of the 5-day postcommunication score, because it referred to tooth-brushing practices prior to exposure to the communication. There were no significant differences among the change scores taken on the immediate postcommunication measure. As Figure 6.1 shows, there was considerable improvement for reported toothbrushing practices within all five conditions 5 days after exposure to the communications. The group hearing the high-fear appeal showed the greatest amount of reported be-

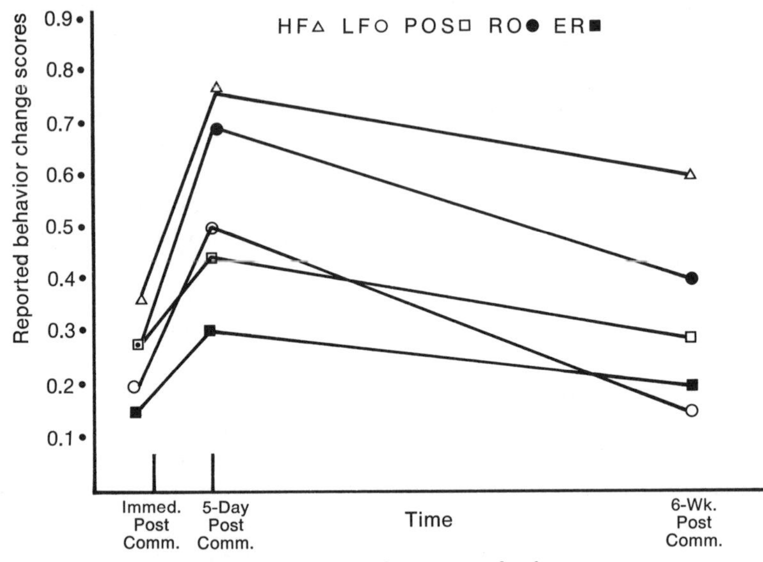

FIG. 6.1. Reported behavior change scores for the treatment groups.

havior change, followed by the recommendations-only group, low-fear, positive-, with the elaborated-recommendations appeal group reporting the least change. In general, the data fail to support the fourth hypothesis. But the change for the high-fear and recommendations-only groups was significantly greater than for the elaborated-recommendations group (high fear versus elaborated recommendations, $t = 3.1$, $p < .01$; recommendations only versus elaborated recommendation, $t = 2.6$, $p < .01$). None of the other t values were significant, however. As Fig. 6.1 shows, there was a marked reduction in reported behavior change between the 5-day and the 6-week postcommunication measure. A significant effect was obtained for time ($F = 21.68$, $df = 2/728$, $p < .001$). All of the appeal groups showed a regression to precommunication reported behavior levels. Six weeks after exposure to the communication the high-fear group again displayed the greatest reported change, and again was followed by the recommendations-only group. Also obtained was a significant interaction effect between time and initial level of cleanliness ($F = 3.5$, $df = 4/728$, $p < .01$).

Behavior change. A significant main effect was obtained for behavior change (tooth cleanliness ratings—$F = 4.92$, $df = 4/364$, $p < .01$). The mean behavior change scores for the five treatment

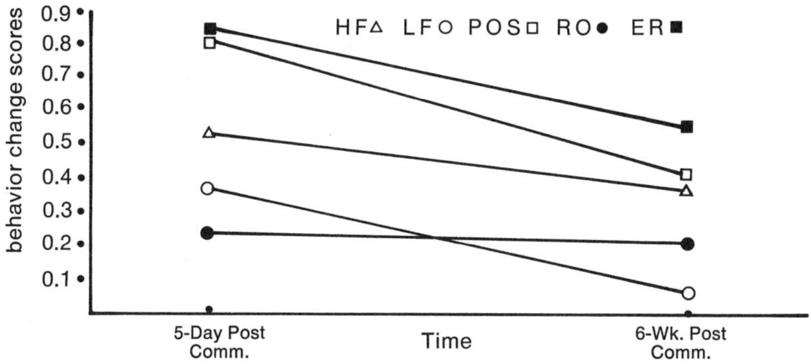

FIG. 6.2. Behavior change scores for the treatment groups.

conditions are presented in Fig. 6.2. Change scores involved only two postcommunication measures, since, unlike that for reported behavior change, the disclosing tablet was not used immediately after exposure to the message. Although all of the groups showed increased tooth cleanliness, the group showing the greatest change from precommunication to 5-day postcommunication was the elaborated-recommendations condition. The positive appeal was second in magnitude of behavior change, followed by the high-fear, low-fear, and recommendations-only conditions, respectively. In partial support of the fifth hypothesis, the positive and high-fear conditions yielded significantly greater change than did the recommendations-only condition (positive versus recommendations only, $t = 3.6$, $p < .001$; high fear versus recommendations only, $t = 2.0$, $p < .05$). Contrary to the fifth hypothesis, the elaborated recommendations condition yielded significantly greater behavior change than did the high-fear, low-fear, and recommendations-only conditions (high fear versus elaborated recommendations, $t = 2.1$, $p < .05$; low fear versus elaborated recommendations, $t = 3.2$, $p < .01$; recommendations only versus elaborated recommendations, $t = 4.2$, $p < .001$). A significant main effect was also obtained for time ($F = 21.01$, $df = 1/364$, $p < .001$). Figure 6.2 shows that 6 weeks after exposure to the communication, all of the treatment groups showed a regression to their precommunication cleanliness levels.

Actual behavior versus reported behavior change. It is important to note that although significant effects of appeals were obtained for both reported behavior and the measure of actual behavior, evidence of their differences as criterion measures is supported by examining Figs. 6.1 and 6.2. The conditions which yielded significant changes in report of behavior were high fear and recommendations only. On the other hand, the conditions which yielded significant changes in the measure of actual behavior were elaborated recommendations and the positive-appeal condition, with the high-fear condition proving to be only moderately effective.

In addition, as would be logically expected, the main effect of the initial level of tooth cleanliness was very large for the reported behavior and actual behavior measures ($F = 13.98$, $df = 2/364$, $p < .01$ and $F = 40.18$, $df = 2/364$, $p < .01$, respectively). This simply indicates that those subjects having cleaner teeth before the experiment both reported and exhibited less change after exposure to the communications than those having dirtier teeth.

DISCUSSION

It appears that in the present investigation as a whole, some very provocative results from the tests of the various hypotheses were obtained which bear on various issues presented by Higbee (1969) concerning the overall problems involved in fear-arousal communication investigations over the past several years.

1. Once again, serious doubt has been cast concerning the generality of any principle which suggests that high fear arousal is or is not as effective as other appeals. In fact, the findings in the present study which show the surprising effectiveness of a positive motivating appeal, as well as the effectiveness of the elaborated recommendations, raise questions concerning the necessity of using fear arousal at all in order to effect behaviors such as the one sought in the present study. The results involving elaborated recommendations would agree essentially with the observations incorporated in the reports of Leventhal and his coinvestigators.

2. The fact that this investigation was implemented within a natural setting utilizing a unique measure of behavior change provides additional evidence concerning the general theoretical notion that attitude or reported behavior and actual behavior do not necessarily correspond. However, it should be stressed that the measure of reported behavior unfortunately may not be recording the same type of activity as the measure of actual behavior (reported frequency of brushing teeth versus a direct indicator of the cleanliness of teeth). Additionally, it should be pointed out that the recommendations never referred to the frequency of brushing teeth as a desirable response. However, Pearson product-moment correlations between information retention and both reported and actual behavior failed to reach significance within *any* of the appeal groups. Thus, it is difficult to determine whether or not the actual

behavior measure recorded a response that resulted from an information input that differed from the reported behavior measure.

3. The finding of a 6-week postcommunication regression through the utilization of a time-series dimension underlines the limitations of investigations involving only immediate postcommunication measures of the effects of persuasive appeals. It also suggests strongly that such research designs would be enhanced by schedules of repeated presentations or other reinforcers of messages.

The first and second authors of the present report are now completing an investigation which attempts to deal with these variables in another school setting. This investigation also is attempting to validate more precisely the measure of actual behavior and uses a more parallel measure of reported behavior. Responding to the need for evaluating the effects of repeated reinforcement of the message, a technique of interschool competition has been introduced.

SUMMARY

In three junior high schools, students were exposed to high fear arousal, moderate fear arousal, positive affect arousal, elaborated recommendations only, and brief recommendations only directed at improving toothbrushing behavior. Criterion measures of information, anxiety, intention to behave, self-report of behavior, and a new chemical indicator of actual toothbrushing behavior were administered precommunication, immediately postcommunication, 5-days postcommunication, and 6-weeks postcommunication. Results suggest that elaborated recommendations and positive affect were most effective in changing actual behavior, but that high fear and recommendations only were the most effective in changing reported behavior. Effects of all conditions were attenuated over time.

REFERENCES

ALLEN, B. P. The relationships among the effects of persuasive appeals, toothbrushing behavior, attitude toward dental hygiene, intention to behave, and reported behavior. Unpublished doctoral dissertation, University of Houston, 1969.

ARNIM, S. S. The use of disclosing agents for measuring tooth cleanliness. *Journal of Periodontology,* 1963, *34,* 227–245.

CROWNE, D. P., & MARLOWE, D. *The approval motive.* New York: Wiley, 1964.

DEMBROSKI, T. M. Locus of control and the effectiveness of persuasive communications: Changing dental health practices as measured by a chemical agent. Unpublished doctoral dissertation, University of Houston, 1969.

EVANS, R. I., ROZELLE, R. M., LASATER, T. M., DEMBROSKI, T. M., & ALLEN, B. P. New measure of effects of persuasive communications: A chemical indicator of toothbrushing behavior. *Psychological Reports,* 1968, *23,* 731–736.

HIGBEE, K. L. Fifteen years of fear arousal: Research on threat appeals: 1953–1968. *Psychological Bulletin,* 1969, *72,* 426–444.

JANIS, I. L. Effects of fear arousal on attitude: Recent developments in theory and experimental research. *Advances in Experimental Social Psychology,* 1967, *4,* 166–224.

JANIS, I. L., & FESHBACH, S. Effects of fear-arousing communications. *Journal of Abnormal and Social Psychology,* 1953, *48,* 78–92.

LASATER, T. M. An examination of the relationships among dogmatism, cognitive and behavioral changes, and persuasive communications within the context of a dental health program. Unpublished doctoral dissertation, University of Houston, 1969.

LEVENTHAL, H., & SINGER, R. P. Order of affect arousal and recommendations as determinants of attitude change. New Haven, Conn.: Author, 1965. (Mimeo)

LEVENTHAL, H., SINGER, R. P., & JONES, S. Effects of fear and specificity of recommendation upon attitudes and behavior. *Journal of Personality and Social Psychology,* 1965, *2,* 20–29.

ROKEACH, M. *The open and closed mind.* New York: Basic Books, 1960.

ROTTER, J. B. Generalized expectancies for internal vs. external control of reinforcement. *Psychological Monographs,* 1966, *80* (No. 1, Whole No. 609).

WINER, B. J. *Statistical principles in experimental design.* New York: McGraw-Hill, 1962.

7

Persistence and Regression of Changed Attitudes:

Long-Range Studies

Theodore M. Newcomb

One's attitude toward something is not only a resultant of one's previous traffic with one's environment but also a determinant of selective response to present and future environments. Viewed in the latter way, existing attitudes may determine one's selection among alternative environmental settings, and these in turn may serve to preserve or undermine the very attitudes that had been initially responsible for one's selection among the alternatives. Insofar as attitudes are self-preserving, such tendencies to select a supportive environment would, if empirically supported, provide an important explanation of their persistence. In its most general form, the hypothesis would run somewhat as follows: Existing attitudes are most likely to persist, other things equal, when one's environment provides most rewards for their behavioral expression. But this platitudinous proposition ("things persist when conditions are favorable to their persistence") is not very interesting, and is probably not even testable. A more interesting and more testable form of the proposition would take account of both change and persistence, both of attitudes and of environmental supportiveness. In particular, it would say something about a changed selection of

From *Journal of Social Issues,* 1963, *19* (4), 3–14.

[Part VI—autobiographical reference, was omitted with permission from Theodore M. Newcomb.]

environments following attitude change, about the ways in which the recently formed attitude is or is not reinforced by the new environment, and about the persistence of the attitude in both supportive and hostile environments. Such a proposition, in its simplest form, would run somewhat as follows: A recently changed attitude is likely to persist insofar as it leads to the selection of subsequent environments that provide reinforcements for the behavioral expression of the changed attitude.

Among the many possible forms of environmental reinforcements of behavioral expressions of attitudes, I shall consider a single class: behavior on the part of other people that one perceives as supportive of one's own attitudes. With few exceptions, such support comes from persons or groups toward whom one is positively attracted, according to the principles of what is perhaps most frequently known as balance theory (Cf. Heider, 1958; Brown, 1962; Newcomb, 1963). I am, in short, about to defend the limited proposition that a recently changed attitude is most likely to persist if one of its behavioral expressions is the selection of a social environment which one finds supportive of the changed attitude. This proposition differs from the one about autistic hostility primarily in that persistence of a recently acquired attitude depends upon continuing rather than cutting off sources of information about the attitude-object.

II

There are various ways in which such a proposition might be tested in the laboratory. But insofar as one is interested, as I have been, in long-range effects, one will make use of "natural" settings. I shall therefore cite a few findings from two of my own studies, mentioning only briefly the less immediately relevant one (1961), which involved the daily observation of two populations of 17 male students, all initial strangers to one another, who lived intimately together for four-month periods. The only attitudes of these subjects that showed much change, from first to last, were their attractions toward each other—attitudes which had not even existed, of course, before their initial encounters in this research setting. Expressions of interpersonal attraction during the first week or two were highly unstable, but after about the fifth week they showed only slow and slight changes (Cf. Newcomb, 1963).

Under the conditions of this research, imposed environments (in the form of arbitrarily assigned rooms, roommates, and floors) had no consistent effects beyond the first week or two in interpersonal preferences. That is, one could predict little or nothing about interpersonal attraction from the fact of being roommates or floormates. Self-selected interpersonal environment, however, was closely associated with interpersonal attraction. At all times later than the first week or two, pairs of subjects who were reported by others to belong to the same voluntary subgroups were almost invariably pairs whose members chose each other at very high levels of attraction. If this seems to be a commonplace observation (as indeed it is), let me remind you of my reason for reporting it; interpersonal environments are not only consequences of existing attraction but also sources of future attraction. It is an everyday phenomenon that, having developed differential attitudes toward one's several acquaintances, one manipulates one's interpersonal environment, insofar as one can, to correspond with one's interpersonal preferences. And insofar as one is successful, chances are that the preferences will be further reinforced. My data, showing stability both of preferences and of voluntarily associating subgroups following the first month or so, indicate that exactly this was occurring. The fact that it is an everyday occurrence enhances rather than negates the importance of the principle involved, namely, that a recently acquired attitude will persist insofar as it results in the selection of an environment that is supportive of that attitude.

III

I now turn to a totally different set of data, or rather to two sets of data from the same subjects, obtained over an interval of more than 20 years. The earlier responses were obtained between 1935 and 1939 at Bennington College (Newcomb, 1943); the later ones, obtained in 1960 and 1961, were from almost all of the subjects who had been studied for three or more consecutive years during the 1930's. To be specific, out of 141 former students in this category who in 1960 were alive, resident in continental United States, and not hopelessly invalided, 130 (scattered in 28 states) were interviewed, and 9 of the remaining 11 completed more or less parallel questionnaires. The interview dealt primarily with their present attitudes toward a wide range of public-affairs issues, with attitudes of their husbands and other contemporary associates, and with their histories and careers since leaving the College.

Before telling you some of the follow-up findings, I ought to report a few of the original ones. During each of four consecutive years (1935-36 through 1938-39), juniors and seniors were on the average markedly less conservative than freshmen in attitude toward many public issues of the day. Studies of the same individuals over three- and four-year intervals showed the same trend, which was not attributable to selective withdrawal from the College. Comparisons with other colleges showed almost no intercollege differences in freshmen attitudes, but much less conservatism at Bennington than at the other institutions on the part of seniors. Individual studies showed that at Bennington nonconservatism was rather closely associated with being respected by other students, with participation in college activities, and with personal involvement in the College as an institution. The relatively few malcontents were, with surprisingly few exceptions, those who held conservative attitudes toward public issues.

Given these initial findings, one of my concerns in planning the follow-up study was the following: Under what conditions would individuals who had become less conservative during their college years remain relatively nonconservative 20-odd years later, and under what conditions would they "regress" to relatively conservative positions? (As to the problem of comparing attitudes toward one set of issues in the 1930's with those toward quite different issues in the 1960's, I shall for present purposes note only that at both times we used indices of relative, not absolute standing: each subject is compared with the same set of peers.)

By way of noting the general pattern of persistence vs. regression on the part of the total population, I shall first compare one early with one later datum. In the 1940 presidential election, 51% of our interview sample who reported a preference for either major candidate chose the Democrat, F. D. Roosevelt, and 49% the Republican, W. Willkie. Twenty years later, the comparable figures were 60% for J. F. Kennedy and 40% for R. M. Nixon. No single election, of course, provides a very good test of what might be termed "general conservatism concerning public affairs," but at any rate this particular comparison does not suggest any conspicuous regression toward freshman conservatism. This conclusion is also supported by the following finding: In six consecutive presidential elections (1940 through 1960), an outright majority of our interviewees (51%) reported that they had preferred the Republican candidate either once or never, whereas only 27% of them had preferred that candidate as many as five times out of the six times.

The problem of regressive effects can also be approached by comparing relative conservatism on the part of the same individuals over the interval of 20-odd years. In terms of party or candidate preference in 1960, the degree of individual stability is startling. As shown in Table 7.1, individuals who were in the least conservative quartile of the total population, on graduating, preferred Kennedy by frequencies of 30 to 3, and those in the next quartile

Table 7.1—Presidential Preferences in 1960, According to Quartiles of PEP Scores on Leaving College in the Late 1930s

PEP Quartile	Nixon Preferred	Kennedy Preferred	Total
1 (least conservative)	3	30	33
2	8	25	33
3	18	13	31
4 (most conservative)	22	11	33
TOTAL	51	79	130

by 25 to 8; 83% of this half of the population preferred Kennedy 20 years later, while 37% of the initially more conservative half preferred Kennedy after 20 years. Political party preferences, and also an index of general political conservatism, showed about the same relationship to political conservatism more than two decades earlier. These data provide no support for a prediction of general regression—either toward previous conservatism or in the statistical sense of regression toward the mean.

Other evidence concerning the general nonconservatism in this population in the early 1960's includes the following:

77% of them considered themselves "liberal" or "somewhat liberal," as compared with 17% who were "conservative" or "somewhat conservative";
76% "approved" or "strongly approved" of "Medicare" for the aged under Social Security;
61% "approved" or "strongly approved" of admitting Red China into the United Nations.

These and other data suggest that the population as a whole is now far less conservative than is to be expected in view of its demographic characteristics. Its socio-economic level may be judged from these facts: (1) 77% of the 117 respondents who were or had been married were judged by the interviewer to be at least "fairly well-to-do," with annual incomes of not less than $20,000; and (2) of 113 mothers in the population, 65% had sent at least one of their children to a private school. In religious background, about three-quarters of them were Protestants (more than half of whom were Episcopalian), and less than 10% were either Catholic or Jewish. According to information assembled for me by the Survey Research Center of the University of Michigan,* the proportion of Protestant women college graduates at the income level of this population who in 1960 expressed a preference for Kennedy over Nixon was less than 25—as compared with 60% of this alumnae population.

I shall now revert to my earlier theme: If this population is now less conservative than one might expect, to what extent is this explainable in terms of its members' selection of post-college environments that were supportive of nonconservative attitudes? It proves to be very difficult to categorize total environments from this point of view, and so for the present I shall limit myself to a single aspect of post-college environments: husbands. I am making no assumptions here except that (1) husbands were indeed a

* By my colleague Philip Converse, to whom I am most grateful.

part of their wives' environments; (2) wives had had something to do with selecting this part of their environments; and (3) husbands, as environmental objects, were capable of being either supportive or nonsupportive of their wives' attitudes.

Nearly 80% of our respondents both had a husband and were able to report on his attitudes toward most of the issues with which we were concerned, during all or most of the past 20 years; one reason for placing a good deal of confidence in their reports is that they seem highly discriminating, as indicated by such responses as these: "I don't think I know how he'd feel on that particular issue," or "Now on *that* one he doesn't agree with me at all." Here are some summaries concerning all husbands whose wives were willing to attribute attitudes toward them (nearly all wives on most issues):

54% of the husbands in 1960 favored Kennedy over Nixon;
64% of them either "approved" or "strongly approved" of "Medicare" for the aged under Social Security;
57% of them either "approved" or "strongly approved" of admitting Red China into the United Nations.

And so it is almost as true of husbands as of wives that they are less conservative than is to be expected in view of their demographic characteristics: husbands' and wives' demographic characteristics are taken to be identical except for a very few couples differing in religious background, and their present attitudes are highly similar (90% of 1960 presidential preferences by pairs of spouses, for example, being reported as the same in 1960). It would hardly seem to be a matter of sheer chance that a set of men who are less conservative than is to be expected are married to a set of women of whom just the same thing is true. It seems necessary, therefore, to assume that attitudes toward public affairs had something to do with husbands' and wives' reciprocal selection of one another, or with post-marital influence upon one another, or with both. Here is one statistical support for this assumption: the correlation between wives' scores on an instrument labeled Political and Economic Progressivism, as of their graduating from college in the late 1930's, with the number of Republican candidates that their subsequent husbands voted for between 1940 and 1960 was

.32; this does not account for much of the variance, but its p value is $< .0005$.

Another interesting finding has to do with the number of women in our interview sample whose husbands had attended Ivy League colleges; one would expect this proportion to be high, since so many of the women's fathers and brothers had attended these colleges. The actual frequency turned out to be just 50%. These Ivy League husbands' voting preferences in 1960, however, turned out to be much more like their wives' preferences than like their classmates' preferences: 52% of husbands whose wives were able to state a preference were for Kennedy—which is to say that they did not differ at all in voting preferences from all non-Ivy League husbands. This total set of facts can best be interpreted as follows: Our Bennington graduates of the late 1930's found their husbands in the kinds of places where their families expected them to be found, but they selected somewhat atypical members of these "proper" populations of eligibles; they tended not to have conservative attitudes that were then typical of these populations.

One evidence of this atypical selection is to be seen in the occupational distribution of these womens' husbands. Only 38% of all husbands are classifiable as "in management or business," the remaining 62% representing for the most part a wide range of professions (especially college teaching, entertainment, and the arts) and public employment (especially in government). Husbands in these two general categories (management and business vs. all others) differed sharply in their voting preferences in 1960; of the 113 husbands whose wives attributed preferences to them, 26% of those in management and business preferred Kennedy, and 68% of all other husbands preferred Kennedy. In sum, these women's husbands had typically come from "the right" places but a majority of them did not have "the right" attitudes or occupational interests.

If, therefore, I were to select a single factor that contributed most to these women's maintenance of nonconservative attitudes between the late 1930's and early 1960's, I think it would be the fact of selecting husbands of generally nonconservative stripe who helped to maintain for them an environment that was supportive of their existing attributes.

IV

Now I shall turn from the total population of interviewees to some comparisons of subpopulations. The most crucial of these, from the point of view of my proposition about supportive environments, are to be found within the population of nonconservatives on leaving college in the late 1930's: What seems to be the differences between those who do and those who do not remain nonconservative in the early 1960's? Such comparisons will have to be impressionistic, since numbers of cases are small.

Among 22 individuals previously labeled as clearly nonconservative in their third or fourth year of attendance at the College, just half belong in the same category now. Only three of them are clearly conservative today, the remaining eight being classified as intermediate. Here are these wives' descriptions of their husbands' political positions over the years:

3 presently conservative wives: 3 Republican husbands (100%)
7 presently intermediate wives: 3 Republican husbands (42%)
8 presently nonconservative wives: 2 Republican husbands (25%)

Of the three presently conservative women, none mentions having engaged in activities related to political or other public issues; of the eight who are intermediate, six mention some activity of this kind, but they identify their activity only in such general terms as "liberal" or "Democratic Party"; of the 11 still nonconservative women, eight mention such activities, more than half of them specifying such "causes" or organizations as labor unions, civil liberties, the ADA, or the NAACP.

Each interviewee was also asked about the general orientation of "most of your friends" toward political and other public affairs. More than half (12) of the 22 women originally labeled as clearly nonconservative described their environment of friends as "liberal," in spite of the fact that most of them lived in suburbs or other geographical areas not generally renowned for liberalism. Interestingly enough, those who are now relatively conservative answered this question in just about the same way as did those who are still relatively nonconservative. The 16 women originally labeled as clearly conservative, on leaving college, answered this question somewhat differently; more than half of them (9) described their environment of friends as predominantly "conservative," but answers differed with the present attitudes of the respondents. That is, those who are now, in fact, relatively conservative with near-unanimity describe their friends as conservative, whereas those who are now relatively nonconservative consider a substantial proportion or even most of their friends to be "liberal." Thus only those who were quite conservative in the late 1930's and who still remain so see themselves surrounded by friends who are primarily conservative.

In sum, nearly all of the still nonconservative women mention either husbands or public activities (most commonly both) that have served to support and maintain previously nonconservative attitudes, while none of the three formerly nonconservative but presently conservative women mentions either husband or public activities which have served to maintain earlier attitudes.

What about attitude persistence on the part of those who, after three or four years in college, were still relatively conservative? Sixteen of those who were then labeled conservative were interviewed in the early 1960's, ten of them being categorized as still conservative and three as now nonconservative. Only one of the nonchangers reported having a husband who was a Democrat, and in this lone case he turned out to have voted for Nixon in 1960. Two of the three changers, on the other hand, report husbands who were Democrats and Kennedy voters in 1960. Only two of the persistent conservatives mentioned public activities presumably supportive of their attitudes (in behalf of the Republican Party, in both cases); eight of the ten described most of their friends either as conservative or as Republicans. The conditions that favor the persistence of conservatism over the 20-odd years are thus about the same as those that favor the persistence of nonconservatism: supportive environments in the form of husbands, local friends, and (for the nonconservatives but not the conservatives) in the form of associates in activities related to public issues.

There is a special sub-population of students who, as of graduating in the late 1930's, were candidates for regression; that is, they became much less conservative during their college years. Of these, about one-third (9 of 28) were among the most conservative half of the same population in the early 1960's, and may be regarded as regressors, in some degree at least. Eight of these potential regressors were, for various reasons, unable to report on husbands' preferences. Among the remaining 19 respondents, five were actual regressors, four of whom reported their husbands to be Republicans or "conservative Republicans." Among 14 actual non-regressors reporting, ten described their husbands as Democrats or "liberal Democrats," two referred to them as "Republicans who have been voting Democratic," and only two call their husbands Republicans. These are highly significant differences: the actual regressors can pretty well be differentiated from the nonregressors merely by knowing their husbands' present attitudes. By this procedure only 3 of 19, or 16% of all predictions would not have been correct.

This total set of data suggests that either regression and persistence of attitudes as of leaving college are, over the years, influenced by husbands' attitudes, or early post-college attitudes had something to do with the selection of husbands, or both. In either case, both regression and persistence are facilitated by the supportiveness of husbands.

V

If there is any very general principle that helps to account for this whole range of phenomena (both my 1946 and my 1963 versions), I believe that it is to be found in an extended version of "balance theory," as originally outlined by Heider (1946, 1958). Heider's formulations are formulated in individual and phenomenological terms; a balanced state is a strictly intrapersonal, psychological state. But it is also possible to conceptualize an objective, multi-person state of balance, referring to the actual relationships among different persons' attitudes, regardless of the person's awareness of each other. Such a concept is psychologically useful not only because it describes an actual, existing situation—an environment of which each person is himself a part, as suggested by Asch (1952)—but also because it describes a relationship which, given reasonably full and accurate communication, comes to be accurately perceived. My own recent work on the acquaintance process has been interesting to me primarily because it inquires into the processes by which and the conditions under which *intra*-personal states of balance come to correspond with *inter*personal ones. As outlined by Heider, and subsequently by many others (Cf. Brown, 1962), the processes by which imbalanced states serve as goals toward the attainment of balanced ones include both internal, psychological changes and external modifications of the environment. Thus, one may achieve a balanced state with the important figures in one's social environment—whether by selecting those figures, by modifying one's own attitudes, or by influencing others' attitudes—and at the same time continue to perceive that environment accurately.

According to such an extended, *inter*personal concept of balance, an imbalanced state under conditions of continued interaction is likely to be an unstable one, simply because when it is discovered it arouses *intra*personal imbalance on the part of one or more of the interactors, and this state arouses forces toward change. Given marked attitude change on the part of one but not the other member of a dyad actually in balance with respect to that attitude, imbalance results. This was what typically happened to students at Bennington College vis-à-vis their parents, in the 1930's. A common way in which they attempted to reduce imbalance was by avoidance—not necessarily of parents but of the divisive issues as related to parents. As Heider might say, unit formation between issue and parents was broken up, and psychological imbalance thus reduced. Such a "solution" resembles autistic hostility in that it involves a marked restriction of communication.

But this solution, as many of my subjects testified, was not a particularly comfortable one. Hence, it would hardly be surprising if many of them, during early post-college years, were in search of environments that would provide less uncomfortable solutions—or, better yet, more positively rewarding ones. An ideal one, of course, would be a husband who was rewarding as a supporter of one's own attitudes as well as in other ways.

And so, vis-à-vis parents and fellow-students at first, and later vis-à-vis husbands (or perhaps working associates), forces toward balance were at work. Specifically, support from important people concerning important issues came to be the rule, and its absence the exception. Support sometimes came about by changing one's own attitudes toward those of needed supporters, or, more commonly, by selecting supporters for existing attitudes. The latter stratagem represented not merely an automatic tendency for attitudes to perpetuate themselves. More significantly, I believe, it represents an adaptation to a world that includes *both* persons and issues. Such a dual adaptation can be made, of course, by sacrificing one's stand on the issues (regression). But if the dual adaptation is to be made without this sacrifice, then an interpersonal world must be selected (or created) that is supportive—in which case we can say that the attitude has been expressed by finding a supportive environment.

According to my two themes (of *1946* and *1963*) an existing attitude may be maintained by creating environments in which *either* new information can be avoided *or* in which other persons support one's own information. In either case, the fate of an attitude is mediated by the social environment in which the individual attempts to maintain or to restore balance regarding that same attitude. Insofar as that environment excludes disturbing information or provides reinforcing information, the attitude persists. And insofar as the selection or the acceptance of that environment is a consequence of holding the attitude, we have a steady-state, self-maintaining system.

REFERENCES

ASCH, S. E. *Social Psychology*. New York: Prentice-Hall, 1952.

BROWN, R. Models of attitude change. In Brown, R., Galanter, E., Hess, E. H., & Mandler, G. *New Directions in Psychology*. New York: Holt, Rinehart & Winston, 1962.

HEIDER, F. Attitudes and cognitive organization. *J. Psychol.*, 1946, *21*, 107–112.

———. *The Psychology of Interpersonal Relations*. New York: Wiley, 1958.

NEWCOMB, T. M. *Personality and Social Change*. New York: Holt, Rinehart & Winston, 1943.

———. Autistic hostility and social reality. *Human Relations,* 1947, *1,* 69–86.
———. *The Acquaintance Process.* New York: Holt, Rinehart & Winston, 1961.
———. Stabilities underlying changes in interpersonal attraction. *J. abnorm. soc. Psychol.,* 1963, *66,* 376-386.

8

Persistence of Attitude Change as a Function of Conclusion Reexposure:

A Laboratory-Field Experiment

Thomas D. Cook and Chester A. Insko

As Watts and McGuire (1964) have pointed out, the literature on the persistence of attitude change is highly inconsistent. Some studies have found complete decay, some have found partial persistence, some have found complete or near complete persistence, and some have found delayed action effects in which attitude

From *Journal of Personality and Social Psychology,* 1968, *9,* 322–328.

This research was supported by a grant to the second author from the Research Council of the University of North Carolina.

change increased over time. Although classification of findings is difficult because of the differing time intervals investigated, some studies which have found complete decay are Chen (1936), Insko, Arkoff, and Insko (1965), Kelman (1958, 1960), and Sims (1938). Some studies which have found partial persistence are Annis and Maier (1934), Cherrington and Miller (1933), Dietrich (1946), Dillehay, Insko, and Smith (1966), Hall (1938), Kelman (1960), McGuire (1957, 1960), Mitnick and McGinnies (1958), Papageorgis (1963), Peterson and Thurstone (1933), Smith (1943), Stotland, Katz, and Patchen (1959), Watts and McGuire (1964), and Weiss (1953). Studies which have found complete or near complete persistence are Cohen (1957), Elms (1966), Kelman (1958, 1960), Newcomb (1963), Peterson and Thurstone (1933), and Watts (1967). Finally, studies which have found delayed action effects are Hovland, Lumsdaine, and Sheffield (1949), Hovland and Weiss (1951), Insko et al. (1965), Kelman and Hovland (1953), Peterson and Thurstone (1933), Stotland et al. (1959), Stotland and Patchen (1961), and Weiss (1953).

Such seeming conflict is an open invitation to search for interactive variables which may help to clarify matters. Quite possibly there are a large number of such variables. The present investigation focuses upon two such variables. The first of these is reexposure to the conclusion of the communication (communication reexposure). That an informational environment which produces such reexposure should facilitate the persistence of attitude change is not at all remarkable. Despite this fact, the literature contains no studies which unambiguously point to the importance of this variable. Watts (1967) found that subjects who reported reading about, as well as discussing, a communication topic showed greater persistence effects. Peterson and Thurstone (1933) found their greatest persistence effects in a condition in which an experimental movie was shown entertainment-deprived children who spent considerable time discussing the film. And Newcomb (1963) reported that after 25 years the Bennington students who show the greatest persistence in their liberal attitude are the ones whose husbands and friends have similar liberal attitudes. These results could, of course, be attributed to a number of variables in addition to conclusion reexposure, namely, exposure to supporting arguments, group or social support from other like-minded individuals, or the initial differences that led to the differential reexposure.

Demonstrating the importance of conclusion reexposure requires manipulating the subjects exposure to communication-relevant material after they have left the laboratory and before they return for the delayed assessment. In the present approach, after exposure to the persuasive communication in an initial laboratory situation, subjects were sent postcards reminding them of the time and place for the second laboratory session and either reinstating or not reinstating the communication topic. For the subjects in the reexposure condition, the postcards served as a conclusion reexposure in a field situation. Subjects in this condition undoubtedly differed in the extent to which they placed the postcard in a prominent place or repeatedly consulted the reminder on the postcards, but it can be assumed that the reexposure subjects were exposed to the communication topic to a greater extent than were the remaining subjects. Hence, it is predicted that these subjects will show greater persistence.

The second variable that may have an important effect upon persistence is the extent to which the newly acquired attitude is positively linked to existing values. If the newly acquired attitude has a large number of links to other values, assuming consistency is to be maintained, then change in the original attitude would necessitate change in a large number of additional links (cognitions) or in the affect associated with the related values (Abelson & Rosenberg, 1958). Extrapolating from Rosenberg and Abelson's (1960) principle of least effort, one might thus expect that a newly acquired attitude with a large number of value linkages would be more resistant to erosion than would a newly acquired attitude with a smaller number of value linkages. The differences in structural strength should lead to differences in persistence. Kelman (1960) reported some findings which provide suggestive support for this hypothesis. He found that a communication which linked acceptance of the advocated point of view to an important value resulted in a greater persistence than a communication which linked acceptance of the advocated point of view to positive and negative reference groups. What is being proposed here, of course, goes somewhat further in postulating a difference in the number of linkages, not just in the presence or absence of a single important linkage.

The authors propose to test this hypothesis by using persuasive communications that differ in terms of the number of value-linking arguments, two or six. Admittedly a simple comparison between two and six value-linking arguments is somewhat crude. Since various value-linking arguments may differ in their persistence-conferring potency, it may be hazardous to propose that superior persistence effects for the six-argument communication are due simply to a greater number of value linkages. Such a difference, however, would be consistent with the hypothesis. Also, the inclusion of an additional communication in the experimental design provides the opportunity to test for further generality with regard to the reexposure findings.

METHOD

Subjects

The subjects were 289 students obtained from the introductory psychology class at the University of North Carolina. Of the 218 subjects who were in the delay conditions, 20 (9.2%) failed to return for the second session. These nonreturning subjects were fairly well distributed over the various delay conditions. The actual number of nonreturning subjects in each condition is given in Table 8.1.

Communications

The two experimental communications were 2,300- and 1,900-word tape-recorded arguments that the President of the United States should be elected by Congress. One communication presented brief statements to the effect that Congressional election of the President would facilitate the attainment of six values (strong checks and balances, effectiveness in implementing policy, savings in costs and personnel, dignity in the election process, assurance that a proper person would be elected, similarity to the workable

British example). The other communication presented a thoroughly developed and well-documented statement that Congressional election of the President would facilitate the attainment of two values (strong checks and balances, assurance that a proper person would be elected.) Hereafter, the former of these communications will be referred to as the six-value communication and the latter as the two-value communication.

The experimental procedure called for the use of a cover communication. This communication, also tape-recorded, was a 700-word argument to the effect that having no sibling of the opposite sex has a slightly disadvantageous effect on marital adjustment during the first years of marriage. The communicator was female for the cover communication and male for the experimental communications.

Independent and Dependent Variables

Three independent variables were manipulated in an incomplete factorial design: communications (six value or two value), time (0, 4, 7, or 11 days), and reexposure (present or absent). The communications variable was manipulated by presenting the subjects with either the six-value or two-value communication. This variable was used to provide some generality to the reexposure results. Time was manipulated by taking the only assessment of attitude toward Congressional election of the president either immediately after, 4 days after, 7 days after, or 11 days after exposure to one of the two experimental communications. Reexposure was manipulated by the nature of the information contained on the postcard sent to subjects in the delay conditions. In the reexposure conditions the postcards read:

> You recently heard two messages in a person perception experiment. The first listed some consequences of not having [a] sibling of the opposite sex, and the second argued that the President should be elected by Congress. Please report . . . for the second part of the experiment to. . . .

In the no-reexposure condition the postcards simply requested that the subjects return at a certain time and place ". . . for the second part of the person-perception experiment." All postcards were mailed 1 day after the initial session and thus were presumably in the subjects' possession for 2, 5, or 8 days. Since reexposure makes no sense in the no-delay condition, this variable is absent in that condition. That entire experimental design is summarized in Table 8.1. All three independent variables involved between-subjects manipulations.

The dependent variable was assessed with the question, "How much do you agree or disagree that the President should be elected by Congress?" [1] Subjects responded by checking an 11-point scale ranging from "totally disagree" to "totally agree." High numbers on the scale indicate agreement with the communication.

Procedure

The subjects were led to believe that the experiment was concerned with evaluating an "unseen speaker." At the initial session they were told that they would listen to two speeches, one delivered by a female and the other by a male, and then they would answer a number of questions about the speakers. After listening to the cover communication, which argued that having no sibling of the opposite sex has a slightly disadvantageous effect on marital adjustment during the first years of marriage, the subjects rated the speaker on a number of dimensions: age, self-assurance, knowledgeableness on the topic, modesty, warmth, considerateness, and good temperament. Following these ratings they were asked to indicate how many brothers or sisters they have, since this may have influenced their previous ratings.

After listening to the second communication (either the six-value or two-value communication), the subjects rated the speakers on the same dimensions that were used for the cover communication. Assessment of the dependent variable was introduced by a written statement explaining that it would be helpful to know how they felt about Congressional election of the President, since their

[1] The authors had originally also intended to assess the dependent variable with the question, "How justified is the present policy of having the President elected by direct vote?" However, some of the subjects noted that, after all, the president is not currently elected by direct vote, but by the electoral college.

Table 8.1—Mean Attitude Scores and Number of Subjects in Each Experimental Condition

	6-value communication								2-value communication							
	Time (in days)								Time (in days)							
	0		4		7		11		0		4		7		11	
	M	N	*M*	N	*M*	N	*M*	N	*M*	N	*M*	N	*M*	N	*M*	N
Reexposure			3.44	16	3.93	15	4.60	15			2.78	20	3.69	16	3.36	14
				(1)[a]		(2)		(2)				(1)		(3)		(3)
No reexposure	4.31	35	3.50	16	3.29	17	3.00	16	4.25	36	3.25	20	2.28	13	2.27	15
				(2)		(0)		(1)				(2)		(1)		(2)

Note.—No-communication control: *M* = 2.0 (N = 12).

[a] Number of subjects who failed to return.

ratings may have been influenced by such feelings. Assessment of the dependent variable was made either immediately after rating the "unseen speaker" or at the beginning of the second session that was either 4, 7, or 11 days later.

At the end of the initial session subjects were given blank postcards and asked to write their names and addresses on them. It was explained that if they were to be needed in a second session these postcards, filled in with information as to time and place, would be mailed to them. (Since at the beginning of the semester there was a shortage of experiments, all or almost all subjects wanted to participate in the second session. It was stressed that the first part of the person-perception experiment was unrelated to the second.) Subjects who were asked in the initial session for their attitude toward Congressional election of the President were not asked to return, although they too filled out postcards. Subjects in the initial sessions were randomly assigned to one of seven conditions (no-reexposure and 0-, 4-, 7-, or 11-day, delay or reexposure and 4-, 7-, or 11-day delay). The initial session differed in whether the six-value or two-value communication was presented to the subjects.

RESULTS

The mean attitude scores in each of the experimental conditions are presented in Table 8.1. Mean attitude in a no-communication control (2.0) is significantly less than the mean in the no-delay communication for both the six-value communication ($t = 2.96$, $p < .01$, $df = 45$) and the two-value communication ($t = 2.78$, $p < .01$, $df = 46$). These significant differences indicate that both communications produced an immediate persuasive impact.

A two-factor unweighted-means analysis of variance (Communications $\times$ Time) of the no-reexposure conditions across all four time intervals is presented in Table 8.2. The only significant F is the one for time. This F indicates that the persuasive impact of both communications decreased significantly over time. A trend analysis for (randomly produced) equal Ns revealed that the decrement is significantly rectilinear ($F = 6.29$, $p < .05$, $df = 1/112$).

Table 8.2—Unweighted-Means Analysis of Variance for All Four Time Intervals

Source	df	MS	F
Communications (C)	1	9.19	1.28
Time (T)	3	19.45	2.71*
C × T	3	1.65	
Within	165	7.17	

* $p < .05$.

Table 8.3—Unweighted-Means Analysis of Variance for the Three Delay Time Intervals

Source	df	MS	F
Communications (C)	1	23.18	4.48*
Reexposure (R)	1	24.08	4.65*
Time (T)	2	.08	
C × R	1	.03	
C × T	2	1.20	
R × T	2	11.86	2.29
C × R × T	2	2.06	
Within	186	5.18	

* $p < .05$.

A three-factor unweighted-means analysis of variance (Communications × Reinstatement × Time) for just the delay conditions is presented in Table 8.3. The only significant *F*s are the ones for communications and reexposure. The communications *F* indicates that in the delay conditions the six-value communication had a greater persuasive impact than did the two-value communication. The reexposure *F* indicates that, as predicted, reexposure produced a greater persistence effect than did no reexposure. Examination of the means in Table 8.1 reveals that the effect is evident for both communications. The Reexposure × Time interaction approaches but does not reach significance. This interaction is significant, however, if the 7- and 11-day intervals are collapsed ($F = 4.78$, $p < .05$, $df = 1/190$) or if the 7-day interval is dropped ($F = 4.40$, $p < .05$, $df = 1/124$). Also a trend analysis (for equal

Ns) reveals a significant rectilinear interaction for the Reexposure × Time effect ($F = 4.65$, $p < .05$, $df = 1/168$). These three significant *Fs* indicate that the reexposure effect was greater for the 7- and 11-day intervals than for the 4-day intervals.

DISCUSSION

The main effect for reexposure in the delay conditions supports the initial hypothesis that reexposure to the communication point of view contributes to the persistence of attitude change. Furthermore, the Time × Reexposure interaction indicates that in the delay conditions the effect of reexposure increased with time. Why should this be? One possibility is the fact that the simple reexposure manipulation would have the most opportunity to be effective after sufficient time had elapsed to allow some decay in the initial persuasive impact. However, the fact that within the reexposure condition alone attitude change *increased* over time (although nonsignificantly, $F < 1$) leads one to conclude that this explanation is not by itself entirely sufficient. An additional possibility is that the number of exposures to the postcard with the conclusion increased over time. This seems likely if the postcard were displayed in a prominent place as a reminder of the second session. We do know that many of the subjects were carrying their postcards when they appeared for the second session.

But why should a number of exposures or even a single exposure to the conclusion facilitate persistence? Possibly because such reexposure stimulates rehearsal and retention of the supporting arguments or rehearsal and retention of the communication point of view. Watts and McGuire (1964) found that both recall of supporting arguments and recall of the side taken by a communication were positively related to persistence at 1 and 6 weeks. Another possibility is that communication reexposure produced what Greenwald (1967) referred to as "recipient-generated thoughts," that is, thoughts occurring in the context of a persuasive communication but not directly reflecting actual communication content. Greenwald found evidence indicating a positive relation between recipient-generated thoughts and persistence.

The results with regard to the second hypothesis are encouraging, but by no means confirmatory. The six-value communication produced significantly more change than the two-value communication in the delay condition but not in the no-delay condition. In order to be able to state unequivocally that the six-value communication resulted in greater persistence than the two-value communication, however, one would need to obtain a significant Communications $\times$ Time interaction. Unfortunately, the incomplete factorial design does not allow for a test of this interaction that uses all of the data. It is true, though, that within the no-reexposure condition this interaction is not significant.

Let us suppose for the sake of argument that the six-value communication did show significantly greater persistence than the two-value communication, and that this effect is a result of the difference in number of value-linking arguments and not to a difference in the persistence-conferring potency of the individual arguments. After granting this, there is still a question as to whether the greater persistence of the six-value communication is due to the effort involved in changing the larger number of initially established linkages, as was initially proposed, or to the fact that the comprehension and acceptance of six-value linking arguments may require more time than the acceptance of two-value linking arguments. The more complex six-value communication may have required more time to "sink in" than the less complicated two-value communication. The authors do not think it reasonable that, in general, complex communications will show greater persistence than simple ones. However, when the complexity is created in such a way that the more thoroughly the communication is understood the greater the number of consistent cognitive linkages supporting the advocated point of view, it is definitely possible that such complexity will facilitate persistence. This type of theoretical possibility is not necessarily antagonistic to the effort explanation. It is conceivable that "sinking in" and avoidance of effort both facilitate persistence.

Finally, the authors would like to call attention to the fact that within the no-reexposure condition the persuasive impact of both communications decreased rectilinearly over time. In view of the pervasiveness of the negatively decelerated curve for various memory assessments, such a straight-line function stands out by contrast. Watts and McGuire (1964) obtained a negatively decelerated function for several recall and recognition assessments and, in agreement with the present findings, a straight-line function for opinion. Such a difference in function suggests that any assumption of a simple functional relation between memory and opinion is at best oversimplified. The same conclusion is implied by Greenwald's (1968) finding that 1 week after reading a persuasive communication there was significant decrease in the number of recalled arguments, but no corresponding loss of initial attitude change.

SUMMARY

An experiment was conducted which demonstrated that conclusion reexposure facilitates the persistence of attitude change. After initial exposure to a communication in a laboratory setting, *S*s were sent postcards reminding them of the time and place for a 2nd laboratory session. For approximately ½ of the *S*s the postcards also mentioned the communication topic. Over the most extreme time intervals *S*s in this reinstatement condition showed significantly greater persistence effects.

REFERENCES

ABELSON, R. P., & ROSENBERG, M. J. Symbolic psycho-logic: A model of attitudinal cognition. *Behavioral Science,* 1958, *3,* 1–13.

ANNIS, A. D., & MAIER, N. C. The induction of opinion through suggestion by means of "planted content." *Journal of Social Psychology,* 1934, *5,* 65–81.

CHEN, W. K. C. Retention of the effects of oral propaganda. *Journal of Social Psychology,* 1936, *7,* 479–483.

CHERRINGTON, B. M., & MILLER, L. W. Changes in attitude as a result of a lecture and of reading similar materials. *Journal of Social Psychology,* 1933, *4,* 479–484.

COHEN, A. R. Need for cognition and order of communication as a determinant of opinion change. In C. I. Hovland (Ed.), *Order of presentation in persuasion.* New Haven: Yale University Press, 1957.

DIETRICH, J. E. The relative effectiveness of two modes of radio delivery in influencing attitudes. *Speech Monographs,* 1946, *13,* 58–65.

DILLEHAY, R. C., INSKO, C. A., & SMITH, M. B. Logical consistency and attitude change. *Journal of Personality and Social Psychology,* 1966, *3,* 646–654.

ELMS, A. C. Influence of fantasy ability on attitude change through role playing. *Journal of Personality and Social Psychology,* 1966, *4,* 36–43.

GREENWALD, A. G. An amended learning model of persuasion. Paper presented at the meeting of the American Psychological Association, Washington, D.C., September 1967.

GREENWALD, A. G. Persuasion as a function of communication content learning. Unpublished manuscript, Ohio State University, 1968.

HALL, W. The effect of defined social stimulus material upon the stability of attitudes towards labor unions, capital punishment, social insurance, and Negroes. *Purdue University Studies in Higher Education,* 1938, *34,* 7–19.

HOVLAND, C. I., LUMSDAINE, A. A., & SHEFFIELD, F. D. *Experiments on mass communications.* Princeton University Press, 1949.

HOVLAND, C. I., & WEISS, W. The influence of source credibility on communication effectiveness. *Public Opinion Quarterly,* 1951, *15,* 635–650.

INSKO, C. A., ARKOFF, A., & INSKO, V. Effects of high and low fear-arousing communications upon opinions toward smoking. *Journal of Experimental Social Psychology,* 1965, *1,* 256–266.

KELMAN, H. C. Compliance, identification, and internalization: Three processes of opinion change. *Journal of Conflict Resolution,* 1958, *2,* 51–60.

KELMAN, H. C. Effects of role orientation and value orientation on the nature of attitude change. Paper presented at the meeting of the Eastern Psychological Association, New York, April 1960.

KELMAN, H. C., & HOVLAND, C. I. "Reinstatement" of the communicator in delayed measurement of opinion change. *Journal of Abnormal and Social Psychology,* 1953, *48,* 327–335.

MCGUIRE, W. J. Order of presentation as a factor in "conditioning" persuasiveness. In C. I. Hovland (Ed.), *Order of presentation in persuasion.* New Haven: Yale University Press, 1957.

MCGUIRE, W. J. A syllogistic analysis of cognitive relationships. In C. I. Hovland & M. J. Rosenberg (Eds.), *Attitude organization and change.* New Haven: Yale University Press, 1960.

MITNICK, L. L., & MCGINNIES, E. Influencing ethnocentrism in small discussion groups through a film communication. *Journal of Abnormal and Social Psychology,* 1958, *56,* 82–90.

NEWCOMB, T. M. Persistence and regression of changed attitudes: Long-range studies. *Journal of Social Issues,* 1963, *4,* 3–13.

PAPAGEORGIS, D. Bartlett effect and the persistence of induced opinion change. *Journal of Abnormal and Social Psychology,* 1963, *67,* 61–67.

PETERSON, R. C., & THURSTONE, L. L. *The effect of motion pictures on the social attitudes of high school children.* Chicago: University of Chicago Press, 1933.

ROSENBERG, M. J., & ABELSON, R. P. An analysis of cognitive balancing. In C. I. Hovland & M. J. Rosenberg (Eds.), *Attitude organization and change.* New Haven: Yale University Press, 1960.

SIMS, V. M. Factors influencing attitude toward the TVA. *Journal of Abnormal and Social Psychology,* 1938, *33,* 34–56.

SMITH, F. T. An experiment in modifying attitudes toward the Negro. *Teachers College Contribution to Education,* 1943, No. 887.

STOTLAND, E., KATZ, D., & PATCHEN, M. The reduction of prejudice through the arousal of self-insight. *Journal of Personality,* 1959, *27,* 507–531.

STOTLAND, E., & PATCHEN, M. Identification and changes in prejudice and in authoritarianism. *Journal of Abnormal and Social Psychology,* 1961, *62,* 265–274.

WATTS, W. A. Relative persistence of opinion change induced by active compared to passive participation. *Journal of Personality and Social Psychology,* 1967, *5,* 4–15.

WATTS, W. A., & MCGUIRE, W. J. Persistence of induced opinion change and retention of inducing message content. *Journal of Abnormal and Social Psychology,* 1964, *68,* 233–241.

WEISS, W. A. A sleeper effect in opinion change. *Journal of Abnormal and Social Psychology,* 1953, *48,* 173–180.

V

Attraction

There are various factors which tend to maximize individual attraction toward other people and objects in the environment. A deduction from cognitive dissonance theory, an approach that has generated much research since its formal statement by Festinger in 1957, is that the more effort in any form a person exerts to achieve a goal, the more he should like it. Early support for this prediction was found in a laboratory study by Aronson and Mills (Chapter 9). Persons who underwent an unpleasant membership initiation found the group more attractive than did individuals who became members without experiencing a severe initiation. Alternative explanations for this finding suggested by other investigators generally were eliminated by subsequent laboratory research. The applicability of this deduction from cognitive dissonance theory to other settings such as a marketing situation was tested by Doob, Carlsmith, Freedman, Landauer, and Tom, Jr. (Chapter 10) in several field experiments. As expected, when the initial price of a product was high, subsequent sales were higher than when the initial price was low. However, the researchers indicated that an explanation derived from adaptation level theory fitted the data as well as the one from cognitive dissonance theory. It seems that alternative explanations are more viable in the field than in the laboratory.

Much of the experimental work on attraction, however, has focused on personal characteristics of individuals. In a study by Byrne, Ervin and Lamberth (Chapter 11), independent variables previously identified in laboratory studies (attitude similarity, personality similarity, and physical attractiveness) were varied in a laboratory-field situation. The investigators selected couples on the basis of maximal or minimal similarity of responses to a questionnaire of attitudes and personality traits and brought them together as part of a "Computer Dating" study. Each couple was introduced and given differential information about the basis for their matching under controlled conditions in a laboratory setting. The couples then were asked to spend 30 minutes together on a coke date in the natural setting of the student center. When they returned from the date, the participants were assessed on a series of measures. Attraction was found to be a joint function of similarity and physical attractiveness. It is important to note that whereas in the previously illustrated laboratory-field experiments (Evans *et al.,* Chapter 6; Cook & Insko, Chapter 8), investigators had little or no control over the natural setting of their subjects, the requirements of the Byrne *et al.* experiment for the couples to have a close to first-impression relationship necessitated a design where the time they spent in the natural setting was quite limited.

9

The Effect of Severity of Initiation on Liking For a Group

Elliot Aronson and Judson Mills

It is a frequent observation that persons who go through a great deal of trouble or pain to attain something tend to value it more highly than persons who attain the same thing with a minimum of effort. For example, one would expect persons who travel a great distance to see a motion picture to be more impressed with it than those who see the same picture at a neighborhood theater. By the same token, individuals who go through a severe initiation to gain admission to a club or organization should tend to think more highly of that organization than those who do not go through the severe initiation to gain admission.

Two questions are relevant here: 1. Is this "common observation" valid, that is, does it hold true when tested under controlled conditions? 2. If the observation is valid, how can it be accounted for? The relationship might be simply a result of differences in initial motivation. To take the case of initiations, persons who initially have a strong desire to join a particular club should be more willing to undergo unpleasantness to gain admission to it than persons who are low in initial interest. Therefore, a club that requires a severe initiation for admission should be joined

From *Journal of Abnormal and Social Psychology,* 1959, *59,* 177–181.

This research was partially supported by a grant from the National Science Foundation, administered by Leon Festinger. The authors are grateful to Leon Festinger for his help and encouragement during the planning and execution of the study.

only by those people with a strong desire to become members. On the other hand, a club that does not require a severe initiation should be joined by some individuals who like it very much, and by others who are relatively uninterested. Because of this self-selection, one would expect persons who are members of clubs with severe initiations to think more highly of their club, on the average, than members of clubs without severe initiations.

But is there something in the initiation itself that might account for this relationship? Is severity of initiation positively related to group preference when motivation for admission is held constant? Such a relationship is strongly implied by Festinger's (1957) theory of cognitive dissonance. The theory of cognitive dissonance predicts this relationship in the following manner. No matter how attractive a group is to a person it is rarely completely positive, i.e., usually there are some aspects of the group that the individual does not like. If he has undergone an unpleasant initiation to gain admission to the group, his cognition that he has gone through an unpleasant experience for the sake of membership is dissonant with his cognition that there are things about the group that he does not like. He can reduce this dissonance in two ways. He can convince himself that the initiation was not very unpleasant, or he can exaggerate the positive characteristics of the group and minimize its negative aspects. With increasing severity of initiation it becomes more and more difficult to believe that the initiation was not very bad. Thus, a person who has gone through a painful initiation to become a member of a group should tend to reduce his dissonance by over estimating the attractiveness of the group. The specific hypothesis tested in the present study is that individuals who undergo an unpleasant initiation to become members of a group increase their liking for the group; that is, they find the group more attractive than do persons who become members without going through a severe initiation.

METHOD

In designing the experiment it was necessary to have people join groups that were similar in every respect except for the severity of the initiation required for admission—and then to measure each individual's evaluation of the group. It was also necessary to randomize the initial motivation of subjects (*S*s) to gain admission to the various groups in order to eliminate systematic effects of differences in motivation. These requirements were met in the following manner: Volunteers were obtained to participate in group discussions. They were assigned randomly to one of three experimental conditions: A *Severe* initiation condition, a *Mild* initiation condition, and a *Control* condition. In the Severe condition, *S*s were required to read some embarrassing material before joining the group; in the Mild condition the material they read in order to join the group was not very embarrassing; in the Control condition, *S*s were not required to read any material before becoming group members. Each *S* listened to the same tape recording which was ostensibly an ongoing discussion by the members of the group that he had just joined. *S*s then evaluated the discussion.

The *S*s were 63 college women. Thirty-three of them volunteered to participate in a series of group discussions on the psychology of sex. The remaining 30, tested at a somewhat later date, were "captive volunteers" from a psychology course who elected to participate in the group discussions on the psychology of sex in preference to several other experiments. Since the results obtained from these two samples were very similar, they were combined in the analysis presented here.

Each *S* was individually scheduled to "meet with a group." When she arrived at the experimental room, she was told by the experimenter *(E)* that he was conducting several group discussions on the psychology of sex. *E* informed her that she was joining a group that had been meeting for several weeks and that she was taking the place of a girl who had to leave the group because of scheduling difficulties. *E* stated that the discussion had just begun and that she would join the other members of the group after he had explained the nature of the experiment to her. The purpose of the foregoing instructions was to confront *S* with an ongoing group and thus make plausible the recorded discussion to which she was to be exposed.

E then "explained" the purpose of the experiment. He said that he was interested in investigating the "dynamics of the group discussion process." Sex was chosen as the topic for the groups to discuss in order to provide interesting subject matter so that volunteers for the discussion groups could be obtained without much difficulty. *E* continued as follows:

> But the fact that the discussions are concerned with sex has one major drawback. Although most people are interested in sex, they tend to be a little shy when it comes to discussing it. This is very bad from the point of view of the experiment; if one or two people in a group do not participate as much as they usually do in group discussions because they are embarrassed about sex, the picture we get of the group discussion process is distorted. Therefore, it is extremely important to arrange things so that the members of the discussion group can talk as freely and frankly as possible. We found that the major inhibiting factor in the discussions was the presence of the other people in the room. Somehow, it's easier to talk about embarrassing things if other people aren't staring at you. To get around this, we hit upon an idea which has proved very successful. Each member of the group is placed in a separate room, and the participants communicate through an intercom system using headphones and a microphone. In this way, we've helped people relax, and have succeeded in bringing about an increase in individual participation.

The foregoing explanation set the stage for the tape recording, which could now be presented to the *S* as a live discussion conducted by three people in separate rooms.

E then mentioned that, in spite of this precaution, occasionally some persons were still too embarrassed to engage in the discussions and had to be asked to withdraw from the discussion group. *S* was asked if she thought she could discuss sex freely. She invariably answered affirmatively. In the Control condition *S* was told, at this point, that she would be a member of the group.

In the other two conditions, *E* went on to say that it was difficult for him to ask people to leave the group once they had become members. Therefore, he had recently decided to screen new people before admitting them to the discussion groups. The screening device was described as an "embarrassment test" which consists of reading aloud some sexually oriented material in the presence of *E*. *S* was told that *E* would make a clinical judgment of her degree of embarrassment, based upon hesitation, blushing, etc. and would determine whether or not she would be capable of participating in the discussion group. He stressed that she was not obligated to take this test, but that she could not become a member unless she did. Only one *S* declined to take the test. She was excluded from the experiment. It was also emphasized, at this point, that the "embarrassment test" was a recent innovation and that the other members had joined the group before it was required for admission. These instructions were included in order to counteract any tendency to identify more strongly with the group as a result of feelings of having shared a common unpleasant experience. Such a process could conceivably bring about a greater preference for the discussion group on the part of *S*s in the Severe condition, introducing ambiguity in the interpretation of the results.

In the Severe condition, the "embarrassment test" consisted of having *S*s read aloud, from 3 × 5 cards, 12 obscene words, e.g., fuck, cock, and screw. *S*s also read aloud two vivid descriptions of sexual activity from contemporary novels. In the Mild condition, *S*s read aloud five words that were related to sex but not obscene, e.g., prostitute, virgin, and petting. In both the Severe and the Mild conditions, after each *S* finished reading the material, she was told that she had performed satisfactorily and was, therefore, a member of the group and could join the meeting that was now in progress.

It was of the utmost importance to prevent the *S* from attempting to participate in the discussion, for if she did, she would soon find that no one was responding to her statements and she would probably infer that the discussion was recorded. To insure their silence, all *S*s were told that, in preparation for each meeting, the group reads an assignment which serves as the focal point of the discussion; for this meeting, the group read parts of the book, *Sexual Behavior in Animals*. After the *S* had indicated that she had never read this book, *E* told her that she would be at a disadvantage and would, consequently, not be able to participate as fully in this discussion as she would had she done the reading. He continued, "Because the presence of a participant who isn't contributing optimally would result in an inaccurate picture of the dynamics of the group discussion process, it would be best if you wouldn't participate at all today, so that we may get an undistorted picture of the dynamics of the other three members of this group. Meanwhile, you can simply listen to the discussion, and get an idea of how the group operates. For the next meeting, you can do the reading and join in the discussion." *S*s were invariably more than willing to comply with this suggestion. The above instructions not only prevented *S* from attempting to participate in the discussion but also served to orient her toward the actual content of discussion.

Under the guise of connecting the *S*'s headphones and microphone, *E* went into the next room and turned on the tape recorder. He then returned to the experimental room, put on the headphones, picked up the microphone, and pretended to break into the discussion which supposedly was in progress. After holding a brief conversation with the "members of the group," he introduced the *S* to them. Then he handed the headphones to her. The tape was timed so that at the precise moment that *S* donned her headphones, the "group members" introduced themselves and then continued their discussion.

The use of a tape recording presented all *S*s with an identical group experience. The recording was a discussion by three female undergraduates. It was deliberately designed to be as dull and banal as possible in order to maximize the dissonance of the *S*s in the Severe condition. The participants spoke dryly and haltingly on secondary sex behavior in the lower animals, "inadvertently" contradicted themselves and one another, mumbled several *non sequiturs,* started sentences that they never finished, hemmed, hawed, and in general conducted one of the most worthless and uninteresting discussions imaginable.

At the conclusion of the recording, *E* returned and explained that after each meeting every member of the group fills out a questionnaire expressing her reactions to the discussion. The questionnaire asked the *S* to rate the discussion and the group members on 14 different evaluative scales, e.g., dull–interesting, intelligent–unintelligent, by circling a number from 0 to 15. After completing the questionnaire, *S* made three additional ratings, orally, in response to questions from *E*. Nine of the scales concerned the *S*'s reactions to the discussion, while the other eight concerned her reactions to the participants.

At the close of the experiment, *E* engaged each *S* in conversation to determine whether or not she was suspicious of the procedure. Only one *S* entertained definite suspicions; her results were discarded.

Finally, the true nature of the experiment was explained in detail. None of the *S*s expressed any resentment or annoyance at having been misled. In fact, the majority were intrigued by the experiment and several returned at the end of the academic quarter to ascertain the results.

RESULTS AND DISCUSSION

The sum of the ratings for the 17 different scales provides an index of each *S*'s liking for the discussion group. The means and *SD*s for the three experimental conditions for this measure are presented in Table 9.1. Means and *SD*s are also presented in Table 9.1 separately for the eight scales which tapped the *S*s' attitudes toward the discussion and the seven scales which tapped their attitudes toward the participants. The significance of the differences between the means for the different conditions were determined by *t* tests. The *t* values and significance levels are presented in Table 9.2.

Examination of Table 9.1 shows that *S*s in the Severe condition rated both the discussion and the participants higher than did those in the Control and Mild conditions. The over-all difference between the ratings by *S*s in the Severe condition and *S*s in the Control condition reaches the .01% level of significance. The over-all difference between the ratings by *S*s in the Severe initiation condition and *S*s in the Mild initiation condition reaches the .05 level.

These differences cannot be explained by differences in initial motivation to become members of the group, since *S*s (with varying degrees of motivation) were randomly assigned to the three experimental conditions. The differences in liking for the group must be considered a consequence of the unpleasant experience. The results clearly substantiate the hypothesis: persons who undergo a severe initiation to attain membership in a group increase their liking for the group. This hypothesis follows directly from Festin-

Table 9.1—Means of the Sum of Ratings for the Different Experimental Conditions

Rating Scales	Experimental Conditions		
	Control (N = 21)	Mild (N = 21)	Severe (N = 21)
Discussion [9]			
M	80.2	81.8	97.6
SD	13.2	21.0	16.6
Participants [8]			
M	89.9	89.3	97.7
SD	10.9	14.1	13.2
Total [17]			
M	166.7	171.1	195.3
SD	21.6	34.0	31.9

Table 9.2—Significance Levels of the Differences Between Experimental Conditions

Rating Scales	Differences Between Conditions		
	Control-Severe	Mild-Severe	Control-Mild
Discussion [9]	$t = 3.66$ $P < .001$*	$t = 2.62$ $P < .02$	$t = .29$ N.S.
Participants [8]	$t = 2.03$ $P < .05$	$t = 1.97$ $P < .10$	$t = .15$ N.S.
Total [17]	$t = 3.32$ $P < .01$	$t = 2.33$ $P < .05$	$t = .49$ N.S.

* The *P* values given are based on both tails of the *t* distribution.

ger's theory of cognitive dissonance. According to the theory, *S*s in the Severe initiation condition held the cognition that they had undergone a painful experience to become members of the discussion group. Then they listened to a dull, banal discussion. Negative cognitions about the discussion which they formed from listening to it were dissonant with the cognition that they had undergone a painful experience to gain membership in this group. The presence of dissonance leads to pressures to reduce it. *Ss* in this condition could reduce their dissonance either by denying the severity of the initiation or by distorting their cognitions concerning the group discussion in a positive direction. The initiation of the *Ss* in the Severe condition was apparently too painful for them to deny—hence, they reduced their dissonance by overestimating the attractiveness of the group.

There was no appreciable difference between the ratings made by *Ss* in the Control condition and those made by *Ss* in the Mild condition. It would seem that the Mild condition was so devoid of unpleasantness as to constitute little investment in the group. Hence, little dissonance was created. If any dissonance did occur in this situation it would be more realistic for the *S* to reduce it by minimizing the pain of the initiation, than by distorting her cognitions concerning the discussion. Thus, it is not an initiation per se that leads to increase in liking for a group. The initiation must be severe enough to constitute a genuine investment and to render it difficult to reduce dissonance by playing down the extent of the pain involved.

An examination of Table 9.1 shows that the rating scales concerning the discussion show greater differences between the conditions than the scales dealing with the evaluations of the participants in the discussion. There are at least two possible explanations for this result: (*a*) It may be easier for people to express negative criticism about an impersonal discussion than about the people involved. Thus, *Ss* in the Control and Mild conditions may have inflated their ratings of the participants to avoid making negative statements about fellow college students. (*b*) It is possible that *Ss* in the Severe condition had less need to distort their perception of the participants than of the discussion itself. The dissonance of the *Ss* in the Severe condition resulted from the actual discussion: they experienced dissonance between going through an unpleasant experience and taking part in worthless uninteresting discussions. The most direct way for them to reduce this dissonance would be to change their perceptions of the discussion in a positive direction. The participants in the discussion were peripheral to the cause of dissonance. If *Ss* in the Severe condition had less need to distort their perceptions of the participants than their perception of the discussion, their evaluations of the participants could be expected to be closer to the evaluations of the participants made by *S*s in the Control and Mild conditions.

SUMMARY AND CONCLUSIONS

An experiment was conducted to test the hypothesis that persons who undergo an unpleasant initiation to become members of a group increase their liking for the group; that is, they find the group more attractive than do persons who become members without going through a severe initiation. This hypothesis was derived from Festinger's theory of cognitive dissonance.

College women who volunteered to participate in discussion groups were randomly assigned to one of three experimental conditions: A *Severe* initiation condition, a *Mild* initiation condition, and a *Control* condition. In the Severe condition, subjects were required to read some embarrassing material before joining the group; in the Mild condition the material they read in order to join the group was not very embarrassing; in the Control condition, subjects were not required to read any material before becoming group members. Each subject listened to a recording that appeared to be an ongoing discussion being conducted by the group which she had just joined. Afterwards, subjects filled out a questionnaire evaluating the discussion and the participants. The results clearly verified the hypothesis. Subjects who underwent a severe initiation perceived the group as being significantly more attractive than did those who underwent a mild initiation or no initiation. There was no appreciable difference between ratings by subjects who underwent a Mild initiation and those by subjects who underwent no initiation.

REFERENCE

FESTINGER, L. *A theory of cognitive dissonance*. Evanston: Row, Peterson, 1957.

10

Effect of Initial Selling Price on Subsequent Sales

Anthony N. Doob, J. Merrill Carlsmith, Jonathan L. Freedman, Thomas K. Landauer, and Soleng Tom, Jr.

The "introductory low price offer" is a common technique used by marketers. A new product is offered at a low price for a short period of time, and the price is subsequently raised to its normal level. Since the goal naturally is to maximize final sales of the product, the assumption behind this technique is that it will accomplish this goal. An economic model based entirely on supply and demand would of course predict that the eventual sales would not be affected by the initial price. The lower price would be expected to attract many marginal buyers and produce greater sales; but as soon as the price is raised, these buyers should drop out of the market. The hope of the marketer, however, is that some of these marginal buyers will learn to like the product enough so that they will continue to purchase it even at the higher price.

Unfortunately for the marketer, this may be a vain hope. There are various psychological reasons why we might expect the introductory low price to have an opposite effect from that which the marketers intend, such that the introductory low price would reduce rather than increase eventual sales. Since this technique is so widespread, it provides an unusual opportunity to investigate

From *Journal of Personality and Social Psychology*, 1969, *11*, 345–350. Copyright 1969 by the American Psychological Association, and reprinted with permission.

This study was supported in part by National Science Foundation grants to Carlsmith and to Freedman. The authors are grateful to management and personnel of the discount chain for their cooperation in this research.

the applicability of social psychology in a natural setting, and to compare the marketer's predictions with that of social psychology.

The most interesting analysis of this situation is based on the theory of cognitive dissonance (Festinger, 1957). One of the clearest deductions from the theory is that the more effort in any form a person exerts to attain a goal, the more dissonance is aroused if the goal is less valuable than expected. The individual reduces this dissonance by increasing his liking for the goal, and therefore the greater the effort, the more he should like the goal. The prediction has received some substantiation in laboratory experimentation (e.g., Aronson & Mills, 1959; Gerard & Mathewson, 1966). Its applicability to the marketing situation is straightforward: the theory predicts that the higher the price a person initially pays for a product, the more he will come to like it. Presumably this greater liking will produce "brand loyalty" in the form of repeat purchases. Thus, when the initial price is high, a higher *proportion* of buyers should continue to purchase the product than when the initial price is low. Accordingly, although the introductory price will initially attract more customers, we may expect the sales curves for the two conditions to cross at some later point, and the higher brand loyalty induced by the dissonance involved in paying a high price to manifest itself in higher final sales in that condition.

Five experiments were performed to demonstrate that introducing a new brand of a product at a low price for a short time and then raising it to the normal selling price leads to lower sales in the long run than introducing the product at its normal selling price. The general design of all the experiments was to introduce the new brand at a low price in one set of stores and, after the price is raised to the normal selling price, compare sales with matched stores where the product was introduced at the normal selling price and held there throughout the course of the experiment.

All of the experiments that are to be reported here were done in a chain of discount houses. All sales figures have been multiplied by a constant in order to maintain confidentiality.

This chain of discount houses differs from most others in a number of important ways. They do not advertise much, and what advertising they do does not include prices on specific items. Price changes occur very seldom in these stores and are usually not advertised. In most cases, prices are lowered because an item is overstocked, and unless the customer remembers the regular selling price, he has no way of knowing that the price is lower than usual. Management in most of these stores is under direct control of the central office. When the manager receives orders from the central office, he has little or no power to change them.

The chain sells a large number of "house brands" at prices lower than the equivalent name brands. These house brands have the same registered trademark, and constitute a brand which customers can easily identify with the store. Generally, the quality of the house brand item is as high as the equivalent name brand, the differences usually being in characteristics which do not directly affect the usefulness of the item (e.g., mouthwash bottles are not as attractive as those of the name brand; the average grain size of powdered detergent is larger than that of the name brand which is chemically equivalent).

The products used in the studies reported here were house brands. All were being introduced into the stores at the time when the study was being run. The particular products used and the price differential were both determined by management.

EXPERIMENT I

Method

Twelve pairs of discount houses, matched on gross sales, were randomly assigned to one of two experimental conditions. In one store of each pair, the house brand of mouthwash was introduced at $.25 per quart bottle. The price was held at this level for 9 days (two weekends and the intervening days), and then the price was brought up to $.39 for all stores. In the other store, it was introduced at its normal selling price of $.39.

None of the managers had any reason to believe that the price of mouthwash at his store was not the same as in all other stores in the chain. No one was given any special instructions beyond the place in the store where the item was to be sold and its selling price. The location was essentially identical for all stores. In stores where mouthwash was introduced at the low price, the manager received a memo at the end of the first week instructing him to change the price to $.39 after that weekend.

Results

Sales were recorded by the sundries buyer as he replenished stock. At the end of each week these figures were sent to the central office and then relayed to the experimenters. Average sales for the 12 matched stores in each condition are shown in Fig. 10.1. It is estimated that at least 2 weeks had to pass before customers would return to buy more mouthwash, and, therefore, one would not expect there to be any difference between the height of the curves until the third week. In fact, the curves cross at this point, and after this point, it is clear that the stores where the initial selling price was high were selling more mouthwash than stores where the initial price was low. This is true in spite of the fact that more mouthwash was sold the first week in stores where the price was low. Unfortunately, for a variety of reasons, the authors were not able to collect continuous data. They were able, however, to check sales 19 weeks after the price change, and clearly the difference still existed. When sales for Weeks 3, 4, 5, and 20 are com-

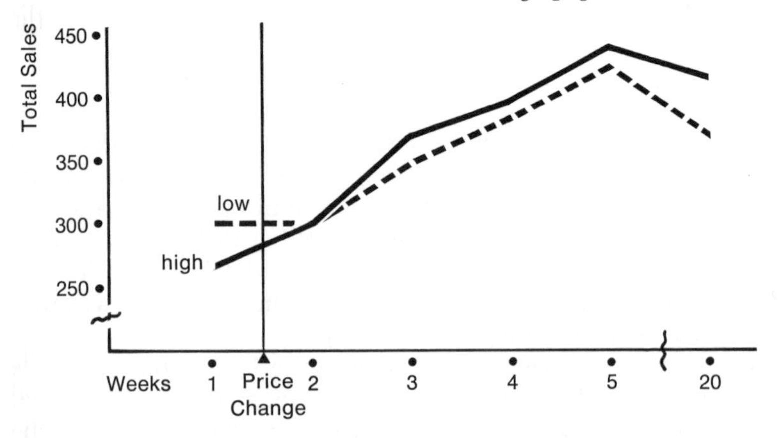

Fig. 10.1. Mouthwash sales.

bined, sales of mouthwash were higher in the store where the initial selling price was high in 10 of the 12 pairs of stores ($p = .02$).

Sales in the two sets of stores during Weeks 3, 4, 5, and 20 (pooled) were also compared by use of a t test, resulting in a t of 2.11 ($df = 11$, $p < .10$). Thus, stores where the initial selling price was low sold less mouthwash than did stores where the initial selling price was the same as the final selling price.

REPLICATIONS

The same experiment was repeated four times, using different products. The procedures were very similar in all cases. In each experiment, the stores were rematched and randomly assigned independent of all other replications.

Experiment II: Toothpaste

Six pairs of stores were matched on the basis of sundries sales and randomly assigned to conditions in which the selling price for the first 3 weeks was either \$.41 or \$.49 for a "family size" tube of toothpaste. After 3 weeks, the price in all stores was set at \$.49. The results are presented in Fig. 10.2. When the sales for the last 4

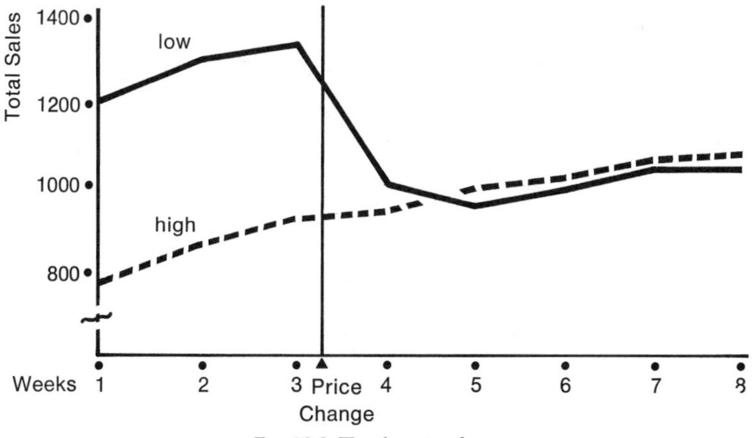

FIG. 10.2. Toothpaste sales.

weeks are combined as in the previous experiment, four of the six pairs show differences in the predicted direction ($p = .34$). When the more sensitive t test is done on the data from these 4 weeks, the t is 2.26 ($df = 5$, $p < .10$).

Experiment III: Aluminum Foil

Seven pairs of stores were matched on the basis of grocery sales and randomly assigned to conditions in which the selling price for the first 3 weeks was either $.59 or $.64 for a 75-foot roll of foil. After 3 weeks, the price in all stores was set at $.64. The results are presented in Fig. 10.3. For Weeks 5–8 combined, all seven pairs ($p = .01$) show differences in the predicted direction ($t = 5.09$, $df = 6$, $p < .005$).

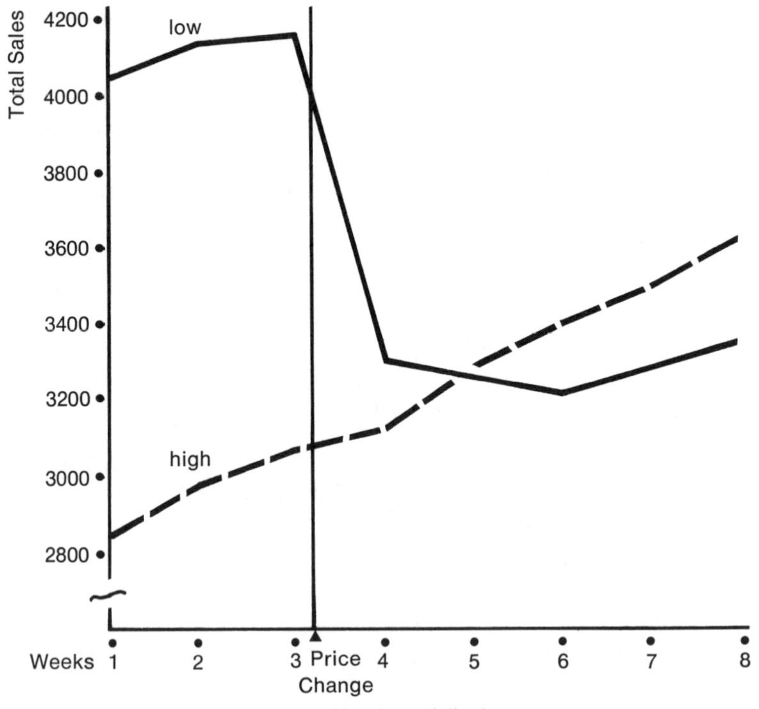

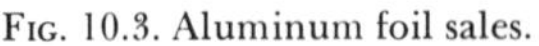
FIG. 10.3. Aluminum foil sales.

Experiment IV: Light Bulbs

Eight pairs of stores were matched on the basis of hardware sales and randomly assigned to conditions in which selling price for the first week was either \$.26 or \$.32 for a package of light bulbs. After 1 week, the price was brought up to \$.32 in all stores. The results are presented in Figure 10.4. For Weeks 3 and 4 combined, six of the eight pairs ($p = .15$) show differences in the predicted direction ($t = .837$, $df = 7$). Although this difference is not significant, it might be noted in Fig. 10.4 that there was the predicted reversal, even though initial sales were almost 50% higher at the low price.

Experiment V: Cookies

Eight pairs of stores were matched on the basis of grocery sales and randomly assigned to conditions in which the selling price for

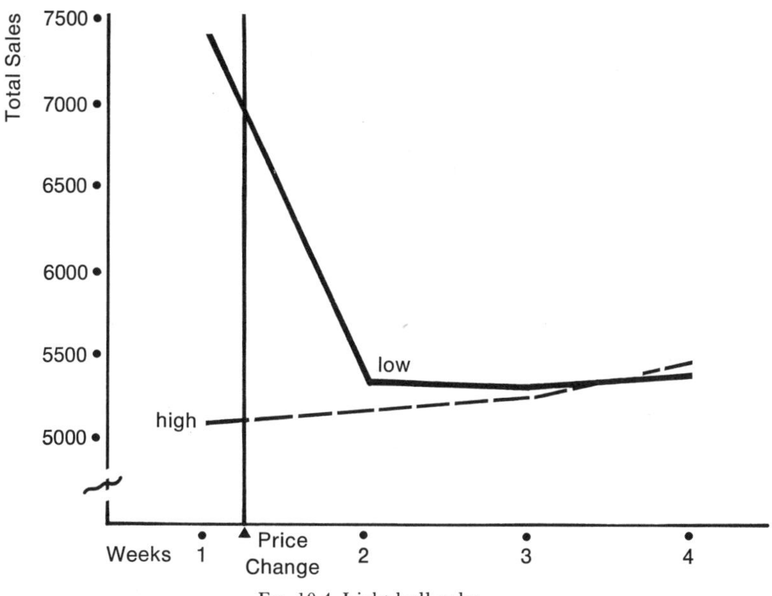

FIG. 10.4. Light bulb sales.

the first 2 weeks was \$.24 or \$.29 for a large bag of cookies. After 2 weeks, the price was at \$.29 for all stores. The results are presented in Fig. 10.5. For Weeks 4–6 combined, six of the eight pairs show differences in the predicted direction ($t = .625$, $df = 7$).

RESULTS

When the results of all five experiments are combined into one test of the hypothesis, a z of 3.63 ($p < .0002$) is obtained. Clearly, so far as this has been tested, the practice of introducing a product at a low price is not a good strategy for this chain of stores to use.

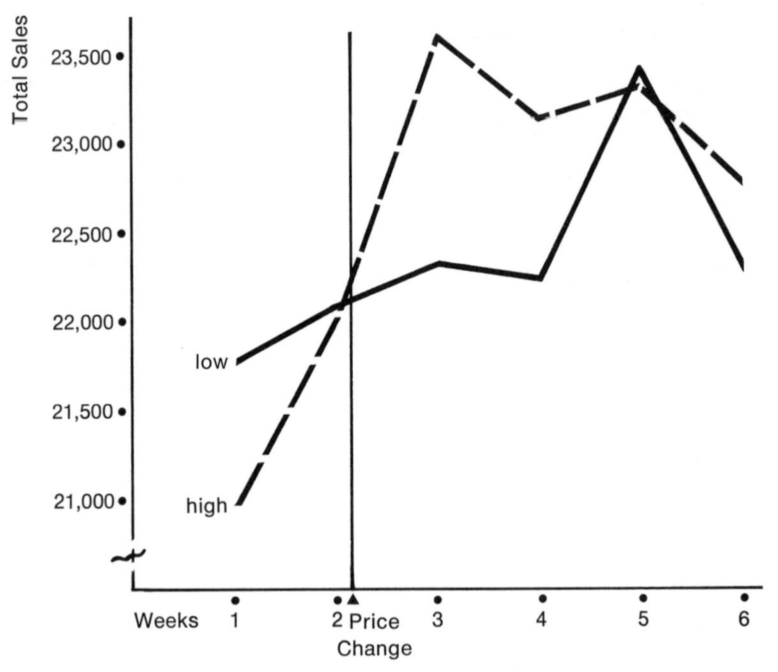

Fig. 10.5. Cookie sales.

DISCUSSION

These studies indicate that introducing products at a lower than usual price is harmful to final sales. It was earlier argued that one possible reason for this is the lower proportion of buyers who return to a product when the initial price is lower than the normal price. Whether or not this causes eventual sales actually to be lower when the initial price is low is not critical to the argument. If, for example, there is an extremely large difference in initial sales, even a lower proportion of returning buyers may produce an advantage for the initial low price. Similarly, if the product has some special feature which would be expected to produce loyalty merely from exposure, it would be beneficial to maximize initial sales by the use of low introductory offers. In the experiments reported here, neither of these possibilities seems to have been present. For the range of prices studied, even a 50% increase in sales due to the lower price was not enough to overcome the increased consumer loyalty engendered by the higher price. Because of the presence of other identical brands, differing only in price, exposure alone was not enough to produce loyalty.

Whether or not eventual sales are actually lower when the initial price is low is not critical to the argument. From a theoretical point of view, the only essential comparison is the relative proportion of repurchases in the two condtions. A stringent method of showing that this proportion is higher when the initial price is high is to demonstrate that the absolute volume of eventual sales is greater for the high-price condition, even though initial sales are lower. For the products and prices studied here, this was true.

There are at least two alternative explanations of this result. The first is that in the low-initial-price stores the market is glutted after the first few weeks, and it takes a long time for there to be any need to repurchase the product. This might be a partial explanation of the difference between the conditions, but seems implausible as a total explanation. For all the products except light bulbs the length of time that the sales curves were followed exceeded by a goodly margin the marketer's estimate of the normal time until repurchase. Indeed, with mouthwash, for which the repurchase period is about 2 weeks, the difference between conditions is still present 19 weeks after the price switch. Customers might have stocked up by buying more than their usual supply of a product, but pricing practices of this chain of stores makes this unlikely. These stores have rarely used low introductory price offers and they were not advertised as such for the products studied. Buyers therefore had no reason to believe that the "low price" was a special price and accordingly had little reason to stock up on the product. Thus, although one cannot entirely rule out this "glutting the market" explanation, it is not convincing.

A second and more interesting alternative is in terms of what might be called the customers' adaptation level regarding the particular product. When mouthwash is put on sale at $.25, customers who buy it at that price or notice what the price is may tend to think of the product in terms of $.25. They say to themselves that this is a $.25 bottle of mouthwash. When, in subsequent weeks, the price increases to $.39, these customers will tend to see it as overpriced, and are not inclined to buy it at this much higher price. Therefore, sales drop off considerably. In the $.39 steady condition, initial sales are lower, but there is no reason for them to drop off due to this effect. Therefore, introducing it at the ultimate price results in greater sales in the long run than does introducing it at the low price. This explanation fits the data as nicely as does the one in terms of cognitive dissonance. In many ways, they are quite similar and are difficult to distinguish experimentally.

It should be noted that the adaptation level and dissonance explanations are by no means mutually exclusive. It is entirely possible that both mechanisms are operating to some extent. In any case, the basic result stands—the introduction of a product at a low price tended to decrease subsequent sales, and this effect lasted for at least 20 weeks.

SUMMARY

Five field experiments investigated the effect of initial selling price on subsequent sales of common household products. Matched pairs of discount houses sold the same product at either a discounted price or the regular price for a short period of time. The prices were then made the same for all stores. The results were consistent with the prediction from dissonance theory that subsequent sales would be higher where the initial price was high.

REFERENCES

ARONSON, E., & MILLS, J. The effect of severity of initiation on liking for a group. *Journal of Abnormal and Social Psychology*, 1959, *59*, 177–181.

FESTINGER, L. *A theory of cognitive dissonance*. Stanford, Calif.: Stanford University Press, 1957.

GERARD, H. B., & MATHEWSON, G. C. The effects of severity of initiation on liking for a group: A replication. *Journal of Experimental Social Psychology*, 1966, *2*, 278–287.

11

Continuity Between The Experimental Study of Attraction and Real-Life Computer Dating

Donn Byrne, Charles R. Ervin, and John Lamberth

From *Journal of Personality and Social Psychology*, 1970, *16*, 157–165. [A reference originally listed as in press was amended to show date of publication. Ed.]

This research was supported in part by Research Grant MH-11178-04 from

A familiar but never totally resolved problem with any experimental findings is the extent to which they may be generalized to the nonlaboratory situation. At least three viewpoints about the problem may be discerned. First, and perhaps most familiar, is instant generalization from the specific and often limited conditions of an experiment to any and all settings which are even remotely related. This tendency is most frequently seen at cocktail parties after the third martini and on television talk shows featuring those who popularize psychology. Second, and almost as familiar, is the notion that the laboratory is a necessary evil. It is seen as an adequate substitute for the real world, only to the extent that it reproduces the world. For example, Aronson and Carlsmith (1968) ask, "Why, then, do we bother with these pallid and contrived imitations of human interaction when there exist rather sophisticated techniques for studying the real thing [p. 4]?" They enumerate the advantages of experiments over field study, but emphasize that good experiments must be realistic in order to involve the subject and have an "impact" on him. Concern with experimental realism often is expressed in the context of positing qualitative differences between the laboratory and the outside world; it is assumed that in moving from simplicity to complexity, new and different principles are emergent. Third, and least familiar in personality and social psychology, is a view which is quite common in other fields. Laboratory research is seen not as a necessary evil but as an essential procedure which enables us to attain isolation and control of variables and thus makes possible the formulation of basic principles in a setting of reduced complexity. If experiments realistically reproduce the nonlaboratory complexities, they provide little advantage over the field study. Continuity is assumed between the laboratory and the outside world, and complexity is seen as quantitative and not qualitative. To move from a simple situation to a complex one requires detailed knowledge about the relevant variables and their interaction. Application and the attainment of a technology depend upon such an approach.

---

the National Institute of Mental Health and in part by Research Grant GS-2752 from the National Science Foundation. The authors wish to thank James Hilgren, Royal Masset, and Herman Mitchell for their help in conducting this experiment.

With respect to a specific psychological phenomenon, the problem of nonlaboratory generalization and application may be examined more concretely. The laboratory investigation of interpersonal attraction within a reinforcement paradigm (Byrne, 1969) has followed a strategy in which the effect of a variety of stimulus variables on a single response variable was the primary focus of interest. A model has evolved which treats all relevant stimuli as positive or negative reinforcers of differential magnitude. Attraction toward any stimulus object (including another person) is then found to be a positive linear function of the proportion of weighted positive reinforcements associated with that object. Attitude statements have been the most frequently employed reinforcing stimuli, but other stimulus elements have included personality variables (e.g., Griffitt, 1966), physical attractiveness (e.g., Byrne, London & Reeves, 1968), economic variables (Byrne, Clore, & Worchel, 1966), race (e.g., Byrne & Ervin, 1969), behavioral preferences (Huffman, 1969), personal evaluations (e.g., Byrne & Rhamey, 1965), room temperature (Griffitt, 1970), and sexual arousal (Picher, 1966).

Considering just one of those variables, attitude similarity-dissimilarity, why is it not reasonable to propose an immediate and direct parallel between laboratory and nonlaboratory responses? One reason is simple and quite obvious, but it seems often to be overlooked. Laboratory research is based on the isolation of variables so that one or a limited number of independent variables may be manipulated, while, if possible, all other stimulus variables are controlled. In the outside world, multiple uncontrolled stimuli are present. Thus, if all an experimental subject knows about a stranger is that he holds opinions similar to his own on six out of six political issues, the stranger will be liked (Byrne, Bond, & Diamond, 1969). We cannot, however, assume that any two interacting individuals who agree on these six issues will become fast friends because (*a*) they may never get around to discussing those six topics at all, and (*b*) even if these topics are discussed, six positive reinforcements may simply become an insignificant portion of a host of other positive and negative reinforcing elements in the interaction. A second barrier to immediate applicability of a laboratory finding lies in the nature of the response. It is good research strategy to limit the dependent variable (in this instance, the sum of two 7-point rating scales), but nonlaboratory responses may be as varied and uncontrolled as the stimuli. The relationship between that paper-and-pencil measure of attraction and other interpersonal responses is only beginning to be explored (e.g., Byrne, Baskett, & Hodges, 1969; Efran, 1969). The third barrier lies in the nature of the relationship investigated. For a number of quite practical reasons, the laboratory study of attraction is limited in its time span and hence might legitimately be labeled the study of first impressions. Whether the determinants of first impressions are precisely the same as the determinants of a prolonged friendship, of love, or of marital happiness is an empirical question and one requiring a great deal of research.

In view of these barriers to extralaboratory application of experimental findings, how may one begin the engineering enterprise? The present research suggests one attempt to seek a solution. Specifically, a limited dating situation is created in which the barriers to application are minimized. Independent variables identified in the laboratory (attitude similarity, personality similarity, and physical attractiveness) are varied in a real-life situation, and an attempt is made to make the variables salient and to minimize the occurrence of other stimulus events. Even though similarity has been the focus of much of the experimental work on attraction, the findings with respect to physical attractiveness have consistently demonstrated the powerful influence of appearance on responses to those of the opposite sex and even of the same sex. Both field studies (Megargee, 1956; Perrin, 1921; Taylor, 1956; Walster, Aronson, Abrahams, & Rottmann, 1966) and laboratory investigations (Byrne et al., 1968; McWhirter, 1969; Moss, 1969) have shown that those who are physically attractive elicit more positive responses than do those who are unattractive. The laboratory response measure was retained so that a common reference point was available, but additional response variables were also used in order to extend the generality and meaning of the attraction construct. Finally, in this experiment, the interaction was deliberately limited in time so that it remained close to a first-impression relationship. Given these deliberately limited conditions, it was proposed that the positive relationship between the proportion of weighted positive reinforcements and attraction is directly applicable to a nonlaboratory interaction. Specifically, it was hypothesized that in a computer dating situation (*a*) attraction is a joint function of similarity and physical attractiveness, and (*b*) the greater the extent to which the specific elements of similarity are made salient, the greater is the relationship between similarity and attraction.

The variety of ways in which similarity and attraction could be investigated in a field situation raises an interesting question of strategy. It should be kept in mind that there is no magic about the similarity effect. Similarity does not exude from the pores; rather, specific attitudes and other characteristics must be expressed overtly. It would be relatively simple to design a computer dating experiment in which no similarity effects would be found. For example, one could lie about the degree of similarity, and in a brief interaction, the subjects would not be likely to discover the deception. Another alternative would be to provide no information about similarity and then to forbid the subjects to talk during their date. Negative results in such studies would be of no importance as a test since they are beyond the boundary conditions of the theory. Another possible study would give no initial similarity information and then require an extended interaction period, but that has already been done. That is, people in the real world do this every day, and numerous correlational studies indicate that under such conditions, similarity is associated with attraction. The strategy of the present research was frankly to maximize the possibility of securing a precise similarity attraction effect in a real-life setting; in subsequent research, the limiting conditions of the effect may be determined.

METHOD

Attitude-Personality Questionnaire

In order to provide a relatively broad base on which to match couples for the dating process, a 50-item questionnaire was constructed utilizing five variables. In previous research, a significant similarity effect has been found for authoritarianism (Sheffield &

Byrne, 1967), repression-sensitization (Byrne & Griffitt, 1969; Byrne, Griffitt, & Stefaniak, 1967), attitudes (Byrne, 1961, 1969), EPPS items,[1] and self-concept (Griffitt, 1966, 1969). Each variable was represented by 10 items which were chosen to represent the least possible intercorrelations within dimensions; the rationale here was the desire to maximize the number of *independent* scale responses on which matching could be based.

Simulated Stranger Condition

In order to provide a base line for the similarity effect under controlled conditions, a simulated stranger condition was run in which the other person was represented only by his or her purported responses to the attitude-personality questionnaire. The study was described as an investigation of the effectiveness of the matching procedures of computer dating organizations. Subjects were told, "Instead of arranging an actual date, we are providing couples with information about one another and asking for their reactions." The simulated scales were prepared to provide either a .33 or .67 proportion of similar responses between stranger and subject. The subject was asked to read the responses of an opposite-sex stranger and then to make a series of evaluations on an expanded version of the Interpersonal Judgment Scale. This scale consists of ten 7-point scales. The measure of attraction within this experimental paradigm (Byrne, 1969) consists of the sum of two scales: liking and desirability as a work partner. This attraction index ranges from 2 to 14 and has a split-half reliability of .85. In addition, four buffer scales deal with evaluations of the other person's intelligence, knowledge of current events, morality, and adjustment. These variables are found to correlate positively with attraction, but they have somewhat different antecedents and are included in the analysis simply as supplemental information. Three new scales, added for the present study in order to explore various responses to the opposite sex, asked the subject to react to the other person as a potential date, as a marriage partner, and as to sexual attractiveness. Finally, a tenth scale was added in order

[1] Unpublished data collected by Donn Byrne and John Lamberth.

to assess a stimulus variable, the physical attractiveness of the other person. In addition, the physical attractiveness of each subject was rated by the experimenter on the same 7-point scale on which the subjects rated one another.

Computer Dating Condition

Selection of dating couples: The attitude-personality questionnaire was administered to a group of 420 introductory psychology students at the University of Texas, and each item was scored in a binary fashion. By means of a specially prepared program, the responses of each male were compared with those of each female; for any given couple, the number of possible matching responses could theoretically range from 0 to 50. The actual range was from 12 to 37. From these distributions of matches, male-female pairs were selected to represent either the greatest or the least number of matching responses. There was a further restriction that the male be as tall as or taller than the female. Of the resulting pairs, a few were eliminated because (*a*) one of the individuals was married, (*b*) the resulting pair was racially mixed, or (*c*) because of a failure to keep the experimental appointment. The remaining 88 subjects formed 24 high-similar pairs, whose proportion of similar responses ranged from .66 to .74, and 20 low-similar pairs, whose proportion of similar responses ranged from .24 to .40.

Levels of information saliency: The experiment was run with one of the selected couples at a time. In the experimental room, they were introduced to one another and told:

> In recent years, there has been a considerable amount of interest in the phenomenon of computer dating as a means for college students to meet one another. At the present time, we are attempting to learn as much as possible about the variables which influence the reactions of one individual to another.

In order to create differential levels of saliency with respect to the matching elements, subjects in the salient condition were told:

> Earlier this semester, one of the test forms you filled out was

> very much like those used by some of the computer dating organizations. In order to refresh your memory about this test and the answers you gave, we are going to ask you to spend a few minutes looking over the questions and your answers to them.
>
> The answers of several hundred students were placed on IBM cards and run through the computer to determine the number of matching answers among the 50 questions for all possible pairs of male and female students. According to the computer, the two of you gave the same answers on approximately 67% (33%) of those questions.

In the nonsalient condition, they were told:

> Imagine for the purposes of the experiment that you had applied to one of the computer dating organizations and filled out some of their information forms. Then, imagine that the two of you had been notified that, according to the computer, you match on approximately 67% (33%) of the factors considered important.

All subjects were then told:

> For our experiment, we would like to create a situation somewhat like that of a computer date. That is, you answered a series of questions, the computer indicated that you two gave the same responses on some of the questions, and now we would like for you to spend a short time together getting acquainted. Specifically, we are asking you to spend the next 30 minutes together on a "coke date" at the Student Union. Here is 50¢ to spend on whatever you would like. We hope that you will learn as much as possible about each other in the next half hour because we will be asking you a number of questions about one another when you return.

Measures of attraction: When they returned from the date to receive their final instructions, an unobtrusive measure of attraction was obtained: the physical distance between the two subjects while standing together in front of the experimenter's desk. The distance was noted on a simple ordinal scale ranging from 0 (touching one another) to 5 (standing at opposite corners of the desk). The subjects were then separated and asked to evaluate their date on the Interpersonal Judgment Scale.

Follow-up measures: At the end of the semester (2–3 months after the date), it was possible to locate 74 of the 88 original subjects who were willing to answer five additional questions. Each was asked to write the name of his or her computer date and to indicate whether or not they had talked to one another since the experiment, dated since the experiment, and whether a date was desired or planned in the future. Finally, each was asked whether the evaluation of the date was influenced more by physical attractiveness or by attitudes.

RESULTS

Simulated Stranger Condition

The mean attraction responses of two simulated stranger conditions [2] which were run separately from the computer dating experiment are shown in Table 11.1 Analysis of variance indicated that the similarity variable yielded the only significant effect ($F = 4.00$, $df = 1/46$, $p =$ approximately .05).

On the remaining items of the Interpersonal Judgment Scale, the only other significant similarity effect was on the intelligence rating ($F = 7.30$, $df = 1/46$, $p < .01$). Interestingly enough, there were several differences between the differently labeled experiments on the other Interpersonal Judgment Scale items. More positive responses were given in the "computer dating" experiment than in

[2] Originally, the plan was to run the simulated stranger groups just after the computer dating groups. An unexpected finding was that almost all of the responses were positive and that the subjects were attired more attractively than is usual among undergraduates reporting for experimental sessions. From anecdotal olfactory evidence, even the perfume and shaving lotion level was noticeably elevated. In retrospect, it seemed clear that because the computer dating study was widely discussed and because this experiment was so labeled, the overwhelming majority of the 34 subjects were expecting to go on a date as part of their task. It then became necessary to rerun the simulated stranger groups at the end of the semester when the expectations of dates had diminished. The two levels of similarity were run under two different experimental titles, "Computer Dating" and "Evaluational Processes." The data reported in this paper are from these latter two experiments.

the "evaluational processes" experiment with respect to knowledge of current events ($F = 8.07$, $df = 1/46$, $p < .01$), adjustment ($F = 6.10$, $df = 1/46$, $p < .02$), and desirability as a marriage partner ($F = 6.57$, $df = 1/46$, $p < .02$). The sexual atractiveness item yielded a significant interaction effect ($F = 4.93$, $df = 1/46$, $p < .03$), with the dissimilar stranger rated as more sexually attractive in the computer dating experiment and the similar stranger as more sexually attractive in the evaluational processes experiment. While these latter findings are gratuitous, they suggest the importance of minor variations in the stimulus context and the sensitivity of the Interpersonal Judgment Scale items to such variations.

Predicting Attraction in the Computer Dating Condition

The mean attraction responses for male and female subjects at two levels of information saliency and two levels of response similarity are shown in Table 11.2. Analysis of variance indicated the

Table 11.1—Mean Attraction Responses toward Similar and Dissimilar Simulated Strangers with Two Different Titles for Experiment

Title of experiment	*Proportion of similar responses*	
	.33	.67
Evaluational processes	9.47	10.78
Computer dating	10.21	11.33
M	9.84	11.06

Note.—The mean attraction responses were 10.12 and 10.77 for the evaluational processes and computer dating experiments, respectively.

only significant effect to be that of proportion of similar responses ($F = 13.67$, $df = 1/40$, $p < .001$). The attempt to make the matching stimuli differentially salient did not affect attraction, and there were no sex differences.

The other variable which was expected to influence attraction

Table 11.2—Mean Attraction Responses of Males and Females with Similar and Dissimilar Dates at Two Levels of Saliency Concerning Matching Information

Level	Proportion of similar responses	
	Low	High
Male Ss		
Information		
Salient	10.00	11.91
Nonsalient	10.56	11.38
Female Ss		
Information		
Salient	10.73	11.82
Nonsalient	10.33	12.15

was the physical attractiveness of the date. Is is interesting to note in the simulated stranger condition that while the manipulation of similarity influenced attraction, it had no effect on guesses as to the other person's physical attractiveness ($F < 1$). Thus, data in the computer dating condition indicating a relationship between attractiveness and attraction would seem to result from the effect of the former on the latter. Two measures of attractiveness were available: ratings by the experimenter when the subjects first arrived and by each subject of his or her own date following their interaction. The correlation between these two measures was significant; the correlation between the experimenter's ratings of male subjects and the females' ratings of their dates was .59 ($p < .01$) and between the experimenter's ratings of female subjects and the males' ratings of their dates was .39 ($p < .01$). As might be expected, the subject's own ratings proved to be better predictors than did the experimenter's ratings. In Table 11.3 are shown those correlations between physical attractiveness ratings and Interpersonal Judgment Scale responses which were consistent across sexes.

Thus, the first hypothesis was clearly confirmed, but there was no support for the second hypothesis.

Table 11.3—Correlations between Ratings of Physical Attractiveness of Date and Evaluations of Date

Variable	Attractiveness of Date Rated by Ss		Attractiveness of Date Rated by E	
	Male Ss	Female Ss	Male Ss	Female Ss
Attraction	.39**	.60**	.07	.32*
Dating	.66**	.57**	.21	.33*
Marriage	.56**	.55**	.18	.34*
Sex	.77**	.70**	.53**	.44**

* $p < .05$.
** $p < .01$.

With respect to the prediction of attraction, it seems likely that a combination of the similarity and attractiveness variables would provide the optimal information. In Table 11.4 are shown the mean attraction responses toward attractive (ratings of 5–7) and unattractive (ratings of 1–4) dates at two levels of response similarity. For both sexes, each of the two independent variables was found to affect attraction.[3] The physical attractiveness variable was significant for both males ($F = 3.85$, $df = 1/39$, $p < .05$) and for females ($F = 10.44$, $df = 1/40$, $p < .01$). The most positive response in each instance was toward similar attractive dates, and the least positive response was toward dissimilar unattractive dates. An additional analysis indicated no relationship between an individual's own physical attractiveness (as rated by the date) and response to the other person's physical attractiveness.

[3] The use of the term "independent variable" for physical attractiveness may be a source of confusion. In this experiment, there was obviously no manipulation of physical appearance, but attractiveness was conceptualized as one of the stimuli determining attraction. In other experiments, attractiveness has been successfully manipulated as an independent variable (e.g., Byrne et al., 1968; McWhirter, 1969; Moss, 1969). In the absence of any evidence that attraction determines perception of physical attractiveness (and some evidence to the contrary), it seems reasonable to consider attractiveness as an antecedent variable in studies such as the present one and that of Walster et al. (1966).

Other Effects of Similarity and Attractiveness

On the additional items of the Interpersonal Judgment Scale, similarity was found to have a significant positive effect on ratings of the date's intelligence ($F = 4.37$, $df = 1/40$, $p < .05$), desirability as a date ($F = 8.92$, $df = 1/40$, $p < .01$), and desirability as a marriage partner ($F = 4.76$, $df = 1/40$, $p < .05$).

The simplest and least obtrusive measure of attraction was the proximity of the two individuals after the date, while receiving their final instructions from the experimenter. If physical distance can be considered as an alternative index of attraction, these two dependent variables should be correlated. For females, the correlation was $-.36$ ($p < .01$) and for males, $-.48$, ($p < .01$); in each instance the greater the liking for the partner, the closer together they stood. Another way of evaluating the proximity variable is to determine whether it is influenced by the same independent variables as is the paper-and-pencil measure. For both sexes, physical separation was found to correlate $-.49$ ($p < .01$) with similarity. Thus, the more similar the couples, the closer they stood. Because similarity and proximity are necessarily identical for each member of a pair, it is not possible to determine whether the males, the females, or both are responsible for the similarity-proximity relationship. When the physical attractiveness measure was examined, however, there was indirect evidence that proximity in this situation was controlled more by the males than by the females. For females, there was no relationship between ratings of the male's appearance and physical separation ($r = -.06$). For males, the correlation was $-.34$ ($p < .05$).

In the follow-up investigation at the end of the semester, 74 of the 88 original subjects were available and willing to participate. For this analysis, each subject was placed in one of three categories with respect to the two stimulus variables of similarity and attractiveness. On the basis of the same divisions as were used in the analysis in Table 11.4, subjects were either in a high-similarity condition with a physically attractive date, a low-similarity condition with a physically unattractive date, or in a mixed condition of high-low or low-high. To maximize the possible effect, frequency analysis was used in comparing the two homogeneous groups (N

= 40).[4] In response to the question about the date's name, the more positive the stimulus conditions at the time of the date, the more likely was the subject to remember correctly the date's name ($x^2 = 8.47$, $df = 1$, $p < .01$). With respect to talking to the other

Table 11.4—Mean Attraction Responses of Males and Females with Similar and Dissimilar Dates Who Are Relatively Attractive and Unattractive

Physical Attractiveness of Date	*Proportion of Similar Responses*	
	Low	*High*
Male Ss		
Attractive	10.55	12.00
Unattractive	9.89	10.43
Female Ss		
Attractive	11.25	12.71
Unattractive	9.50	11.00

individual during the period since the experiment, the relationship was again significant ($x^2 = 4.95$, $df = 1$, $p < .05$). The same effect was found with regard to whether the individual would like or not like to date the other person in the future ($x^2 = 5.38$, $df = 1$, $p < .05$). The only follow-up question which failed to show a significant effect for the experimental manipulation was that dealing with actual dating; even here, it might be noted that the only dates reported were by subjects in the high-similarity, high-attractiveness condition.

The only other question in the follow-up survey represented an attempt to find out whether the subjects could accurately verbalize the stimuli to which they had been found to respond. Of the 74 respondents, about one-third indicated that both attitudes and physical attractiveness determined their response to the partner, while about one-sixth of the subjects felt they had responded to

[4] When the 33 individuals who were heterogeneous with respect to similarity and attractiveness were included in the analysis, they fell midway between the similar-attractive and dissimilar-unattractive groups on each item. The probability levels were consequently reduced to the .02 level on remembering the date's name and to the .10 level on the talking and desire to date items.

neither variable. With the remaining half of the sample, an interesting sex difference emerged. Physical attractiveness was identified as the most important stimulus by 14 of the 18 males, while attitudes were seen as the most important stimulus by 16 of the 19 females ($x^2 = 14.30$, $df = 1$, $p < .001$). The present subjects seemed to have accepted Bertrand Russell's observation that "On the whole, women tend to love men for their character, while men tend to love women for their appearance." In contrast to these verbal sentiments, it might be noted that the date's physical attractiveness correlated .60 with attraction responses of female subjects and only .39 among male subjects. A further analysis compared the similarity-attraction effect and the attractiveness-attraction effect for those subjects who indicated one or the other stimulus variable as the more important. The similarity-attraction effect did not differ between the two groups ($z < 1$). It has been reported previously that awareness of similarity is not a necessary component of the similarity effect (Byrne & Griffitt, 1969). There was, however, a difference in the attractiveness effect. For the subjects identifying attractiveness as the major determinant, physical attractiveness correlated .63 ($p < .01$) with attraction responses; for the subjects identifying similarity as the major determinant, attractiveness correlated —.04 (*ns*) with attraction. The difference was a significant one ($z = 2.16$, $p < .05$).

CONCLUSIONS

Perhaps the most important aspect of the present findings is the evidence indicating the continuity between the laboratory study of attraction and its manifestation under field conditions. At least as operationalized in the present investigation, variables such as physical attractiveness and similarity of attitudes and personality characteristics are found to influence attraction in a highly predictable manner.

The findings with respect to the physical distance measure are important in two respects. First, they provide further evidence that voluntary proximity is a useful and unobtrusive measure of interpersonal attraction. Second, the construct validity and generality of the paper-and-pencil measure of attraction provided by the Interpersonal Judgment Scale is greatly enhanced. The significant relationship between two such different response measures is comforting to users of either one. In addition, the follow-up procedure provided evidence of the lasting effect of the experimental manipulations and of the relation of the attraction measures to such diverse responses as remembering the other person's name and engaging in conversation in the weeks after the termination of the experiment.

The failure to confirm the second hypothesis is somewhat puzzling. It is possible that present procedures, designed to vary the saliency of the elements of similarity, were inadequate and ineffective, that the actual behavioral cues to similarity and dissimilarity were sufficiently powerful to negate the effects of the experimental manipulation, or that the hypothesis was simply incorrect. There is no basis within the present experiment on which to decide among these alternatives.

In conclusion, it must be emphasized that striking continuity has been demonstrated across experiments using paper-and-pencil materials to simulate a stranger and to measure attraction (Byrne, 1961), more realistic audio and audiovisual presentations of the stimulus person (Byrne & Clore, 1966), elaborate dramatic confrontations in which a confederate portrays the stimulus person (Byrne & Griffitt, 1966), and a quasi-realistic experiment such as the present one, in which two genuine strangers interact and in which response measures include nonverbal behaviors. Such findings suggest that attempts to move back and forth between the controlled artificiality of the laboratory and the uncontrolled natural setting are both feasible and indicative of the potential applications of basic attraction research to a variety of interpersonal problems.

SUMMARY

As a test of the nonlaboratory generalizability of attraction research, a computer dating field study was conducted. A 50-item questionnaire of attitudes and personality was administered to a

420-student pool, and 44 male-female pairs were selected on the basis of maximal or minimal similarity of responses. Each couple was introduced, given differential information about the basis for their matching, and asked to spend 30 minutes together at the Student Union on a "coke date." Afterward, they returned to the experimenter and were independently assessed on a series of measures. It was found that attraction was significantly related to similarity and to physical attractiveness. Physical attractiveness was also significantly related to ratings of desirability as a date, as a spouse, and to sexual attractiveness. Both similarity and attractiveness were related to the physical proximity of the two individuals while they were talking to the experimenter after the date. In a follow-up investigation at the end of the semester, similarity and physical attractiveness were found to predict accurate memory of the date's name, incidence of talking to one another in the interim since the coke date, and desire to date the other person in the future.

REFERENCES

ARONSON, E., & CARLSMITH, J. M. Experimentation in social psychology. In G. Lindzey & E. Aronson (Eds.), *The handbook of social psychology.* Vol. 2. (2nd ed.) Reading, Mass.: Addison-Wesley, 1968.

BYRNE, D. Interpersonal attraction and attitude similarity. *Journal of Abnormal and Social Psychology,* 1961, *62,* 713–715.

BYRNE, D. Attitudes and attraction. In L. Berkowitz (Ed.), *Advances in experimental social psychology.* Vol. 4. New York: Academic Press, 1969.

BYRNE, D., BASKETT, G. D., & HODGES, L. Behavioral indicators of interpersonal attraction. Paper presented at meeting of the Psychonomic Society, St. Louis, November 1969.

BYRNE, D., BOND, M. H., & DIAMOND, M. J. Response to political candidates as a function of attitude similarity-dissimilarity. *Human Relations,* 1969, *22,* 251–262.

BYRNE, D., & CLORE, G. L., JR. Predicting interpersonal attraction toward strangers presented in three different stimulus modes. *Psychonomic Science,* 1966, *4,* 239–240.

BYRNE, D., CLORE, G. L., JR., & WORCHEL, P. Effect of economic similarity-dissimilarity on interpersonal attraction. *Journal of Personality and Social Psychology,* 1966, *4,* 220–224.

BYRNE, D., & ERVIN, C. R. Attraction toward a Negro stranger as a function of prejudice, attitude similarity, and the stranger's evaluation of the subject. *Human Relations,* 1969, *22,* 397–404.

BYRNE, D., & GRIFFITT, W. Similarity versus liking: A clarification. *Psychonomic Science,* 1966, *6,* 295–296.

BYRNE, D., & GRIFFITT, W. Similarity and awareness of similarity of personality characteristics as determinants of attraction. *Journal of Experimental Research in Personality,* 1969, *3,* 179–186.

BYRNE, D., GRIFFITT, W., & STEFANIAK, D. Attraction and similarity of personality characteristics. *Journal of Personality and Social Psychology,* 1967, *5,* 82–90.

BYRNE, D., LONDON, O., & REEVES, K. The effects of physical attractiveness, sex, and attitude similarity on interpersonal attraction. *Journal of Personality,* 1968, *36,* 259–271.

BYRNE, D., & RHAMEY, R. Magnitude of positive and negative reinforcements as a determinant of attraction. *Journal of Personality and Social Psychology,* 1965, *2,* 884–889.

EFRAN, M. G. Visual interaction and interpersonal attraction. Unpublished doctoral dissertation, University of Texas, 1969.

GRIFFITT, W. B. Interpersonal attraction as a function of self-concept and personality similarity-dissimilarity. *Journal of Personality and Social Psychology,* 1966, *4,* 581–584.

GRIFFITT, W. B. Environmental effects of interpersonal affective behavior: Ambient affective temperature and attraction. *Journal of Personality and Social Psychology,* 1970, *15,* 240–244.

GRIFFITT, W. B. Personality similarity and self-concept as determinants of interpersonal attraction. *Journal of Social Psychology,* 1969, *78,* 137–146.

HUFFMAN, D. M. Interpersonal attraction as a function of behavioral similarity. Unpublished doctoral dissertation, University of Texas, 1969.

MCWHIRTER, R. M., JR. Interpersonal attraction in a dyad as a function of the physical attractiveness of its members. Unpublished doctoral dissertation, Texas Tech University, 1969.

MEGARGEE, E. I. A study of the subjective aspects of group membership at Amherst. Unpublished manuscript, Amherst College, 1956.

MOSS, M. K. Social desirability, physical attractiveness, and social choice. Unpublished doctoral dissertation, Kansas State University, 1969.

PERRIN, F. A. C. Physical attractiveness and repulsiveness. *Journal of Experimental Psychology,* 1921, *4,* 203–217.

PICHER, O. L. Attraction toward Negroes as a function of prejudice, emotional arousal, and the sex of the Negro. Unpublished doctoral dissertation, University of Texas, 1966.

SHEFFIELD, J., & BYRNE, D. Attitude similarity-dissimilarity, authoritarianism, and interpersonal attraction. *Journal of Social Psychology,* 1967, *71,* 117–123.

TAYLOR, M. J. Some objective criteria of social class membership. Unpublished manuscript, Amherst College, 1956.

WALSTER, E., ARONSON, V., ABRAHAMS, D., & ROTTMANN, L. Importance of physical attractiveness in dating behavior. *Journal of Personality and Social Psychology,* 1966, *4,* 508–516.

VI

Social Influence

An individual can be induced to conform to the wishes of others by applying pressure which weakens his confidence in his beliefs while strengthening his confidence in the correctness of the others' views. In a laboratory study where subjects were individually placed in a room with "experimental confederates" instructed to give the wrong answers, Asch found that greater conformity occurred when the assistants were unanimous in their incorrect judgments and where the stimulus conditions were unclear. Deutsch and Gerard (Chapter 12) indicated that although Asch used the term "group" influence, each subject acted in the physical presence of others rather than functioning as a member of a group faced with a common task requiring cooperative effort to achieve a solution. Extending Asch's study in another laboratory setting, they found that an individual was more likely to conform as a group member than when only in the physical presence of others. An ancillary finding was that once an individual conforms he is more susceptible to further social influence. However, Freedman and Fraser (Chapter 13) pointed out that there are times when, for moral, ethical or practical reasons, factors other than external pressure are necessary to promote compliance. One assumption that often has been made is that if a person can be induced to comply with a small request he is more likely to comply with a larger demand. They indicated that the most relevant experimental evidence for the "foot-in-the-door" idea comes from Deutsch and Gerard's findings pertaining to future conformity. Freedman and Fraser designed two field experiments to provide a more direct test of their notion. As predicted, carrying out a small request increased the likelihood that the subject would agree to a larger demand. The effect was strong even when a different person made the larger request, and the two demands were dissimilar.

12

A Study of Normative and Informational Social Influences Upon Individual Judgment

Morton Deutsch and Harold B. Gerard

By now, many experimental studies (e.g., 1, 3, 6) have demonstrated that individual psychological processes are subject to social influences. Most investigators, however, have not distinguished among different kinds of social influences; rather, they have carelessly used the term "group" influence to characterize the impact of many different kinds of social factors. In fact, a review of the major experiments in this area—e.g., those by Sherif (6), Asch (1), Bovard (3)—would indicate that the subjects (*Ss*) in these experiments as they made their judgments were *not* functioning as *mem-*

From *Journal of Abnormal and Social Psychology*, 1955, *51*, 629–636.

This research was conducted under a grant from the Office of Naval Research, Contract No. NONR 285(10).

bers of a group in any simple or obvious manner. The *S*, in the usual experiment in this area, made perceptual judgments in the physical presence of others after hearing their judgments. Typically, the *S* was not given experimental instructions which made him feel that he was a member of a group faced with a common task requiring cooperative effort for its most effective solution. If "group" influences were at work in the foregoing experiments, they were subtly and indirectly created rather than purposefully created by the experimenter.

HYPOTHESES

The purpose of this paper is to consider two types of social influence, "normative" and "informational," which we believe were operative in the experiments mentioned above, and to report the results of an experiment bearing upon hypotheses that are particularly relevant to the former influence. We shall define a *normative social influence* as an influence to conform with the positive expectations [1] of another.[2] An *informational social influence* may be defined as an influence to accept information obtained from another as *evidence* about reality. Commonly these two types of influence are found together. However, it is possible to conform behaviorally with the expectations of others and say things which one disbelieves but which agree with the beliefs of others. Also, it is possible that one will accept an opponent's beliefs as evidence about reality even though one has no motivation to agree with him, per se.

Our hypotheses are particularly relevant to normative social influence upon individual judgment. We shall not elaborate the theoretical rationales for the hypotheses, since they are for the

[1] By positive expectations we mean to refer to those expectations whose fulfillment by another leads to or reinforces positive rather than negative feelings, and whose nonfulfillment leads to the opposite, to alienation rather than solidarity; conformity to negative expectations, on the other hand, leads to or reinforces negative rather than positive feelings.

[2] The term *another* is being used inclusively to refer to "another person," to a "group," or to one's "self." Thus, a normative social influence can result from the expectations of oneself, or of a group, or of another person.

most part obvious and they follow from other theoretical writings (e.g., 4, 5).

Hypothesis I

Normative social influence upon individual judgments will be greater among individuals forming a group than among an aggregation of individuals who do not compose a group.[3]

That is, even when susceptibility to informational social influence is equated, we would predict that the greater susceptibility to normative social influence among group members would be reflected in the greater group influence upon individual judgment. This is not to say that individuals, even when they are not group members, may not have some motivation to conform to the expectations of others—e.g., so as to ingratiate themselves or so as to avoid ridicule.

Hypothesis II

Normative social influence upon individual judgment will be reduced when the individual perceives that his judgment cannot be identified or, more generally, when the individual perceives no pressure to conform directed at him from others.

Hypothesis III

Normative social influence to conform to one's own judgment will reduce the impact of the normative social influence to conform to the judgment of others.

[3] Generally one would also expect that group members would be more likely to take the judgments of other group members as trustworthy evidence for forming judgments about reality and, hence, they would be more susceptible to informational social influence than would nongroup members. The greater trustworthiness usually reflects more experience of the reliability of the judgments of other members and more confidence in the benevolence of their motivations. However, when group members have had no prior experience together and when it is apparent in both the group and nongroup situations that the others are motivated and in a position to report correct judgments, there is no reason to expect differential susceptibility to informational social influence among group and nongroup members.

Hypothesis IV

Normative social influence to conform to one's own judgment from another as well as from oneself will be stronger than normative social influence from oneself.

Normative social influence from oneself to conform to one's own judgment may be thought of as an internalized social process in which the individual holds expectations with regard to his own behavior; conforming to positive self-expectations leads to feelings of self-esteem or self-approval while nonconformity leads to feelings of anxiety or guilt. In general one would expect that the strength of these internalized self-expectations would reflect the individual's prior experiences with them as sources of need satisfaction—e.g., by conforming to his own judgments or by self-reliance he has won approval from such significant others as his parents. As Hypothesis IV indicates, we believe that contemporaneous social pressure to conform to one's own judgment may supplement, and perhaps be even stronger than, the individual's internalized pressure to conform to his own judgment.

Two additional hypotheses, dealing with the effect of difficulty of judgment, are relevant to one of the experimental variations. They follow:

Hypothesis V

The more uncertain the individual is about the correctness of his judgment, the more likely he is to be susceptible to both normative and informational social influences in making his judgment.

Hypothesis VI

The more uncertain the individual is about the correctness of the judgment of others, the less likely he is to be susceptible to informational social influence in making his judgment.[4]

[4] Although we have no data relevant to this hypothesis, we present it to qualify Hypothesis V and to counteract an assumption in some of the current social psychological literature. Thus, Festinger (5) has written that where no physical reality basis exists for the establishment of the validity of one's belief,

METHOD

Subjects

One hundred and one college students from psychology courses at New York University were employed as *Ss*. The study was defined for the *Ss* as an experimental study of perception.

Procedure

We employed the experimental situation developed by Asch (1) with certain modifications and variations which are specified below. For detailed description of the procedures utilized by Asch and replicated in this experiment, Asch's publication should be consulted. The basic features of the Asch situation are: (*a*) the *Ss* are instructed that they are participating in a perceptual experiment, wherein they have to match accurately the length of a given line with one of three lines; (*b*) correct judgments are easy to make; (*c*) in each experimental session there is only one *naive S*, the other participants, while ostensively *Ss*, are in fact "stooges" who carry out the experimenter's instructions; (*d*) each participant (i.e., the naive *S* and the stooges) has to indicate his judgments publicly; (*e*) on 12 of the 18 perceptual judgments the

---

one is dependent upon social reality (i.e., upon the beliefs of others). Similarly, Asch (2) has indicated that group influence grows stronger as the judgmental situation diminishes in clarity. The implication of Hypothesis VI is that if an individual perceives that a situation is objectively difficult to judge—that others as well as he experience the situation in the same way (i.e., as being difficult and as having uncertainty about their judgments)—he will not trust their judgments any more than he trusts his own. It is only as his confidence in their judgments increases (e.g., because he deems that agreement among three uncertain judges provides more reliable evidence than one uncertain judge) that the judgments of others will have informational social influence. However (at any particular level of confidence in the judgment of others), one can predict that as his confidence in his own judgment decreases he will be more susceptible to normative social influence. With decreasing self-confidence there is likely to be less of a commitment to one's own judgment and, hence, less influence not to conform to the judgments of others.

stooges announce wrong and unanimous judgments, the errors of the stooges are large and clearly in error; (*f*) the naive *S* and the stooges are in a face-to-face relationship and have been previously acquainted with one another.[5]

To test the hypotheses set forth in the foregoing section, the following experimental variations upon Asch's situation were employed:

1. The face-to-face situation. This was an exact replication of Asch's situation except for the following minor modifications: (*a*) Only three stooges, rather than eight, were employed,[6] (*b*) the *S* and the stooges were unacquainted prior to the experiment; and (*c*) two series of 18 judgments were employed. In one series (the visual series), the lines were physically present when the *S* and the stooges announced their judgments; in the other series (the memory

[5] Inspection of the Asch situation would suggest that informational social influence would be strongly operative. As Asch has put it (2, p. 461):

> The subject knows (a) that the issue is one of fact; (b) that a correct result is possible; (c) that only one result is correct; (d) that the others and he are oriented to and reporting about the same objectively given relations; (e) that the group is in unanimous opposition at certain points with him.

He further, perceives that the others are motivated to report a correct judgment. In such a situation, the subject's accumulated past experience would lead him to expect that he could rely on the judgments of others, especially if they all agreed. That is, even if his eyes were closed he might feel that he could safely risk his life on the assumption that the unanimous judgments of the others were correct. This is a strong informational social influence and one would expect it to be overriding except for the fact that the subject has his eyes open and receives information from a source which he also feels to be completely trustworthy—i.e., from his own perceptual apparatus. The subject is placed in strong conflict because the evidences from two sources of trustworthy information are in opposition.

In the Asch situation, it is apparent that, in addition to informational social influence, normative social influence is likely to be operating. The naive *S* is in a face-to-face situation with acquaintances and he may be motivated to conform to their judgments in order to avoid being ridiculed, or being negatively evaluated, or even possibly out of a sense of obligation. While it may be impossible to remove completely the impact of normative social influence upon any socialized being, it is evident that the Asch situation allows much opportunity for this type of influence to operate.

[6] Asch found that three stooges were about as effective in influencing the *S*s as eight.

series) the lines were removed before any one announced his judgment. In the memory series, approximately three seconds after the lines were removed the first stooge was asked to announce his judgment. The sequences of visual and memory series were alternated so that approximately half the *S*s had the memory series first and half had the visual series first.

2. The anonymous situation. This situation was identical with the face-to-face situation except for the following differences: (*a*) Instead of sitting in the visual presence of each other, the *S*s were separated by partitions which prevented them from talking to each other or seeing one another; (*b*) Instead of announcing their judgments by voice, the *S*s indicated their judgments by pressing a button; (*c*) No stooges were employed. Each *S* was led to believe he was Subject No. 3, and the others were No. 1, No. 2, and No. 4. He was told that when the experimenter called out "Subject No. 3" he was to indicate his judgment by pressing one of three buttons (A, B, or C) which corresponded to what he thought the correct line was. When an *S* pressed a given button, a corresponding bulb lit on his own panel and on a hidden master panel. Presumably the appropriate bulb also lit on the panels of each of the other *S*s, but, in fact, the bulbs on any *S*'s panel were not connected to the buttons of the other *S*s. When the experimenter called for the judgments of Subject No. 1, of Subject No. 2, and of Subject No. 4, a concealed accomplice manipulated master switches which lit bulbs on each of the *S*'s panels that corresponded to judgments presumably being made by these respective *S*s. Subjects No. 1, No. 2, and No. 4 were, in effect, "electrical stooges" whose judgments were indicated on the panels of the four naive *S*s (all of whom were Subject No. 3) by an accomplice of the experimenter who manipulated master switches controlling the lights on the panels of the naive *S*s. The pattern of judgments followed by the "electrical stooges" was the same as that followed by the "live stooges" in the face-to-face situation. (*d*) In providing a rationale for being labeled Subject No. 3 for each of the naive *S*s, we explained that due to the complicated wiring setup, the *S*'s number had no relation to his seating position. Implicitly, we assumed that each *S* would realize that it would be impossible for the others to identify that a judgment was being made by him rather than by any of two

others. However, it is apparent from postexperiment questionnaires that many of the *Ss* did not realize this. It seems likely that if we had made the anonymous character of the judgments clear and explicit to the *Ss*, the effects of this experimental variation would have been even more marked.

3. The group situation. This situation was identical to the anonymous situation except that the subjects were instructed as follows:

> This group is one of twenty similar groups who are participating in this experiment. We want to see how accurately you can make judgments. We are going to give a reward to the five best groups—the five groups that make the fewest errors on the series of judgments that you are given. The reward will be a pair of tickets to a Broadway play of your own choosing for each member of the winning group. An error will be counted any time one of you makes an incorrect judgment. That is, on any given card the group can make as many as four errors if you each judge incorrectly or you can make no errors if you each judge correctly. The five groups that make the best scores will be rewarded.

4. The self-commitment variation. This variation was employed in both the face-to-face and anonymous situations. In it, each *S* was given a sheet of paper on which to write down his judgment before he was exposed to the judgments of the others. He was told not to sign the sheet of paper and that it would not be collected at the end of the experiment. After the first series of 18 judgments, the *Ss* threw away their sheets. The *Ss* did not erase their recorded judgments after each trial as they did in the Magic Pad self-commitment variation.

4A. The Magic Pad self-commitment variation. This variation was employed in the anonymous situation. In it, each *S* was given a Magic Writing Pad on which to write down his judgment before he was exposed to the judgments of the others. After each *S* had been exposed to the judgment of the others and had indicated his own judgment, he erased his judgment on the Magic Writing Pad by lifting up the plastic covering. It was made convincingly clear to the *S* that only he would ever know what he had written down on the pad.

5. The public commitment variation. This variation was employed in both the face-to-face situation and in the anonymous situation.

In it, the *S*s followed the same procedure as in the self-commitment variation except that they wrote down their initial judgments on sheets of paper which they signed and which they knew were to be handed to the experimenter after each series of 18 judgments.

RESULTS

The primary data used in the analysis of the results are the errors made by the *S*s which were in the direction of the errors made by the stooges. We shall present first the data which are relevant to our hypotheses; later we shall present other information.

Hypothesis I

The data relevant to the first hypothesis are presented in Table 12.1. The table presents a comparison of the anonymous situation in which the individuals were motivated to act as a group with the anonymous situation in which there was no direct attempt to induce membership motivation; in both situations, no self or public commitment was made. The data provide strong support for the prediction that the normative social influence upon individual judgments will be greater among individuals forming

Table 12.1—Mean Number of Socially Influenced Errors in Individual Judgment Among Group Members and Among Nonmembers

Experimental Treatment	*N*	*Memory Series*	*Visual Series*	*Total*
Group, anonymous, no commitment	15	6.87	5.60	12.47
Nongroup, anonymous, no commitment	13	3.15	2.77	5.92
			*p values**	
		.01	.05	.001

* Based on a *t* test, using one tail of the distribution.

a group than among individuals who do not compose a group. The average member of the group made more than twice as many errors as the comparable individual who did not participate in the task as a member of a group.

Qualitative data from a postexperimental questionnaire, in which we asked the *S* to describe any feelings he had about himself or about the others during the experiment, also support Hypothesis I. Seven out of the fifteen *S*s in the "group" condition spontaneously mentioned a felt obligation to the other group members; none of the individuals in the non-group condition mentioned any feeling of obligation to go along with the others.

Hypothesis II

To test the second hypothesis, it is necessary to compare the data from the face-to-face and anonymous situations among the individuals who were otherwise exposed to similar experimental treatments. Tables 12.2 and 12.3 present the relevant data. It is

Table 12.2—Mean Number of Socially Influenced Errors in Individual Judgment in the Anonymous and in the Face-to-face Situations

Situation	No Commitment				Self-Commitment				Public Commitment			
	Visual	Memory	Total	N	Visual	Memory	Total	N	Visual	Memory	Total	N
Face-to-face	3.00	4.08	7.08	13	.92	.75	1.67	12	1.13	1.39	2.52	13
Anonymous	2.77	3.15	5.92	13	.64	.73	1.37	11	.92	.46	1.38	13

apparent that there was less social influence upon individual judgment in the anonymous as compared with the face-to-face situation. This lessening of social influence is at the .001 level of statistical confidence even when the comparisons include the "commitment variations" as well as both the visual and the memory series of judgments. The interaction between the commitment variations and the anonymous, face-to-face variations, which is statistically significant, is such as to reduce the over-all differences between the anonymous and face-to-face situation; the differences between the face-to-face and the anonymous situations are most strongly brought out when there is no commitment. Similarly, if we compare the anonymous and face-to-face situations, employing the memory rather than the visual series, the effect of the normative influence upon judgments in the face-to-face situation is increased somewhat, but not significantly. That is, as we eliminate counter-normative influences (i.e., the "commitment") and as we weaken reality restraints (i.e., employ the "memory" rather than "visual" series), the normative influences in the face-to-face situation operate more freely.

The support for Hypothesis II is particularly striking in light

Table 12.3—p Values* for Various Comparisons of Socially Influenced Errors in the Anonymous and Face-to-Face Situations

Comparison	Total Errors
A vs. F	.001
A vs. F, no commitment	.001
A vs. F, self-commitment	.10
A vs. F, public commitment	.001
Interaction of commitment with A-F	.01

* *p* values are based on *t* tests, using one tail of distribution, derived from analyses of variation.

Table 12.4—p Values* for Various Comparisons of Socially Influenced Errors in the Different Commitment Treatments

Comparison	Total Errors	Errors on Visual Series	Errors on Memory Series
No commitment vs. public commitment, F	.001	.01	.001
No commitment vs. self-commitment, F	.001	.01	.001
Self-commitment vs. public commitment, F	.01	NS	NS
No commitment vs. self-commitment, A	.001	.01	.01
No commitment vs. public commitment, A	.001	.01	.002
Self-commitment vs. public commitment, A	NS	NS	NS

* *p* values are based on *t* tests, using one tail of the distribution, and derived from analyses of variation.

of the fact that, due to faulty experimental procedure, the "anonymous" character of the anonymous situation was not sufficiently impressed on some of the *S*s. For these *S*s, the anonymous situation merely protected them from the immediate, visually accessible pressure to conform arising from the lifted eyebrows and expressions of amazement by the stooges in the face-to-face situation. Complete feeling of anonymity would probably have strengthened the results.

Hypotheses III and IV

Tables 12.4, 12.5, and 12.6 present results showing the influence of the different commitment variations. The public and the self-commitment variations markedly reduce the socially influenced errors in both the face-to-face and anonymous situations. In other words, the data provide strong support for Hypothesis III which asserts that normative social influence to conform to one's own judgment will reduce the impact of the normative influence to conform to the judgment of others.

The data with regard to the influence of self-commitment are ambiguous in implication since the results of the two self-commitment variations—i.e., the "Magic Pad self-commitment" and the "self-commitment"—are not the same. The first self-commitment variation produced results which are essentially the same as the public commitment variation, markedly reducing socially influenced errors. The Magic Pad self-commitment variation produced results which were different from the no commitment variation, reducing the errors to an extent which is statistically significant; however, unlike the first self-commitment variation, the Magic Pad self-commitment was significantly less effective than the public commitment in reducing socially influenced errors.

Our hunch is that the *S*s in the first self-commitment variation perceived the commitment situation as though it were a public commitment and that this is the explanation of the lack of differences between these two variations. That is, writing their judgments indelibly supported the belief that "others can see what I have written." The *S*s in the Magic Pad self-commitment variation, on the other hand, were literally wiping their initial judgments

Table 12.5—Mean Number of Socially Influenced Errors in Judgments in the Anonymous Situation as Affected by the Commitment Variations

No Commitment				Magic Pad Self-Commitment				Self-Commitment				Public Commitment			
Visual	*Memory*	*Total*	N	*Visual*	*Memory*	*Total*	N	*Visual*	*Memory*	*Total*	N	*Visual*	*Memory*	*Total*	N
2.77	3.15	5.92	13	1.63	2.27	3.90	11	.64	.73	1.37	11	.92	.46	1.38	13

Table 12.6—p Values for Various Comparisons of Socially Influenced Errors in the Different Commitment Variations*

Comparison	Total Errors	Errors on Visual Series	Errors on Memory Series
No commitment vs. Magic Pad self-commitment	.05	NS	NS
Magic Pad self-commitment vs. self-commitment	.005	NS	.05
Magic Pad self-commitment vs. public commitment	.001	NS	.01

* *p* values are based on *t* tests using one tail of the distribution.

away in such a manner that they would be inaccessible to anyone. Hence, in the Magic Pad variation, the normative influences to conform to one's own judgment had to be sustained by the *S* himself. Normative influences from the *S*'s self (to be, in a sense, true to himself) were undoubtedly also operating in the noncommitment variation. What the Magic Pad did was to prevent the *S* from distorting his recollection of his independent judgment after being exposed to the judgments of the others. Further, there is a theoretical basis for assuming that the commitment to a judgment or decision is increased following the occurrence of behavior based upon it. Hence, the behavior of writing one's judgment down on the Magic Pad makes the original decision less tentative and less subject to change. However, it is apparent that this internally sustained influence to conform with one's own judgment was not as strong as the combination of external and self-motivated influences. These results support our fourth hypothesis.

Hypothesis V

Table 12.7 presents a comparison of the errors made on the visual and on the memory series of judgments. It is apparent that the *Ss* were less influenced by the judgments of others when the judgments were made on a visual rather than on a memory basis. It is also evident from the data of Table 12.2 that the differences

Table 12.7—Socially Influenced Errors in Individual Judgments as Affected by the Stimulus to be Judged (Visual or Memory)

	N	*Mean Number of Errors*	*"p" value*
Errors on visual series	99	2.20	.005*
Errors on memory series	99	2.60	
Total errors when visual series was first	51	4.12	.005
Total errors when memory series was first	48	5.71	

* Based on a *t* test of differences between visual and memory series for each subject.

between the visual and memory series were reduced or disappeared when the *Ss* wrote down their initial, independent judgments. These results support our fifth hypothesis which asserts that the more uncertain the individual is about the correctness of his judgment, the more likely he is to be susceptible to social influences in making his judgment. Further support comes from the questionnaire data. Out of the 90 *Ss* who filled out questionnaires, 51 indicated that they were more certain of their judgment when the lines were visually present, 2 were more certain when they were absent, and 39 were equally certain in both instances.

Being exposed first to the memory series rather than the visual series had the effect of making the *Ss* more susceptible to social influence upon their judgments throughout both series of judgments. In other words, an *S* was more likely to make socially influenced errors on the memory series and, having allowed himself to be influenced by the others on this first series of judgments, he was more likely to be influenced on the visual series than if he had not previously participated in the memory series. It is as though once having given in to the social influence (and it is easier to give in when one is less certain about one's judgment), the *S* is more susceptible to further social influences.

DISCUSSION

A central thesis of this experiment has been that prior experiments which have been concerned with "group" influence upon individual judgment have, in fact, only incidentally been concerned with the type of social influence most specifically associated with groups, namely "normative social influence." Our results indicate that, even when normative social influence in the direction of an incorrect judgment is largely removed (as in the anonymous situation), more errors are made by our *S*s than by a control group of *S*s making their judgments when alone.[7] It seems reasonable to conclude that the *S*, even if not normatively influenced, may be influenced by the others in the sense that the judgments of others are taken to be a more or less trustworthy source of information about the objective reality with which he and the others are confronted.

It is not surprising that the judgments of others (particularly when they are perceived to be motivated and competent to judge accurately) should be taken as evidence to be weighed in coming to one's own judgment. From birth on, we learn that the perceptions and judgments of others are frequently reliable sources of evidence about reality. Hence, it is to be expected that if the perceptions by two or more people of the same objective situation are discrepant, each will tend to re-examine his own view and that of the others to see if they can be reconciled. This process of mutual influence does not necessarily indicate the operation of normative social influence as distinct from informational social influence. Essentially the same process (except that the influence is likely to be unilateral) can go on in interaction with a measuring or computing machine. For example, suppose one were to judge which of two lines is longer (as in the Müller-Lyer illusion) and then were given

[7] Asch (2) reports that his control group of *S*s made an average of considerably less than one error per *S*.

information that a measuring instrument (which past experience had led one to believe was infallible) came up with a different answer; certainly one might be influenced by this information. This influence could hardly be called a normative influence except in the most indirect sense.

While the results of prior experiments of "group" influence upon perception can be largely explained in terms of non-normative social influence, there is little doubt that normative influences were incidentally operative. However, these were the casual normative influences which can not be completely eliminated from any human situation, rather than normative influences deriving from specific group membership. Our experimental results indicate that when a group situation is created, even when the group situation is as trivial and artificial as it was in our groups, the normative social influences are grossly increased, producing considerably more errors in individual judgment.

The implications of the foregoing result are not particularly optimistic for those who place a high value on the ability of an individual to resist group pressures which run counter to his individual judgment. In the experimental situation we employed, the *S*, by allowing himself to be influenced by the others, in effect acquiesced in the distortion of his judgment and denied the authenticity of his own immediate experience. The strength of the normative social influences that were generated in the course of our experiment was small; had it been stronger, one would have expected even more distortion and submission.

Our findings, with regard to the commitment variations, do, however, suggest that normative social influences can be utilized to buttress as well as to undermine individual integrity. In other words, normative social influence can be exerted to help make an individual be an individual and not merely a mirror or puppet of the group. Groups can demand of their members that they have self-respect, that they value their own experience, that they be capable of acting without slavish regard for popularity. Unless groups encourage their members to express their own, independent judgments, group consensus is likely to be an empty achievement. Group process which rests on the distortion of individual experience undermines its own potential for creativity and productiveness.

SUMMARY AND CONCLUSIONS

Employing modifications of the Asch situation, an experiment was carried out to test hypotheses concerning the effects of normative and informational social influences upon individual judgment. The hypotheses received strong support from the experimental data.

In discussion of our results, the thesis was advanced that prior studies of "group" influence upon individual judgment were only incidentally studies of the type of social influence most specifically associated with groups—i.e., of normative social influence. The role of normative social influence in buttressing as well as undermining individual experience was considered.

REFERENCES

1. ASCH, S. E. Effects of group pressure upon the modification and distortion of judgments. In H. Guetzkow (Ed.), *Groups, leadership and men.* Pittsburgh: Carnegie Press, 1951. Pp. 177–190.
2. ASCH, S. E. *Social psychology.* New York: Prentice-Hall, 1952.
3. BOVARD, E. W. Group structure and perception. *J. abnorm. soc. Psychol.,* 1951, *46,* 398–405.
4. DEUTSCH, M. A theory of cooperation and competition. *Hum. Relat.,* 1949, *2,* 129–152.
5. FESTINGER, L. Informal social communication. *Psychol. Rev.,* 1950, *57,* 271–282.
6. SHERIF, M. A study of some social factors in perception. *Arch. Psychol.,* 1935, *27,* No. 187.

13

Compliance Without Pressure:

The Foot-In-The-Door Technique

Jonathan L. Freedman and Scott C. Fraser

How can a person be induced to do something he would rather not do? This question is relevant to practically every phase of social life from stopping at a traffic light to stopping smoking, from buying Brand X to buying savings bonds, from supporting the March of Dimes to supporting the Civil Rights Act.

One common way of attacking the problem is to exert as much pressure as possible on the reluctant individual in an effort to force him to comply. This technique has been the focus of a considerable amount of experimental research. Work on attitude change, conformity, imitation, and obedience has all tended to stress the importance of the degree of external pressure. The prestige of the communicator (Kelman & Hovland, 1953), degree of discrepancy of the communication (Hovland & Pritzker, 1957), size of the group disagreeing with the subject (Asch, 1951), perceived power of the model (Bandura, Ross, & Ross, 1963), etc., are the kinds of variables that have been studied. This impressive body of work, added to the research on rewards and punishments in learning, has produced convincing evidence that greater external pressure generally leads to greater compliance with the wishes of

From *Journal of Personality and Social Psychology,* 1966, *4,* 195–202.

The authors are grateful to Evelyn Bless for assisting in the running of the second experiment reported here. These studies were supported in part by Grant GS-196 from the National Science Foundation. The first study was conducted while the junior author was supported by an NSF undergraduate summer fellowship.

the experimenter. The one exception appears to be situations involving the arousal of cognitive dissonance in which, once discrepant behavior has been elicited from the subject, the greater the pressure that was used to elicit the behavior, the less subsequent change occurs (Festinger & Carlsmith, 1959). But even in this situation one critical element is the amount of external pressure exerted.

Clearly, then, under most circumstances the more pressure that can be applied, the more likely it is that the individual will comply. There are, however, many times when for ethical, moral, or practical reasons it is difficult to apply much pressure when the goal is to produce compliance with a minimum of apparent pressure, as in the forced-compliance studies involving dissonance arousal. And even when a great deal of pressure is possible, it is still important to maximize the compliance it produces. Thus, factors other than external pressure are often quite critical in determining degree of compliance. What are these factors?

Although rigorous research on the problem is rather sparse, the fields of advertising, propaganda, politics, etc., are by no means devoid of techniques designed to produce compliance in the absence of external pressure (or to maximize the effectiveness of the pressure that is used, which is really the same problem). One assumption about compliance that has often been made either explicitly or implicitly is that once a person has been induced to comply with a small request he is more likely to comply with a larger demand. This is the principle that is commonly referred to as the foot-in-the-door or gradation technique and is reflected in the saying that if you "give them an inch, they'll take a mile." It was, for example, supposed to be one of the basic techniques upon which the Korean brainwashing tactics were based (Schein, Schneier, & Barker, 1961), and, in a somewhat different sense, one basis for Nazi propaganda during 1940 (Bruner, 1941). It also appears to be implicit in many advertising campaigns which attempt to induce the consumer to do anything relating to the product involved, even sending back a card saying he does not want the product.

The most relevant piece of experimental evidence comes from a study of conformity done by Deutsch and Gerard (1955). Some subjects were faced with incorrect group judgments first in a series in which the stimuli were not present during the actual judging and then in a series in which they were present, while the order of the memory and visual series was reversed for other subjects. For both groups the memory series produced more conformity, and when the memory series came first there was more total conformity to the group judgments. It seems likely that this order effect occurred because, as the authors suggest, once conformity is elicited at all it is more likely to occur in the future. Although this kind of conformity is probably somewhat different from compliance as described above, this finding certainly lends some support to the foot-in-the-door idea. The present research attempted to provide a rigorous, more direct test of this notion as it applies to compliance and to provide data relevant to several alternative ways of explaining the effect.

EXPERIMENT I

The basic paradigm was to ask some subjects (Performance condition) to comply first with a small request and then 3 days later with a larger, related request. Other subjects (One-Contact condition) were asked to comply only with the large request. The hypothesis was that more subjects in the Performance condition than in the One-Contact condition would comply with the larger request.

Two additional conditions were included in an attempt to specify the essential difference between these two major conditions. The Performance subjects were asked to perform a small favor, and, if they agreed, they did it. The question arises whether the act of agreeing itself is critical or whether actually carrying it out was necessary. To assess this a third group of subjects (Agree-Only) was asked the first request, but, even if they agreed, they did not carry it out. Thus, they were indentical to the Performance group except that they were not given the opportunty of performing the request.

Another difference between the two main conditions was that at the time of the larger request the subjects in the Performance condition were more familiar with the experimenter than were the other subjects. The Performance subjects had been contacted twice, heard his voice more, discovered that the questions were not dangerous, and so on. It is possible that this increased familiarity would serve to decrease the fear and suspicion of a strange voice on the phone and might accordingly increase the likelihood of the subjects agreeing to the larger request. To control for this a fourth condition was run (Familiarization) which attempted to give the subjects as much familiarity with the experimenter as in the Performance and Agree-Only conditions with the only difference being that no request was made.

The major prediction was that more subjects in the Performance condition would agree to the large request than in any of the other conditions, and that the One-Contact condition would produce the least compliance. Since the importance of agreement and familiarity was essentially unknown, the expectation was that the Agree-Only and Familiarization conditions would produce intermediate amounts of compliance.

METHOD

The prediction stated above was tested in a field experiment in which housewives were asked to allow a survey team of five or six men to come into their homes for 2 hours to classify the household products they used. This large request was made under four different conditions: after an initial contact in which the subject had been asked to answer a few questions about the kinds of soaps she used, and the questions were actually asked (Performance condition); after an identical contact in which the questions were not actually asked (Agree-Only condition); after an initial contact in which no request was made (Familiarization condition); or after no initial contact (One-Contact condition). The dependent measure was simply whether or not the subject agreed to the large request.

Procedure

The subjects were 156 Palo Alto, California, housewives, 36 in each condition, who were selected at random from the telephone directory. An additional 12 subjects distributed about equally among the three two-contact conditions could not be reached for the second contact and are not included in the data analysis. Subjects were assigned randomly to the various conditions, except that the Familiarization condition was added to the design after the other three conditions had been completed. All contacts were by telephone by the same experimenter who identified himself as the same person each time. Calls were made only in the morning. For the three groups that were contacted twice, the first call was made on either Monday or Tuesday and the second always 3 days later. All large requests were made on either Thursday or Friday.

At the first contact, the experimenter introduced himself by name and said that he was from the California Consumers' Group. In the Performance condition he then proceeded:

> We are calling you this morning to ask if you would answer a number of questions about what household products you use so that we could have this information for our public service publication, "The Guide." Would you be willing to give us this information for our survey?

If the subject agreed, she was asked a series of eight innocuous questions dealing with household soaps (e.g., "What brand of soap do you use in your kitchen sink?") She was then thanked for her cooperation, and the contact terminated.

Another condition (Agree-Only) was run to assess the importance of actually carrying out the request as opposed to merely agreeing to it. The only difference between this and the Performance condition was that, if the subject agreed to answer the questions, the experimenter thanked her, but said that he was just lining up respondents for the survey and would contact her if needed.

A third condition was included to check on the importance of the subject's greater familiarity with the experimenter in the two-contact conditions. In this condition the experimenter introduced himself, described the organization he worked for and the survey it was conducting, listed the questions he was asking, and then said that he was calling merely to acquaint the subject with the existence of his organization. In other words, these subjects were contacted, spent as much time on the phone with the experimenter as the Performance subjects did, heard all the questions, but neither agreed to answer them nor answered them.

In all of these two-contact conditions some subjects did not agree to the requests or even hung up before the requests were made. Every subject who answered the phone was included in the analysis of the results and was contacted for the second request regardless of her extent of cooperativeness during the first contact. In other words, no subject who could be contacted the appropriate number of times was discarded from any of the four conditions.

The large request was essentially identical for all subjects. The experimenter called, identified himself, and said either that his group was expanding its survey (in the case of the two-contact conditions) or that it was conducting a survey (in the One-Contact condition). In all four conditions he then continued:

> The survey will involve five or six men from our staff coming into your home some morning for about 2 hours to enumerate and classify all the household products that you have. They will have to have full freedom in your house to go through the cupboards and storage places. Then all this information will be used in the writing of the reports for our public service publication, "The Guide."

If the subject agreed to the request, she was thanked and told that at the present time the experimenter was merely collecting names of people who were willing to take part and that she would be contacted if it were decided to use her in the survey. If she did not agree, she was thanked for her time. This terminated the experiment.

RESULTS

Apparently even the small request was not considered trivial by some of the subjects. Only about two thirds of the subjects in the Performance and Agree-Only conditions agreed to answer the questions about household soaps. It might be noted that none of those who refused the first request later agreed to the large request, although as stated previously all subjects who were contacted for the small request are included in the data for those groups.

Our major prediction was that subjects who had agreed to

and carried out a small request (Performance condition) would subsequently be more likely to comply with a larger request than would subjects who were asked only the larger request (One-Contact condition). As may be seen in Table 13.1, the results support the prediction. Over 50% of the subjects in the Performance condition agreed to the larger request, while less than 25% of the One-Contact condition agreed to it. Thus it appears that obtaining compliance with a small request does tend to increase subsequent compliance. The question is what aspect of the initial contact produces this effect.

Table 13.1—Percentage of Subjects Complying with Large Request in Experiment I

Condition	%
Performance	52.8
Agree-Only	33.3
Familiarization	27.8*
One-Contact	22.2**

Note.—$N = 36$ for each group. Significance levels represent differences from the Performance condition.

* $p < .07$.
** $p < .02$.

One possibility is that the effect was produced merely by increased familiarity with the experimenter. The Familiarization control was included to assess the effect on compliance of two contacts with the same person. The group had as much contact with the experimenter as the Performance group, but no request was made during the first contact. As the table indicates, the Familiarization group did not differ appreciably in amount of compliance from the One-Contact group, but was different from the Performance group ($x^2 = 3.70$, $p < .07$). Thus, although increased familiarity may well lead to increased compliance, in the present situation the differences in amount of familiarity apparently were not great enough to produce any such increase; the effect that was obtained seems not to be due to this factor.

Another possibility is that the critical factor producing increased compliance is simply agreeing to the small request (i.e., carrying it out may not be necessary). The Agree-Only condition was identical to the Performance condition except that in the former the subjects were not asked the questions. The amount of compliance in this Agree-Only condition fell between the Performance and One-Contact conditions and was not significantly different from either of them. This leaves the effect of merely agreeing somewhat ambiguous, but it suggests that the agreement alone may produce part of the effect.

Unfortunately, it must be admitted that neither of these control conditions is an entirely adequate test of the possibility it was designed to assess. Both conditions are in some way quite peculiar and may have made a very different and extraneous impression on the subject than did the Performance condition. In one case, a housewife is asked to answer some questions and then is not asked them; in the other, some man calls to tell her about some organization she has never heard of. Now, by themselves neither of these events might produce very much suspicion. But several days later, the same man calls and asks a very large favor. At this point it is not at all unlikely that many subjects think they are being manipulated, or in any case that something strange is going on. Any such reaction on the part of the subjects would naturally tend to reduce the amount of compliance in these conditions.

Thus, although this first study demonstrates that an initial contact in which a request is made and carried out increases compliance with a second request, the question of why and how the initial request produces this effect remains unanswered. In an attempt to begin answering this question and to extend the results of the first study, a second experiment was conducted.

There seemed to be several quite plausible ways in which the increase in compliance might have been produced. The first was simply some kind of commitment to or involvement with the particular person making the request. This might work, for example, as follows: The subject has agreed to the first request and perceives that the experimenter therefore expects him also to agree to the second request. The subject thus feels obligated and does not want to disappoint the experimenter; he also feels that he needs a good reason for saying "no"—a better reason than he would need if he had never said "yes." This is just one line of causality—the particular process by which involvement with the experimenter operates might be quite different, but the basic idea would be similar. The commitment is to the particular person. This implies that the increase in compliance due to the first contact should occur primarily when both requests are made by the same person.

Another explanation in terms of involvement centers around the particular issue with which the requests are concerned. Once the subject has taken some action in connection with an area of concern, be it surveys, political activity, or highway safety, there is probably a tendency to become somewhat more concerned with the area. The subject begins thinking about it, considering its importance and relevance to him, and so on. This tends to make him more likely to agree to take further action in the same area when he is later asked to. To the extent that this is the critical factor, the initial contact should increase compliance only when both requests are related to the same issue or area of concern.

Another way of looking at the situation is that the subject needs a reason to say "no." In our society it is somewhat difficult to refuse a reasonable request, particularly when it is made by an organization that is not trying to make money. In order to refuse, many people feel that they need a reason—simply not wanting to do it is often not in itself sufficient. The person can say to the requester or simply to himself that he does not believe in giving to charities or tipping or working for political parties or answering questions or posting signs, or whatever he is asked to do. Once he has performed a particular task, however, this excuse is no longer valid for not agreeing to perform a similar task. Even if the first thing he did was trivial compared to the present request, he cannot say he never does this sort of thing, and thus one good reason for refusing is removed. This line of reasoning suggests that the similarity of the first and second requests in terms of the type of action required is an important factor. The more similar they are, the more the "matter of principle" argument is eliminated by agreeing to the first request, and the greater should be the increase in compliance.

There are probably many other mechanisms by which the initial request might produce an increase in compliance. The second experiment was designed in part to test the notions described above, but its major purpose was to demonstrate the effect unequivocally. To this latter end it eliminated one of the important problems with the first study which was that when the experimenter made the second request he was not blind as to which condition the subjects were in. In this study the second request was always made by someone other than the person who made the first request, and the second experimenter was blind as to what condition the subject was in. This eliminates the possibility that the experimenter exerted systematically different amounts of pressure in different experimental conditions. If the effect of the first study were replicated, it would also rule out the relatively uninteresting possibility that the effect is due primarily to greater familiarity or involvement with the particular person making the first request.

EXPERIMENT II

The basic paradigm was quite similar to that of the first study. Experimental subjects were asked to comply with a small request and were later asked a considerably larger request, while controls were asked only the larger request. The first request varied along two dimensions. Subjects were asked either to put up a small sign or to sign a petition, and the issue was either safe driving or keeping California beautiful. Thus, there were four first requests: a small sign for safe driving or for beauty, and a petition for the two issues. The second request for all subjects was to install in their front lawn a very large sign which said "Drive Carefully." The four experimental conditions may be defined in terms of the similarity of the small and large requests along the dimensions of issue and task. The two requests were similar in both issue and task for the small-sign, safe-driving group, similar only in issue for the safe-driving-petition group, similar only in task for the small "Keep California Beautiful" sign group, and similar in neither issue nor task for the "Keep California Beautiful" petition group.

The major expectation was that the three groups for which either the task or the issue were similar would show more compliance than the controls, and it was also felt that when both were similar there would probably be the most compliance. The fourth condition (Different Issue-Different Task) was included primarily to assess the effect simply of the initial contact which, although it was not identical to the second one on either issue or task, was in many ways quite similar (e.g., a young student asking for cooperation on a noncontroversial issue). There were no clear expectations as to how this condition would compare to the controls.

METHOD

The subjects were 114 women and 13 men living in Palo Alto, California. Of these, 9 women and 6 men could not be contacted for the second request and are not included in the data analysis. The remaining 112 subjects were divided about equally among the five conditions (see Table 13.2). All subjects were contacted between 1:30 and 4:30 on weekday afternoons.

Two experimenters, one male and one female, were employed, and a different one always made the second contact. Unlike the first study, the experimenters actually went to the homes of the subjects and interviewed them on a face-to-face basis. An effort was made to select subjects from blocks and neighborhoods that were as homogeneous as possible. On each block every third or fourth house was approached, and all subjects on that block were in one experimental condition. This was necessary because of the likelihood that neighbors would talk to each other about the contact. In addition, for every four subjects contacted, a fifth house was chosen as a control but was, of course, not contacted. Throughout this phase of the experiment, and in fact throughout the whole experiment, the two experimenters did not communicate to each other what conditions had been run on a given block nor what condition a particular house was in.

The small-sign, safe-driving group was told that the experimenter was from the Community Committee for Traffic Safety, that he was visiting a number of homes in an attempt to make the citizens more aware of the need to drive carefully all the time, and that he would like the subject to take a small sign and put it in a window or in the car so that it would serve as a reminder of the need to drive carefully. The sign was 3 inches square, said "Be a safe driver," was on thin paper without a gummed backing, and in general looked rather amateurish and unattractive. If the subject agreed, he was given the sign and thanked; if he disagreed, he was simply thanked for his time.

The three other experimental conditions were quite similar with appropriate changes. The other organization was identified as the Keep California Beautiful Committee and its sign said, appropriately enough, "Keep California Beautiful." Both signs were simply black block letters on a white background. The two petition groups were asked to sign a petition which was being sent to California's United States Senators. The petition advocated support for any legislation which would promote either safer driving or keeping California beautiful. The subject was shown a petition, typed on heavy bond paper, with at least 20 signatures already affixed. If she agreed, she signed and was thanked. If she did not agree, she was merely thanked.

The second contact was made about 2 weeks after the initial one. Each experimenter was armed with a list of houses which had been compiled by the other experimenter. This list contained all four experimental conditions and the controls, and, of course, there was no way for the second experimenter to know which condition the subject had been in. At this second contact, all subjects were asked the same thing: Would they put a large sign concerning safe driving in their front yard? The experimenter identified himself as being from the Citizens for Safe Driving, a different group from the original safe-driving group (although it is likely that most subjects who had been in the safe-driving conditions did not notice the difference). The subject was shown a picture of a very large sign reading "Drive Carefully" placed in front of an attractive house. The picture was taken so that the sign obscured much of the front of the house and completely concealed the doorway. It was rather poorly lettered. The subject was told that: "Our men will come out and install it and later come and remove it. It makes just a small hole in your lawn, but if this is unacceptable to you we have a special mount which will make no hole." She was asked to put the sign up for a week or a week and a half. If the subject agreed, she was told that more names than necessary were being gathered and if her home were to be used she would be contacted in a few weeks. The experimenter recorded the subject's response and this ended the experiment.

RESULTS

First, it should be noted that there were no large differences among the experimental conditions in the percentages of subjects agreeing to the first request. Although somewhat more subjects agreed to post the "Keep California Beautiful" sign and somewhat fewer to sign the beauty petition none of those differences approach significance.

The important figures are the number of subjects in each group who agreed to the large request. These are presented in Table 13.2. The figures for the four experimental groups include all subjects who were approached the first time, regardless of whether or not they agreed to the small request. As noted above, a few subjects were lost because they could not be reached for the second request, and, of course, these are not included in the table.

It is immediately apparent that the first request tended to increase the degree of compliance with the second request. Whereas fewer than 20 % of the controls agreed to put the large sign on their lawn, over 55% of the experimental subjects agreed, with

Table 13.2—Percentage of Subjects Complying with Large Request in Experiment II

Issue[a]	*Task*[a]			
	Similar	*N*	*Different*	*N*
Similar	76.0**	25	47.8*	23
Different	47.6*	21	47.4*	19
One-Contact 16.7 (N = 24)				

Note.—Significance levels represent differences from the One-Contact condition.
a Denotes relationship between first and second requests.
* $p < .08$.
** $p < .01$.

over 45% being the lowest degree of compliance for any experimental condition. As expected, those conditions in which the two requests were similar in terms of either issue or task produced significantly more compliance than did the controls (x^2's range from 3.67, $p < .07$ to 15.01, $p < .001$). A somewhat unexpected result is that the fourth condition, in which the first request had relatively little in common with the second request, also produced more compliance than the controls ($x^2 = 3.40$, $p < .08$). In other words, regardless of whether or not the two requests are similar in either issue or task, simply having the first request tends to increase the likelihood that the subject will comply with a subsequent, larger request. And this holds even when the two requests are made by different people several weeks apart.

A second point of interest is a comparison among the four experimental conditions. As expected, the Same Issue-Same Task condition produced more compliance than any of the other two-contact conditions, but the difference is not significant (x^2's range from 2.7 to 2.9). If only those subjects who agreed to the first request are considered, the same pattern holds.

DISCUSSION

To summarize the results, the first study indicated that carrying out a small request increased the likelihood that the subject would agree to a similar larger request made by the same person. The second study showed that this effect was quite strong even when a different person made the larger request, and the two requests were quite dissimilar. How may these results be explained?

Two possibilities were outlined previously. The matter-of-principle idea which centered on the particular type of action was not supported by the data, since the similarity of the tasks did not make an appreciable difference in degree of compliance. The notion of involvement, as described previously, also has difficulty accounting for some of the findings. The basic idea was that once someone has agreed to any action, no matter how small, he tends to feel more involved than he did before. This involvement may center around the particular person making the first request or the particular issue. This is quite consistent with the results of the first study (with the exception of the two control groups which as discussed previously were rather ambiguous) and with the Similar-Issue groups in the second experiment. This idea of involvement does not, however, explain the increase in compliance found in the two groups in which the first and second request did not deal with the same issue.

It is possible that in addition to or instead of this process a more general and diffuse mechanism underlies the increase in compliance. What may occur is a change in the person's feelings about getting involved or about taking action. Once he has agreed to a request, his attitude may change. He may become, in his own eyes, the kind of person who does this sort of thing, who agrees to requests made by strangers, who takes action on things he believes in, who cooperates with good causes. The change in attitude could be toward any aspect of the situation or toward the whole business of saying "yes." The basic idea is that the change in attitude need not be toward any particular issue or person or activity, but may be toward activity or compliance in general. This would imply that an increase in compliance would not depend upon the two contacts being made by the same person, or concerning the same issue or involving the same kind of action. The similarity could be much more general, such as both concerning good causes, or requiring a similar kind of action, or being made by pleasant, attractive individuals.

It is not being suggested that this is the only mechanism operating here. The idea of involvement continues to be extremely plausible, and there are probably a number of other possibilities. Unfortunately, the present studies offer no additional data with which to support or refute any of the possible explanations of the effect. These explanations thus remain simply descriptions of mechanisms which might produce an increase in compliance after agreement with a first request. Hopefully, additional research will test these ideas more fully and perhaps also specify other manipulations which produce an increase in compliance without an increase in external pressure.

It should be pointed out that the present studies employed what is perhaps a very special type of situation. In all cases the requests were made by presumably nonprofit service organizations. The issues in the second study were deliberately noncontroversial, and it may be assumed that virtually all subjects initially sympathized with the objectives of safe driving and a beautiful California. This is in strong contrast to campaigns which are designed to sell a particular product, political candidate, or dogma. Whether the technique employed in this study would be successful in these other situations remains to be shown.

SUMMARY

Two experiments were conducted to test the proposition that once someone has agreed to a small request he is more likely to comply with a larger request. The 1st study demonstrated this effect when the same person made both requests. The 2nd study extended this to the situation in which different people made the 2 requests. Several experimental groups were run in an effort to explain these results, and possible explanations are discussed.

REFERENCES

ASCH, S. E. Effects of group pressure upon the modification and distortion of judgments. In H. Guetzkow (Ed.), *Groups, leadership and men; research in human relations.* Pittsburgh: Carnegie Press, 1951. Pp. 177–190.

BANDURA, A., ROSS, D., & ROSS, S. A. A comparative test of the status envy, social power, and secondary reinforcement theories of identificatory learning. *Journal of Abnormal and Social Psychology,* 1963, *67,* 527–534.

BRUNER, J. The dimensions of propaganda: German short-wave broadcasts to America. *Journal of Abnormal and Social Psychology,* 1941, *36,* 311–337.

DEUTSCH, M., & GERARD, H. B. A study of normative and informational social influences upon individual judgment. *Journal of Abnormal and Social Psychology,* 1955, *51,* 629–636.

FESTINGER, L., & CARLSMITH, J. Cognitive consequences of forced compliance. *Journal of Abnormal and Social Psychology,* 1959, *58,* 203–210.

HOVLAND, C. I., & PRITZKER, H. A. Extent of opinion change as a function of amount of change advocated. *Journal of Abnormal and Social Psycology,* 1957, *54,* 257–261.

KELMAN, H. C., & HOVLAND, C. I. "Reinstatement" of the communicator in delayed measurement of opinion change. *Journal of Abnormal and Social Psychology,* 1953, *48,* 327–335.

SCHEIN, E. H., SCHNEIER, I., & BARKER, C. H. *Coercive pressure.* New York: Norton, 1961.

VII

Leadership

Fiedler and Meuwese (Chapter 14) indicated the need for more research to specify the conditions under which efficient use of the leader's abilities occurs. Drawing on findings from earlier work by Fiedler, they hypothesized that the leader's ability (as measured by intelligence) to influence task effectiveness depends to a considerable extent on group cohesiveness. To test this prediction they applied correlational techniques to data obtained by Fiedler and his colleagues from previous research with groups in laboratory and natural settings. The results consistently showed that the leader's intelligence predicted group performance only in cohesive groups. Thus, Fiedler, pursuing a specific research interest in a variety of settings, had available a data bank for testing a subsequently derived hypothesis.

14

Leader's Contribution to Task Performance in Cohesive and Uncohesive Groups

Fred E. Fiedler and W. A. T. Meuwese

Although a group or a team may be frequently less efficient than individuals working alone (Faust, 1959; McCurdy & Lambert, 1952; Shaw, 1932) when taken on a per man-hour basis, teamwork is essential where the task precludes individuals from independent action. A single individual cannot operate a submarine or represent three widely divergent viewpoints. One of the leader's main functions is the effective use and coordination of his team members' skills and abilities.

Interestingly enough, practically no work has been published on the specific conditions under which efficient utilization of the leader's or his group members' abilities takes place. We have generally assumed that a good group simply consists of abler members than a poor group. Leaders tend to be chosen from among those most competent to perform the job they are to supervise. The present paper attempts to show that the leader's ability to contribute to the task depends to a considerable extent on the cohesiveness of his group.

The underlying hypothesis deriving from earlier work (Fiedler,

From *Journal of Abnormal and Social Psychology*, 1963, *67*, 83–87.

This study was conducted under Contract NR 177-472, Nonr-1834(36), "Group and Organization Factors Influencing Group Creativity," between the Office of Naval Research and the University of Illinois, Fred E. Feidler, Lawrence M. Stolurow, and Harry C. Triandis, coinvestigators.

1958) can be described as follows: The leader's ability to contribute to the group's productivity requires that the group's structure enable him to communicate effectively with all members, and that the members be willing to follow the directions of the leader.

It is probably also necessary that the leader is free to devote his influence to the task rather than having to direct his efforts mainly toward group maintenance. From empirical evidence (Back, 1951; Fiedler, 1958) it may be inferred that these conditions are fulfilled if there is a certain degree of *cohesiveness* in the group. In this paper a group is defined to be cohesive if one or both of the following conditions are present in the group: the members feel attracted to the group, the members are adjusted to the group and free of interpersonal tension. Both of these conditions can be assessed by questionnaires administered to the group members.

We shall here examine data which were obtained in four different studies. The analyses were based on the assumption that a correlation between some person's ability or achievement score and some measure of his group's performance provides a measure of the individual's direct influence on the group's task performance.

The major operational hypothesis to be tested was that: The leader's ability score will correlate positively with a measure of group effectiveness in cohesive groups, but not in uncohesive groups.

METHOD AND RESULTS

Tank Crew Study

A study was conducted on 25 Army tank crews which participated in an experiment comparing tank equipment (Fiedler, 1955). Each crew consisted of five enlisted men, viz., a tank commander (TC) who was the formal leader of the group, a gunner (G), a driver (D), a loader (L), and a bow gunner (BG). All crews remained intact during the course of the study.

Each crew was assigned to work with five different models of tanks and each tank test entailed driving toward, recognizing, and hitting five different targets. A combined criterion was developed

Table 14.1—Correlations (rho) of Army General Classification Test (AGCT) and Proficiency Scores with Tank Crew Criteria (N = 8)

Group	TC	G	D	L	BG
			AGCT Score		
Cohesive	26	05	52	76**	59
Uncohesive	—21	—29	20	23	—21
			Proficiency Score		
Cohesive	94***	38	94***	47	49
Uncohesive	—21	—38	—66*	43	—23

Note.—TC = Tank commander, G = Gunner, D = Driver, L = Loader, BG = Bow gunner.
* $p < .10$, two-tailed.
** $p < .05$, two-tailed.
*** $p < .01$, two-tailed.

which estimated the probability that a tank performing in this manner would emerge victorious in a duel with a similar tank. This score was based on the number of seconds required for each of the three subtasks: time to travel to the target, time to recognize the target, and time to hit the target. Army General Classification Test (AGCT) scores as well as individual proficiency scores were obtained for all crew members prior to the experiment.

The sample was divided into the eight most cohesive and the eight least cohesive groups on the basis of sociometric choices which were obtained from crew members at three points in the experiment. As can be seen from Table 14.1, Column 1, the contribution of the leader is greater in cohesive groups. This trend emerges most clearly when proficiency scores are utilized.

Although this was not hypothesized, it can also be seen from Table 14.1 that the ability of the other crew members generally correlated positively in cohesive teams while zero or negative relations were found in uncohesive teams.

B-29 Bomber Crews

A second set of crew performance and individual proficiency data were obtained in the course of a study on B-29 bomber crews

(Fiedler, 1955). These crews, each consisting of five officers and six enlisted men, were in training at Randolph Air Force Base during the Korean war in 1951.

Ground School Grades (GSG) were available for several crew members. These grades reflect with reasonable accuracy the crew member's competence on his crew tasks. According to research of the Air Force Crew Research Laboratory at Randolph Field, one of the best objective measures of crew effectiveness was the "Radar Bomb Score circular error average" (RBS). The reliability of this score was estimated to be .45 (Knoell & Forgays, 1952).

Several measures were obtained which indicate the cohesiveness or attractiveness of the crew. These were the crew members' ratings of confidence in the aircraft commander, liking for the aircraft commander, liking for fellow crew members, and feeling of crew effectiveness. The median intercorrelation of these measures was .59 and the ratings were, therefore, combined.

On the basis of these combined cohesiveness or attractiveness scores, the crews were divided into those having high, low, and very low attractiveness to crew members.[1] Table 14.2 presents the correlation of ground school scores with the radar bomb score criterion.

The officers' proficiency score correlated positively with radar bomb scores in high and low cohesiveness conditions, but not in very low cohesive groups. The proficiency of the enlisted men correlated zero or negatively with the criterion. In essence, therefore, these findings support those obtained on Army tank crews. This analysis also suggests the possibility that not only the leader's proficiency, but also the proficiency of the key members, in this case the officers, can influence group effectiveness only in cohesive teams.

Research on Antiaircraft Artillery Crews

A study was conducted by Hutchins and Fiedler (1960) on antiaircraft artillery crews, each of which consisted of 8–12 enlisted men. AGCT scores were gathered on all available personnel. As was the case in other studies, complete data could not be obtained

[1] Data for "medium cohesive" crews were too incomplete to be of use.

Table 14.2—Correlations (rho) of Individual Ground School Grades and Radar Bomb Scores under Different Conditions of Attraction to Group (Cohesiveness)

Group	Cohesiveness					
	High		Low		Very low	
	N	r	N	r	N	r
Officers						
Aircraft commander	6	67	7	85*	4	—40
Pilot	6	70	7	43	5	30
Bombardier	5	80	7	22	5	—30
Radar operator	5	48	6	41	5	30
$\bar{r}$		66		48		—02
Enlisted						
Radio operator	5	—20	7	47	5	—18
Left gunner	5	—30	7	—01	5	10
Right gunner	5	—78	7	—87**	5	—70
$\bar{r}$		—43		—14		—26

* $p < .05$, two-tailed.
** $p < .01$, two-tailed.

Table 14.3—Correlation (rho) of AGCT with Effectiveness in Groups High, Medium, and Low on Leader's and Member's General Army Adjustment Score

	High	Medium	Low
	Leader's GAA Score		
	(N = 6)	(N = 9)	(N = 9)
AGCT leader	84*	—21	23
AGCT members	24	—37	—17
	Member's GAA Score		
	(N = 8)	(N = 8)	(N = 8)
AGCT leader	57	26	—05
AGCT members	—48	—01	—07

Note.—Seventeen groups were omitted from the analysis because of missing data.
* $p < .05$, two-tailed.

from all crews in the sample because of sickness, temporary leaves, or duty assignments away from the site of testing.

Crew performance scores were based on crew rankings by officers in charge of companies and platoons. These rankings correlated with objective target acquisition and performance scores which were the accepted crew performance criteria indicating that the guns were accurately aimed on the targets.

The General Army Adjustment (GAA) scores which are indices of morale and crew attractiveness served to indicate the cohesiveness of the group. The groups were divided into crews high, medium, and low on these two criteria. The AGCT score of the leader and the average AGCT score of the members were correlated with the crew's effectiveness. The results are presented in Table 14.3.

Again, it can be seen that the leader's AGCT score correlates with performance in cohesive crews (high GAA) but not in uncohesive crews. Member AGCT, on the other hand, does not correlate with crew performance in either cohesive or uncohesive groups.

Research on Group Creativity

The last study to be described was intended to identify leader attitudes which are conducive to group creativity (Fiedler, Meuwese, & Oonk, 1961). This investigation was conducted in the Netherlands and utilized 32 Catholic and 32 Calvinist university students. Each subject participated in two groups: once in a four-man team having homogeneous membership, and once in a team consisting of two men from each religion. In 16 of the groups the experimenters appointed a chairman, while the other 16 groups worked as "informal" teams.

The task consisted in devising three different stories from the same TAT card, either Card 11 or 19. The creativity expressed in these stories was judged by two raters on the basis of a manual. The correlation between the two judges' ratings was .81 for Card 11 and .88 for Card 19.

A 14-item Analogies test [2] was administered to all subjects and we are here concerned with the relation of performance on this

[2] Constructed by J. C. van Lennep, University of Utrecht. This test is similar in form and content to the Miller Analogies Test.

Table 14.4—Correlations (rho) between Group Creativity and Analogies Scores

	"Cohesive"	"Uncohesive"
Analogies score of:	*No destructive critic (N = 14)*	*Destructive critic (N = 17)*
Informal leader	54*	24
Group members	—02	18

Note.—In one group it was impossible to determine the informal leader on the basis of the sociometric questions.

* $p < .05$, one-tailed.

short intelligence test and group creativity. The groups were divided into those which seemed tense and unpleasant and thus uncohesive, and those which were relaxed and at ease, hence cohesive. This was inferred from sociometric questions which asked the subjects to name individuals who were "destructively critical." The informal leader of the group was determined by means of sociometric questions, e.g., "Which of the group members had most influence on the opinions of others?"

Correlations between creativity and informal leader's Analogies scores and member's average Analogies scores are presented in Table 14.4.

Here again, we find that the leader's intelligence influences the group performance most in cohesive, pleasant groups. The informal leader has little direct influence in groups which are relatively uncohesive. It can thus be concluded that this analysis also confirms the hypothesized relationship.

Significance of Results

To assess the combined probability that this series of results could have been obtained by chance, a set of four independent cases was formed, consisting of the *smallest* correlations for each separate sample from Table 14.5 in which the main results of this study are summarized. The combined probability for these four samples, computed according to Jones and Fiske (1953), was below the .01 level, one-tailed test.

Table 14.5—Correlations of Leader's Ability with Group Effectiveness

Study	Ability score	Effectiveness criterion	Cohesiveness criterion	Correlation (rho)			
				Cohesive groups	N	Uncohesive groups	N
Army tank crews	AGCT	Probability of winning a battle	Sociometric	.26	8	—.21	8
Army tank crews	Proficiency rating	Probability of winning a battle	Sociometric	.94**	8	—.21	8
B-29 bomber crews	Ground School Grade	Radar bomb score	Liking for the group	.67	6	—.40	4
Antiaircraft artillery crews	AGCT	Ratings	Leader's Army Adjustment score	.84*	6	.23	9
Antiaircraft artillery crews	AGCT	Ratings	Member's Army Adjustment score	.57	8	—.05	8
Dutch creativity study	Analogies score	Creativity ratings	Presence of destructive critic	.54*	14	.24	17

* $p < .05$.
** $p < .01$.

DISCUSSION

The results clearly confirm the hypohesis that a leader directly influences the effectiveness of the group only if the group is cohesive. This relationship was found in four entirely different studies and it thus seems to be fairly general.

The results do *not* indicate that the leader does not have *power* in uncohesive groups. He may or may not have power; but if he does, he exerts it in a way that is not directly reflected in the group's product. Thus, the leader of an uncohesive group may be forced into a position in which it is necessary to exert influence mainly on the maintenance of the group. Cohesive groups probably do not require as much of the leader's effort to maintain the group as would be the case in uncohesive groups. The leader may, therefore, be able to influence the level of group task performance by contributing directly to the solution of the problem.

SUMMARY

Army tank crews, B-29 bomber crews, antiaircraft artillery crews, and creative discussion groups provided data which were analyzed to determine the relationship between the leader's intelligence and group performance. Each sample was divided into cohesive and uncohesive groups, and the correlation between the leader's intelligence and group performance was computed. The results indicated consistently that the leader's intelligence predicts group performance in cohesive groups, but not in uncohesive groups.

REFERENCES

BACK, K. Influence through social communication. *J. abnorm. soc. Psychol.*, 1951, *46*, 9–23.

FAUST, W. L. Group versus individual problem-solving. *J. abnorm. soc. Psychol.*, 1959, *59*, 68–72.

FIEDLER, F. E. The influence of leader-keyman relations on combat crew effectiveness. *J. abnorm. soc. Psychol.*, 1955, *51*, 227–235.

FIEDLER, F. E. *Leader attitudes and group effectiveness.* Urbana: Univer. Illinois Press, 1958.

FIEDLER, F. E., MEUWESE, W. A. T., & OONK, SOPHIE. An exploratory study of group creativity in laboratory tasks. *Acta psychol., Amsterdam,* 1961, *18,* 100–119.

HUTCHINS, E. B., & FIEDLER, F. E. Task-oriented and quasi-therapeutic role functions of the leader in small military groups. *Sociometry,* 1960, *23,* 393–406.

JONES, L. V., & FISKE, D. W. Models for testing the significance of combined results. *Psychol. Bull.,* 1953, *50,* 375–382.

KNOELL, DOROTHY, & FORGAYS, D. G. Interrelationships of combat crew performance in the B-29. *USAF Hum. Resour. Res. Cent., Res. Note,* 1952, CCT 52-1.

MCCURDY, H. G., & LAMBERT, W. E. The efficiency of small human groups in the solution of problems requiring genuine cooperation. *J. Pers.,* 1952, *20,* 478–494.

SHAW, MARJORIE E. A comparison of individuals and small groups in the rational solution of complex problems. *Amer. J. Psychol.,* 1932, *44,* 491–504.

VIII

The Individual and Group in the Social and Cultural Environment

The urbanization of American society has been occurring at a rapidly increasing rate. One characteristic of the high population density in an urban setting is that an individual caught in a crisis situation is likely to be observed by others, but in many instances these observers tend to act as a passive audience viewing changing scenes unfolding across a TV screen. Latané and Darley (Chapter 15) were among the first investigators to study systematically bystander behavior in a crisis. In a program of research which included primarily laboratory studies, they found that as the number of bystanders present in an emergency situation increased, the likelihood that any one of them would intervene decreased. However, in a field experiment conducted by Piliavin, Rodin, and Piliavin (Chapter 16), where bystanders were confronted with a face-to-face emergency situation different from those in previous lab studies, the expected decrease in speed of responding as group size increased did not occur. The authors discussed the implications of this difference between laboratory and field results and suggested a model for the prediction of behavior in emergency situations.

Behavior of bystanders in a crisis is only one feature of the urban experience. Milgram (Chapter 17), in an overview of city living, suggested an organizing theory to explain the wide range of situations which compose the urban environment. He indicated that the observed behavior of the urbanite in different situations appears to be determined primarily by a variety of adaptations to *overload.* Drawing on research conducted in natural settings, it was shown how these adaptations created the characteristic tone and behaviors of urban life. Milgram concluded his paper by discussing the differing atmospheres of great cities.

15

Bystander "Apathy"

Bibb Latané and John M. Darley

Do the work that's nearest
  Though it's dull at whiles,
Helping, when you meet them,
  Lame dogs over stiles.

From *American Scientist,* 1969, *57,* 244–268. Reprinted by permission, *American Scientist,* journal of The Society of the Sigma Xi. Copyright 1969 by The Society of the Sigma Xi. [References originally listed as in press were amended to show dates of publication. Ed.]

The experiments reported in this paper were supported by the National Science Foundation grants GS1238 and GS1239. The book on this research (Latané and Darley, *The Unresponsive Bystander,* Appleton-Century-Crofts, 1970) won the 1968 Socio-Psychological Prize awarded by the American Asso-

In the century since it was written, this minor bit of exhortatory doggerel has become sheer camp. We have become too sophisticated to appreciate the style—many believe that we have become too cynical to appreciate the moral. Working at dull tasks is now taken as a sign of dullness, and helping lame dogs is no longer much in vogue. At least, that is the impression we get from the newspapers.

On a March night in 1964, Kitty Genovese was set upon by a maniac as she came home from work at 3 A.M. Thirty-eight of her Kew Gardens neighbors came to their windows when she cried out in terror—none came to her assistance. Even though her assailant took over half an hour to murder her, no one even so much as called the police.

This story became the journalistic sensation of the decade. "Apathy," cried the newspapers. "Indifference," said the columnists and commentators. "Moral callousness," "dehumanization," "loss of concern for our fellow man," added preachers, professors, and other sermonizers. Movies, television specials, plays, and books explored this incident and many more like it. Americans became concerned about their lack of concern.

But can these epithets be correct? We think not. Although it is unquestionably true that witnesses in such emergencies have often done nothing to save the victims, "apathy," "indifference," and "unconcern" are not entirely accurate descriptions of their reactions. The 38 witnesses to Kitty Genovese's murder did not merely look at the scene once and then ignore it. Instead they continued to stare out their windows at what was going on. Caught, fascinated, distressed, unwilling to act but unable to turn away, their behavior was neither helpful nor heroic; but it was not indifferent or apathetic either.

Actually, it was like crowd behavior in many other emergency situations; car accidents, drownings, fires, and attempted suicides all attract substantial numbers of people who watch the drama in helpless fascination without getting directly involved in the action. Are these people alienated and indifferent? Are the rest of us? Obviously not. It seems only yesterday we were being called overconforming. But why, then, don't we act?

---

ciation for the Advancement of Science and the Century Psychology Prize for 1968.

There are certainly strong forces leading us to act. Empathy or sympathy, innate or learned, may cause us to share, at least in part, a victim's distress. If intervention were easy, most of us would be willing to relieve our own discomfort by alleviating another's suffering. As Charles Darwin put it some years ago, "As man is a social animal it is almost certain that . . . he would, from an inherited tendency, be willing to defend, in concert with others, his fellow men; and be ready to aid them in any way, which did not interfere too greatly with his own welfare or his own strong desires."

Even if empathy or sympathy were not strong enough to lead us to help in emergencies, there are a variety of social norms which suggest that each of us has a responsibility to each other, and that help is the proper thing to do. "Do unto others as you would have them do unto you," we hear from our earliest years. Although norms such as these may not have much influence on our behavior in specific situations, they may imbue us with a general predisposition to try to help others.

Indeed, in many non-emergency situations, people seem surprisingly willing to share their time and money with others. According to the Internal Revenue Service, Americans contribute staggering sums to a great variety of charitable organizations each year. Even when tax deductions don't fan the urge to help, people still help others. When Columbia students asked 2,500 people on the streets of New York for 10¢ or 20¢, over half of these people gave it.

If people are so willing to help in non-emergency situations, they should be even more willing to help in emergencies when the need is so much greater. Or should they? Emergencies differ in many ways from other types of situations in which people need help, and these differences may be important. The very nature of an emergency implies certain psychological consequences.

CHARACTERISTICS OF EMERGENCIES

Perhaps the most distinctive characteristic of an emergency is that it involves threat or harm. Life, well-being, or property is in danger. Even if an emergency is successfully dealt with, nobody is better off afterwards than before. Except in rare circumstances, the best that can be hoped for if an emergency occurs is a return to the status quo. Consequently, there are few positive rewards for successful action in an emergency. At worst, an emergency can claim the lives not only of those people who were initially involved in it, but also of anybody who intervenes in the situation. This fact puts pressures on individuals to ignore a potential emergency, to distort their perceptions of it, or to underestimate their responsibility for coping with it.

The second important feature of an emergency is that it is an unusual and rare event. Fortunately, although he may read about them in newspapers, or watch fictionalized accounts on television, the average person probably will encounter fewer than half a dozen serious emergencies in his lifetime. Unfortunately when he does encounter one, he will have had little direct personal experience in handling such a situation. Unlike the stereotyped patterns of his everyday behavior, an individual facing an emergency is untrained and unrehearsed.

In addition to being rare, emergencies differ widely, one from another. There are few common requirements for action between a drowning, a fire, or an automobile accident. Each emergency presents a different problem, and each requires a different type of action. Consequently, unlike other rare events, our culture provides us with little secondhand wisdom about how to deal with emergencies. An individual may cope with the rare event of a formal dinner party by using manners gleaned from late night Fred Astaire movies, but the stereotypes that the late movies provide for dealing with emergencies are much less accurate. "Charge!" "Women and children first!" "Quick, get lots of hot water and towels." This is about the extent of the advice offered for dealing with emergencies and it is singularly inappropriate in most specific real emergency situations.

The fourth basic characteristic of emergencies is that they are unforeseen. They "emerge," suddenly and without warning. Being unexpected, emergencies must be handled without the benefit of forethought and planning and an individual does not have the opportunity to think through in advance what course of action he should take when faced with an emergency. He must do his thinking in the immediacy of the situation, and has no opportunity to consult others as to the best course of action or to alert others who are especially equipped to deal with emergencies. The individual confronted with an emergency is thrown on his own resources. We have already seen that he does not have much in the way of practiced responses or cultural stereotypes to fall back upon.

A final characteristic of an emergency is that it requires instant action. It represents a pressing necessity. If the emergency is not dealt with immediately, the situation will deteriorate. The threat will transform itself into damage; the harm will continue or spread. There are urgent pressures to deal with the situation at once. The requirement for immediate action prevents the individual confronted with an emergency from leisurely considering the possible courses of action open to him. It forces him to come to a decision before he has had time to consider his alternatives. It places him in a condition of stress.

The picture we have drawn is a rather grim one. Faced with a situation in which there is no benefit to be gained for himself, unable to rely on past experience, on the experience of others, or on forethought and planning, denied the opportunity to consider carefully his course of action, the bystander to an emergency is in an unenviable position. It is perhaps surprising that anyone should intervene at all.

A MODEL OF THE INTERVENTION PROCESS

If an individual is to intervene in an emergency, he must make, not just one, but a *series* of decisions. Only one particular set of choices will lead him to take action in the situation. Let us now consider the behavioral and cognitive processes that go on in an individual who is in the vicinity of an emergency. What must he do and decide before he actually intervenes? These may have important implications for predicting whether an individual will act.

Let us suppose that an emergency is actually taking place. A middle-aged man, walking down the street, has a heart attack. He stops short, clutches his chest, and staggers to the nearest building wall, where he slowly slumps to the sidewalk in a sitting position. What is the likelihood with which a passerby will come to his assistance? First, the bystander has to *notice* that something is happening. The external event has to break into his thinking and intrude itself on his conscious mind. He must tear himself away from his private thoughts or from the legs of the pretty girl walking down the street ahead of him and pay attention to this unusual event.

Once the person is aware of the event as something to be explained, it is necessary that he *interpret* the event. Specifically, he must decide that there is something wrong, that this ambiguous event is an emergency. It may be that the man slumped on the sidewalk is only a drunk, beyond any assistance that the passerby can give him. If the bystander decided that something is indeed wrong, he must next decide that he has a *responsibility* to act. Perhaps help is on the way or perhaps someone else might be better qualified to help. Even in an emergency, it is not clear that everybody should immediately intrude himself into the situation.

If the person does decide that he should help, he must decide what *form of assistance* he can give. Should he rush in directly and try to help the victim or should he detour by calling a doctor or the police? Finally, of course, he must decide how to *implement* his choice and form of intervention. Where is the nearest telephone? Is there a hospital nearby? At this point, the person may finally begin to act in the situation. The socially responsible act is the end point of a series of decisions that the person makes.

Obviously, this model is too rational. It seems unlikely that a bystander will run through the series of choice points in a strictly logical and sequential order. Instead, he may consider two or three of them simultaneously and "try on" various decisions and their consequences before he finally arrives at his overall assessment of the situation. Since he has no commitment to any intermediary decision until he has taken final action, he may cycle back and forth through the decision series until he comes up with a set which serves both his needs and the needs of "reality."

Second, the bystander in an emergency is not a detached and objective observer. His decisions have consequences for himself just as much as for the victim. Unfortunately, however, the rewards and penalties for action and inaction are biased in favor of inaction. All the bystander has to gain from intervention is a feeling of pride and the chance to be a hero. On the other hand, he can be made to appear a fool, sued, or even attacked and wounded. By leaving the situation, he has little to lose but his self-respect. There are strong pressures against deciding that an event is an emergency.

Intervention, then, requires choosing a single course of action through a rather complex matrix of possible actions. The failure to intervene may result from failing to notice an event, failing to realize that the event is an emergency, failing to feel personally responsible for dealing with the emergency, or failing to have sufficient skill to intervene.

SOCIAL DETERMINANTS OF BYSTANDER INTERVENTION, I

Most emergencies are, or at least begin as, ambiguous events. A quarrel in the street may erupt into violence, but it may be simply a family argument. A man staggering about may be suffering a coronary or an onset of diabetes; he may simply be drunk. Smoke pouring from a building may signal a fire; on the other hand, it may be simply steam or airconditioner vapor. Before a bystander is likely to take action in such ambiguous situations, he must first define the event as an emergency and decide that intervention is the proper course of action.

In the course of making these decisions, it is likely that an individual bystander will be considerably influenced by the decisions he perceives other bystanders to be taking. If everyone else in a group of onlookers seems to regard an event as nonserious and the proper course of action as non-intervention, this consensus may strongly affect the perceptions of any single individual and inhibit his potential intervention.

The definitions that other people hold may be discovered by discussing the situation with them, but they may also be inferred from their facial expressions or their behavior. A whistling man with his hands in his pockets obviously does not believe he is in the midst of a crisis. A bystander who does not respond to smoke obviously does not attribute it to fire. An individual, seeing the inaction of others, will judge the situation as less serious than he would if alone.

But why should the others be inactive? Unless there were some force inhibiting responses on the part of others, the kind of social influence process described would, by itself, only lead to a convergence of attitudes within a group. If each individual expressed his true feelings, then, even if each member of the group were entirely guided by the reactions of the others, the group should still respond with a likelihood equal to the average of the individuals.

An additional factor is involved, however. Each member of a group may watch the others, but he is also aware that others are watching him. They are an audience to his own reactions. Among American males, it is considered desirable to appear poised and collected in times of stress. Being exposed to the public view may constrain the actions and expressions of emotion of any individual as he tries to avoid possible ridicule and embarrassment. Even though he may be truly concerned and upset about the plight of a victim, until he decides what to do, he may maintain a calm demeanor.

The constraints involved with being in public might in themselves tend to inhibit action by individuals in a group, but in conjunction with the social influence process described above, they may be expected to have even more powerful effects. If each member of a group is, at the same time, trying to appear calm and also looking around at the other members to gauge their reactions, all members may be led (or misled) by each other to define the situation as less critical than they would if alone. Until someone acts, each person sees only other non-responding bystanders, and is likely to be influenced not to act himself. A state of "pluralistic ignorance" may develop.

It has often been recognized (Brown, 1954, 1965) that a crowd can cause contagion of panic, leading each person in the crowd to over-react to an emergency to the detriment of everyone's welfare. What we suggest here is that a crowd can also force inaction on its members. It can suggest, implicitly but strongly, by its passive behavior that an event is not to be reacted to as an emergency, and it can make any individual uncomfortably aware of what a fool he will look for behaving as if it is.

This line of thought suggests that individuals may be less likely to intervene in an emergency if they witness it in the presence of other people than if they see it alone. It suggests that the presence of other people may lead each person to interpret the situation as less serious, and less demanding of action than he would if alone. The presence of other people may alter each bystander's perceptions and interpretations of the situation. We suspect that the presence of other people may also affect each individual's assessment of the rewards and costs involved in taking action, and indeed we will discuss this possibility in some detail later. First, however, let us look at evidence relevant to this initial process. The experiments reported below were designed to test the line of thought presented above.

EXPERIMENT 1. WHERE THERE'S SMOKE, THERE'S (SOMETIMES) FIRE [1]

In this experiment we presented an emergency to individuals either alone, in the presence of two passive others (confederates of the experimenter who were instructed to notice the emergency but remain indifferent to it), or in groups of three. It was our expectation that individuals faced with the passive reactions of the confederates would be influenced by them and thus less likely to take action than single subjects. We also predicted that the constraints on behavior in public combined with social influence processes would lessen the likelihood that members of three-person groups would act to cope with the emergency.

Male Columbia students living in campus residences were invited to an interview to discuss "some of the problems involved in life at an urban university." As they sat in a small room waiting to be called for the interview and filling out a preliminary question-

[1] A more detailed report of this experiment is given in: Latané, B. and Darley, J. M. Group inhibition of bystander intervention in emergencies. *Journal of Personality and Social Psychology,* 1968, *10,* 215–221.

naire, they faced an ambiguous but potentially dangerous situation as a stream of smoke began to puff into the room through a wall vent. Some subjects filled out the questionnaire and were exposed to this potentially critical situation while alone. Others were part of three-person groups consisting of one subject and two confederates acting the part of naive subjects. The confederates attempted to avoid conversation as much as possible. Once the smoke had been introduced, they stared at it briefly, made no comment, but simply shrugged their shoulders, returned to the questionnaires and continued to fill them out, occasionally waving away the smoke to do so. If addressed, they attempted to be as uncommunicative as possible and to show apparent indifference to the smoke. "I dunno," they said, and no subject persisted in talking. In a final condition, three naive subjects were tested together. In general, these subjects did not know each other, although in two groups, subjects reported a nodding acquaintance with another subject. Since subjects arrived at slightly different times and since they each had individual questionnaires to work on, they did not introduce themselves to each other, or attempt anything but the most rudimentary conversation.

As soon as the subjects had completed two pages of their questionnaires, the experimenter began to introduce the smoke through a small vent in the wall. The "smoke" was finely divided titanium dioxide produced in a stoppered bottle and delivered under slight air pressure through the vent. It formed a moderately fine-textured but clearly visible stream of whitish smoke. For the entire experimental period, the smoke continued to jet into the room in irregular puffs. By the end of the experimental period, vision was obscured in the room by the amount of smoke present.

All behavior and conversation was observed and coded from behind a one-way window (largely disguised on the subject's side by a large sign giving preliminary instructions). When and if the subject left the experimental room and reported the smoke, he was told that the situation "would be taken care of." If the subject had not reported the smoke within six minutes of the time he first noticed it, the experiment was terminated.

The typical subject, when tested alone, behaved very reasonably. Usually, shortly after the smoke appeared, he would glance up from his questionnaire, notice the smoke, show a slight but distinct startle reaction, and then undergo a brief period of indecision, and perhaps return briefly to his questionnaire before again staring at the smoke. Soon, most subjects would get up from their chairs, walk over to the vent, and investigate it closely, sniffing the smoke, waving their hands in it, feeling its temperature, etc. The usual Alone subject would hesitate again, but finally walk out of the room, look around outside, and, finding somebody there, calmly report the presence of the smoke. No subject showed any sign of panic; most simply said, "There's something strange going on in there, there seems to be some sort of smoke coming through the wall. . . ." The median subject in the Alone condition had reported the smoke within two minutes of first noticing it. Three-quarters of the 24 people run in this condition reported the smoke before the experimental period was terminated.

The behavior of subjects run with two passive confederates was dramatically different; of ten people run in this condition, only one reported the smoke. The other nine stayed in the waiting room as it filled up with smoke, doggedly working on their questionnaires and waiving the fumes away from their faces. They coughed, rubbed their eyes, and opened the window—but they did not report the smoke. The difference between the response rate of 75% in the Alone condition and 10% in the Two Passive Confederates condition is highly significant ($p < .002$ by Fisher's Exact test, two-tailed).

Because there are three subjects present and available to report the smoke in the Three Naive Bystander condition as compared to only one subject at a time in the Alone condition, a simple comparison between the two conditions is not appropriate. On the one hand, we cannot compare speeds in the Alone condition with the average speed of the three subjects in a group, since, once one subject in a group had reported the smoke, the pressures on the other two disappeared. They legitimately could feel that the emergency had been handled, and that any action on their part would be redundant and potentially confusing. Therefore, we used the speed of the *first* subject in a group to report the smoke as our dependent variable. However, since there were three times as many people available to respond in this condition as in the Alone condition, we would expect an increased likelihood that at least one person would report the smoke by chance alone. Therefore, we mathematically created "groups" of three scores from the Alone condition to serve as a baseline.[2]

In contrast to the complexity of this procedure, the results were quite simple. Subjects in the Three Naive Bystander condition were markedly inhibited from reporting the smoke. Since 75% of the Alone subjects reported the smoke, we would expect over 98% of the three-person groups to include at least one reporter. In fact, in only 38% of the eight groups in this condition did even one person report ($p < .01$). Of the twenty-four people run in these eight groups, only one person reported the smoke within the first four minutes before the room got noticeably unpleasant. Only three people reported the smoke within the entire experimental period. Social inhibition of reporting was so strong that the smoke was reported quicker when only one person saw it than when groups of three were present ($p < .01$).

Subjects who had reported the smoke were relatively consistent in later describing their reactions to it. They thought the smoke looked somewhat "strange," they were not sure exactly what it was or whether it was dangerous, but they felt it was unusual enough to justify some examination. "I wasn't sure whether it was a fire, but it looked like something was wrong." "I thought it might be steam, but it seemed like a good idea to check it out."

Subjects who had not reported the smoke also were unsure about exactly what it was, but they uniformly said that they had rejected the idea that it was a fire. Instead, they hit upon an astonishing variety of alternative explanations, all sharing the common characteristic of interpreting the smoke as a nondangerous event. Many thought the smoke was either steam or airconditioning vapors, several thought it was smog, purposely introduced to simulate an urban environment, and two (from different groups) actually suggested that the smoke was a "truth gas" filtered into the room to induce them to answer the questionnaire accurately

[2] The formula for calculating the expected proportion of groups in which at least one person will have acted by a given time is $1-(1-p)^n$ where p is the proportion of single individuals who act by that time and n is the number of persons in the group.

(surprisingly, they were not disturbed by this conviction). Predictably, some decided that "it must be some sort of experiment" and stoically endured the discomfort of the room rather than overreact.

Despite the obvious and powerful report-inhibiting effect of other bystanders, subjects almost invariably claimed that they had paid little or no attention to the reactions of the other people in the room. Although the presence of other people actually had a strong and pervasive effect on the subjects' reactions, they were either unaware of this or unwilling to admit it.

The results of this study clearly support the predictions. Individuals exposed to a room filling with smoke in the presence of passive others themselves remained passive, and groups of three naive subjects were less likely to report the smoke than solitary bystanders. Our predictions were confirmed—but this does not necessarily mean that our explanation for these results is the correct one. As a matter of fact several alternatives are available.

Two alternative explanations stem from the fact that the smoke represented a possible danger to the subject himself as well as to others in the building. Subjects' behavior might have reflected their fear of fire, with subjects in groups feeling less threatened by the fire than single subjects and thus less concerned to act. It has been demonstrated in studies with humans (Schachter, 1959) and with rats (Latané, 1969; Latané and Glass, 1968) that togetherness reduces fear, even in situations where it does not reduce danger. In addition, subjects may have felt that the presence of others increased their ability to cope with fire. For both these reasons, subjects in groups may have been less afraid of fire and thus less likely to report the smoke than solitary subjects.

A similar explanation might emphasize, not fearfulness, but the desire to hide fear. To the extent that bravery or stoicism in the face of danger or discomfort is a socially desirable trait (as it appears to be for American male undergraduates), we might expect individuals to attempt to appear more brave or more stoic when others are watching than when they are alone. It is possible that subjects in the Group condition saw themselves as engaged in a game of "Chicken," and thus did not react.

Although both of these explanations are plausible, we do not think that they provide an accurate account of subjects' thinking. In the post-experimental interviews, subjects claimed, *not* that they were unworried by the fire or that they were unwilling to endure the danger; but rather that they had decided that there was no fire at all and the smoke was caused by something else. They failed to act because they thought there was no reason to act. Their "apathetic" behavior was reasonable—given their interpretation of the circumstances.

EXPERIMENT 2. A LADY IN DISTRESS [3]

Although it seems unlikely that the group inhibition of bystander intervention observed in Experiment 1 can be attributed entirely to the fact that smoke represents a danger to the individual bystander, it is certainly possible that this is so. Experiment 2 was designed to see whether similar group inhibition effects could be observed in situations where there is no danger to the individual himself for not acting. In addition, a new variable was included: whether the bystanders knew each other.

Male Columbia undergraduates waited either alone, with a friend, or with a stranger to participate in a market research study. As they waited, they heard someone fall and apparently injure herself in the room next door. Whether they tried to help, and how long they took to do so were the main dependent variables of the study. Subjects were telephoned and offered $2 to participate in a survey of game and puzzle preferences conducted at Columbia by the Consumer Testing Bureau (CTB), a market research organization. Each person contacted was asked to find a friend who would also be interested in participating. Only those students who recommended friends, and the friends they suggested, were used as subjects.

Subjects were met at the door by the market research representative, an attractive young woman, and taken to the testing room.

[3] A more detailed description of this experiment is given in: Latané, B. and Rodin, J. A Lady in distress: Inhibiting effects of friends and strangers on bystander intervention, *Journal of Experimental Social Psychology,* 1969, *5,* 189–202.

On the way, they passed the CTB office and through its open door they were able to see a desk and bookcases piled high with papers and filing cabinets. They entered the adjacent testing room which contained a table and chairs and a variety of games, and they were given a preliminary background information and game preference questionnaire to fill out. The representative told subjects that she would be working next door in her office for about 10 minutes while they completed the questionnaires, and left by opening the collapsible curtain which divided the two rooms. She made sure that subjects were aware that the curtain was unlocked and easily opened and that it provided a means of entry to her office. The representative stayed in her office, shuffling papers, opening drawers, and making enough noise to remind the subjects of her presence. Four minutes after leaving the testing area, she turned on a high fidelity sterophonic tape recorder.

The Emergency

If the subject listened carefully, he heard the representative climb up on a chair to reach for a stack of papers on the bookcase. Even if he were not listening carefully, he heard a loud crash and a scream as the chair collapsed and she fell to the floor. "Oh, my God, my foot . . . I . . . can't move . . . it. Oh . . . my ankle," the representative moaned. "I . . . can't get this . . . thing . . . off me." She cried and moaned for about a minute longer, but the cries gradually got more subdued and controlled. Finally, she muttered something about getting outside, knocked over the chair as she pulled herself up, and thumped to the door, closing it behind her as she left. The entire incident took 130 seconds.

The main dependent variable of the study, of course, was whether the subjects took action to help the victim and how long it took him to do so. There were actually several modes of intervention possible: a subject could open the screen dividing the two rooms, leave the testing room and enter the CTB office by the door, find someone else, or, most simply, call out to see if the representative needed help. Four experimental conditions were run. In one condition (Alone, $n = 26$) each subject was by himself in the testing room while he filled out the questionnaire and heard the fall.

In a second condition (Stooge, $n = 14$), a stranger, actually a confederate of the experimenter, was also present. The confederate had instructions to be as passive as possible and to answer questions put to him by the subjects with a brief gesture or remark. During the emergency, he looked up, shrugged his shoulders, and continued working on his questionnaire. Subjects in the third condition (Strangers, $n = 20$ pairs) were placed in the testing room in pairs. Each subject in the pair was unacquainted with the other before entering the room and they were not introduced. Only one subject in this condition spontaneously introduced himself to the other. In a final condition (Friends, $n = 20$ pairs), pairs of friends overheard the incident together.

Mode of Intervention

Across all experimental groups, the majority of subjects who intervened did so by pulling back the room divider and coming into the CTB office (61%). Few subjects came the round-about way through the door to offer their assistance (14%), and a surprisingly small number (24%) chose the easy solution of calling out to offer help. No one tried to find someone else to whom to report the accident. Since experimental conditions did not differ in the proportions choosing various modes of intervention, the comparisons below will deal only with the total proportions of subjects offering help.

Alone vs. Stooge Conditions

Seventy per cent of all subjects who heard the accident while alone in the waiting room offered to help the victim before she left the room. By contrast the presence of a non-responsive bystander markedly inhibited helping. Only 7% of subjects in the Stooge condition intervened. These subjects seemed upset and confused during the emergency and frequently glanced at the passive confederate who continued working on his questionnaire. The difference between the Alone and Stooge response rates is, of course, highly significant ($p < .001$).

Alone vs. Two Strangers

Since 70% of Alone subjects intervened, we should expect that at least one person in 91% of all two-person groups would offer help if members of a pair had no influence upon each other. In fact, members did influence each other. In only 40% of the groups did even one person offer help to the injured woman. Only 8 subjects of the 40 who were run in this condition intervened. This response rate is significantly below the hypothetical baseline ($p < .001$). Social inhibition of helping was so strong, that the victim was actually aided more quickly when only one person heard her distress than when two did ($p < .01$).

Strangers vs. Stooge

The response rate in the Two Strangers condition appears to be somewhat higher than the 7% rate in the Stooge condition. Making a correction similar to that used for the Alone scores, the expected response rate based on the Stooge condition is 13%. This is significantly lower than the response rate in the Strangers condition ($p < .05$).

Alone vs. Two Friends

Pairs of friends often talked about the questionnaire before the accident, and sometimes discussed a course of action after the fall. Even so, in only 70% of the pairs did even one person intervene. While, superficially, this appears as high as the Alone condition, there must again be a correction for the fact that twice as many people are free to act. When compared to the 91% hypothetical base rate, friends do inhibit each other from intervening ($p < .10$). They were also slower to intervene than would be expected from the Alone condition ($p < .05$).

Friends vs. Strangers

Although pairs of friends were inhibited from helping when compared to the Alone condition, they were significantly faster to intervene than were pairs of strangers ($p < .01$). The median latency of the first response from pairs of friends was 36 seconds; the median pair of strangers did not respond at all within the arbitrary 130-second duration of the emergency.

Subjects who intervened usually claimed that they did so either because the fall sounded very serious or because they were uncertain what had occurred and felt they should investigate. Many talked about intervention as the "right thing to do" and asserted they would help again in any situation.

Many of the non-interveners also claimed that they were unsure what had happened (59%), but had decided that it was not too serious (46%). A number of subjects reported that they thought other people would or could help (25%), and three said they refrained out of concern for the victim—they did not want to embarrass her. Whether to accept these explanations as reasons or rationalizations is moot—they certainly do not explain the differences among conditions. The important thing to note is that non-interveners did not seem to feel that they had behaved callously or immorally. Their behavior was generally consistent with their interpretation of the situation. Subjects almost uniformly claimed that, in a "real" emergency, they would be among the first to help the victim.

Interestingly, when subjects were asked whether they had been influenced by the presence of action of their coworkers, they were either unwilling or unable to report that they had. Subjects in the passive confederate condition reported, on the average, that they were "very little" influenced by the stooge. Subjects in the Two Strangers condition claimed to have been only "a little bit" influenced by each other, and friends admitted to "moderate" influence. Put another way, only 14%, 30%, and 70% of the subjects in these three conditions admitted to at least a "moderate" degree of influence. These claims, of course, run directly counter to the experimental results, in which friends were the least inhibited and subjects in the Stooge condition most inhibited by the other's actions.

These results strongly replicate the findings of the Smoke study. In both experiments, subjects were less likely to take action if they were in the presence of passive confederates than if they were alone, and in both studies, this effect showed up even when groups of naive subjects were tested together. This congruence of findings from different experimental settings supports the validity and generality of the phenomenon: it also helps rule out a variety of alternative explanations suitable to either situation alone. For example, the possibility that smoke may have represented a threat to the subject's personal safety and that subjects in groups may have had a greater concern to appear "brave" than single subjects does not apply to the present experiment. In the present experiment, non-intervention cannot signify bravery. Comparison of the two experiments also suggests that the absolute number of non-responsive bystanders may not be a critical factor in producing social inhibition of intervention. One passive confederate in the present experiment was as effective as two in the smoke study; pairs of strangers in the present study inhibited each other as much as did trios in the former study.

How can we account for the differential social inhibition caused by friends and strangers? It may be that people are less likely to fear possible embarrassment in front of friends than before strangers, and that friends are less likely to misinterpret each other's inaction than are strangers. If so, social influence should be less likely to lead friends to decide there is no emergency than strangers. When strangers overheard the accident, they seemed noticeably concerned but confused. Attempting to interpret what they had heard and to decide upon a course of action, they often glanced furtively at one another, apparently anxious to discover the other's reaction yet unwilling to meet eyes and betray their own concern. Friends, on the other hand, seemed better able to convey their concern nonverbally, and often discussed the incident and arrived at a mutual plan of action. Although these observations are admittedly impressionistic, they are consistent with other data. During the emergency, a record was kept of whether the bystanders engaged in conversation. Unfortunately, no attempt was made to code the amount or content of what was said, but it is possible to determine if there was any talking at all. Only 29% of subjects attempted any conversation with the stooge; while 60% of the pairs of strangers engaged in some conversation, it was mostly desultory and often unrelated to the accident. Although the latter rate seems higher than the former, it really is not, since there are two people free to initiate a conversation rather than just one. Friends, on the other hand, were somewhat more likely to talk than strangers—85% of the pairs did so. Friends, then, may show less mutual inhibition than strangers because they are less likely to develop a state of "pluralistic ignorance."

These first experiments show that in two, widely different types of emergency settings, the presence of other people inhibits intervention. Subjects were less likely to report a possible fire when together than alone, and they were less likely to go to the aid of the victim of an accident when others were present. Is this a general effect? Will it apply to all types of emergency? Are there situations in which the presence of other people might actually facilitate bystander intervention? One possible set of circumstances in which we might expect social facilitation of intervention is when an emergency is caused by a villain. People who fail to intervene in real emergencies sometimes claim they were afraid of the consequences of intervention—afraid of direct attack, afraid of later retribution, afraid of having to go to court. In situations involving a villain, even if one person is afraid to take action, the presence of other people as potential risk-sharing allies might embolden him to intervene. Under these circumstances, there might actually be a group facilitation of intervention. To test this possibility, two Columbia undergraduates, Paul Bonnarigo and Malcolm Ross, turned to a life of crime.

EXPERIMENT 3. THE CASE OF THE STOLEN BEER

The Nu-Way Beverage Center in Suffern, New York, is a discount beer store. It sells beer and soda by the case, often to New Jerseyans who cross the state line to find both lowered prices and a lowered legal drinking age. During the spring of 1968 it was the scene of a minor crime wave—within one two-week period, it was robbed 96 times. The robbers followed much the same modus operandi on each occasion. Singly or in a pair, they would enter the store and ask the cashier at the checkout counter "What is the most expensive imported beer that you carry?" The cashier, in cahoots with the robbers, would reply "Lowenbrau. I'll go back and check how much we have." Leaving the robbers in the front of the store, the cashier would disappear into the rear to look for the Lowenbrau. After waiting for a minute, the robbers would pick up a case of beer near the front of the store, remark to nobody in particular, "They'll never miss this," walk out of the front door, put the beer in their car, and drive off. On 46 occasions, one robber carried off the theft; on 46 occasions, two robbers were present.

The robberies were always staged when there were either one or two people in the store, and the timing was arranged so that the one or both customers would be at the checkout counter at the time when the robbers entered. On 46 occasions, one customer was at the checkout counter during the theft; on 46 occasions, two customers were present. Although occasionally the two customers had come in together, more usually they were strangers to each other. Sixty-one per cent of the customers were male, 39% female. Since the checkout counter was about 20 feet from the front door, since the theft itself took less than a minute, and since the robbers were both husky young men, nobody tried directly to prevent the theft. There were, however, other courses of intervention available.

When the cashier returned from the rear of the store, he went to the checkout counter and resumed waiting on the customers there. After a minute, if nobody had spontaneously mentioned the theft, he casually inquired, "Hey, what happened to that man (those men) who was (were) in here? Did you see him (them) leave?" At this point the customer could either report the theft, say merely that he had seen the man or men leave, or disclaim any knowledge of the event whatsoever. Overall 20% of the subjects reported the theft spontaneously, and 51% of the remainder reported it upon prompting. Since the results from each criterion followed an identical pattern, we shall indicate only the total proportion of subjects in each condition who reported the theft, whether spontaneously or not.

Results

Whether there were one or two robbers present made little difference. Customers were somewhat but not significantly more likely to report the theft if there were two robbers (69%) than if there was only one (52%). Sex also made no difference; females were as likely to report as males. The number of customers, on the other hand, made a big difference. Thirty-one of the 48 single customers, or 65%, mentioned the theft. From this, we would expect that 87% of the two-person groups would include at least one reporter. In fact, in only 56% of the two-person groups did even one person report the theft ($p < .01$). Social inhibition of reporting was so strong that the theft was actually somewhat (though not significantly) less likely to be reported when two people saw it than when only one did.

In three widely differing situations the same effect has been observed. People are less likely to take a socially responsible action if other people are present than if they are alone. This effect has occurred in a situation involving general danger, in a situation where someone has been the victim of an accident, and in a situation involving one or more villains. The effect holds in real life as well as in the laboratory, and for members of the general population as well as college students. The results of each of these three experiments clearly support the line of theoretical argument advanced earlier. When bystanders to an emergency can see the reactions of other people, and when other people can see their own reactions, each individual may, through a process of social influence, be led to interpret the situation as less serious than he would if he were alone, and consequently be less likely to take action.

SOCIAL DETERMINANTS OF BYSTANDER INTERVENTION, II

So far we have devoted our attention exclusively to one stage of our hypothesized model of the intervention process: noticing the situation and interpreting it. Once an individual has noticed an emergency and interpreted it as being serious, he still has to decide what, if anything, he will do about it. He must decide that he has a responsibility to help, and that there is some form of assistance that he is in a position to give. He is faced with the choice of whether he himself will intervene. His decision will presumably be made in terms of the rewards and costs of the various alternative courses of action open to him.

In addition to affecting the interpretations that he places on a situation, the presence of other people can also alter the rewards and costs facing an individual bystander. Perhaps most importantly, the presence of other people can alter the cost of not acting. If only one bystander is present at an emergency, he carries all of the responsibility for dealing with it; he will feel all of the guilt for not acting; he will bear all of any blame others may level for non-intervention. If others are present, the onus of responsibility is diffused, and the individual may be more likely to resolve his conflict between intervening and not intervening in favor of the latter alternative.

When only one bystander is present at an emergency, if help is to come it must be from him. Although he may choose to ignore them (out of concern for his personal safety, or desire "not to get involved"), any pressures to intervene focus uniquely on him. When there are several observers present, however, the pressures to intervene do not focus on any one of the observers; instead the responsibility for intervention is shared among all the onlookers and is not unique to any one. As a result, each may be less likely to help.

Potential blame may also be diffused. However much we wish to think that an individual's moral behavior is divorced from considerations of personal punishment or reward, there is both theory and evidence to the contrary. It is perfectly reasonable to assume that, under circumstances of group responsibility for a punishable act, the punishment or blame that accrues to any one individual is often slight or nonexistent.

Finally, if others are known to be present, but their behavior cannot be closely observed, any one bystander may assume that one of the other observers is already taking action to end the emergency. If so, his own intervention would only be redundant—perhaps harmfully or confusingly so. Thus, given the presence of other onlookers whose behavior cannot be observed, any given bystander can rationalize his own inaction by convincing himself that "somebody else must be doing something."

These considerations suggest that, even when bystanders to an emergency cannot see or be influenced by each other, the more bystanders who are present, the less likely any one bystander would be to intervene and provide aid. To test this suggestion, it would be necessary to create an emergency situation in which each subject is blocked from communicating with others to prevent his getting information about their behavior during the emergency. Experiment 4 attempted to fulfill this requirement.

EXPERIMENT 4. A FIT TO BE TRIED [4]

Procedure

Thirteen male and 104 female students in introductory psychology courses at New York University were recruited to take part in an unspecified experiment as part of their class requirement. When a subject arrived in the laboratory, he was ushered into an individual room from which a communication system would enable him to talk to the other participants (who were actually figments of the tape recorder). Over the intercom, the subject was told that the experimenter was concerned with the kinds of personal problems faced by normal college students in a high-pressure, urban environment, and that he would be asked to participate in a discussion about these problems. To avoid possible embarrassment about discussing personal problems with strangers, the experimenter said, several precautions would be taken. First, subjects would remain anonymous, which was why they had been placed in individual rooms rather than face-to-face. Second, the experimenter would not listen to the initial discussion himself, but would only get the subjects' reactions later by questionnaire.

The plan for the discussion was that each person would talk in turn for two minutes, presenting his problems to the group. Next, each person in turn would comment on what others had said, and finally there would be a free discussion. A mechanical switching device regulated the discussion, switching on only one microphone at a time.

[4] Portions of these results have been reported in Darley, J. M. and Latané, B. Bystander intervention in emergencies: Diffusion of responsibility. *Journal of Personality and Social Psychology,* 1968, *8,* 377–383.

The Emergency

The discussion started with the future victim speaking first. He said he found it difficult to get adjusted to New York and to his studies. Very hesitantly and with obvious embarrassment, he mentioned that he was prone to seizures, particularly when studying hard or taking exams. The other people, including the one real subject, took their turns and discussed similar problems (minus the proneness to seizures). The naive subject talked last in the series, after the last prerecorded voice.

When it was again the victim's turn to talk, he made a few relatively calm comments, and then, growing increasingly loud and incoherent, he continued:

> I er um I think I I need er if if could er er somebody er er er er er er give me a little er give me a little help here because er I er I'm er er h-h-having a a a a real problem er right now and I er if somebody could help me out it would it would er er s-s-sure be sure be good . . . because er there er er a cause I er I uh I've got a a one of the er sei-----er er things coming on and and and I could really er use some help so if somebody would er give me a little h-help uh er-er-er-er-er c-could somebody er er help er uh uh uh (choking sounds) . . . I'm gonna die er er I'm . . . gonna die er help er er seizure er (chokes, then quiet).

The major independent variable of the study was the number of people the subject believed also heard the fit. The subject was led to believe that the discussion group was one of three sizes: a two-person group consisting of himself and the victim; a three-person group consisting of himself, the victim and one other person; or a six-person group consisting of himself, the victim, and four other persons.

Varying the kind of bystanders present at an emergency as well as the number of bystanders should also vary the amount of responsibility felt by any single bystander. To test this, several variations of the three-person group were run. In one three-person condition, the other bystander was a female; in another, a male; and in a third, a male who said that he was a premedical student who occasionally worked in the emergency wards at Bellevue Hospital.

Subjects in the above conditions were female college students. To test whether there are sex differences in the likelihood of helping, males drawn from the same subject pool were tested in the three-person, female bystander condition.

Two final experimental variations concerned acquaintanceship relationships between the subject and other bystanders and between the subject and the victim. In one of these conditions, female subjects were tested in the three-person condition, but were tested with a friend that they had been asked to bring with them to the laboratory. In another, subjects were given prior contact with the victim before being run in the six-person group. Subjects underwent a very brief "accidental" encounter with an experimental confederate posing as the future victim. The two met for about a minute in the hall before the experiment began. During this time, they chatted about topics having nothing to do with the experiment.

The major dependent variable of the experiment was the time elapsed from the start of the victim's seizure until the subject left her experimental cubicle. When the subject left her room, she saw the experiment's assistant seated at the end of the hall, and invariably went to the assistant to report the seizure. If six minutes elapsed without the subject's having emerged from her room, the experiment was terminated.

Ninety-five per cent of all the subjects who ever responded did so within the first half of the time available to them. No subject who had not reported within three minutes after the fit ever did so. This suggests that even had the experiment been allowed to run for a considerably longer period of time, few additional subjects would have responded.

Eighty-five per cent of the subjects who thought they alone knew of the victim's plight reported the seizure before the victim was cut off; only 31% of those who thought four other bystanders were present did so. Every one of the subjects in the two-person condition, but only 62% of the subjects in the six-person condition ever reported the emergency. To do a more detailed analysis of the results, each subject's time score was transformed into a "speed" score by taking the reciprocal of the response time in seconds and multiplying by 100. Analysis of variance of these speed scores indicates that the effect of group size was highly significant ($p < .01$), and all three groups differed significantly one from another ($p < .05$).

Effect of Group Composition and Sex of the Subject

Several variations of the three-person group were run. In one pair of variations, the female subject thought the other bystander was either male or female, in another, she thought the other bystander was a premedical student who worked in the emergency ward at Bellevue Hospital. These variations in the sex and medical competence of the other bystander had no important or detectable effect on speed of response. Subjects responded equally frequently and fast whether the other bystander was female, male, or medically experienced.

Coping with emergencies is often thought to be the duty of males, especially when there are females present, but there was no evidence that this is the case in this study. Male subjects responded to the emergency with almost exactly the same speed as did females.

Effects of Friendship and Prior Acquaintance

Friends responded considerably differently from strangers in the three-person condition. When two friends were each aware of the victim's distress, even though they could not see or be seen by each other, they responded significantly faster than subjects in the other three-person groups. In fact, the average speed of response by subjects who thought their friend was also present was not noticeably different from the average speed of response in the two-person condition, where subjects believed that they alone were aware of the emergency. This suggests that responsibility does not diffuse across friends.

The effects of prior acquaintance with the victim were also strong. Subjects who had met the victim, even though only for less than a minute, were significantly faster to report his distress than other subjects in the six-person condition. Subjects in this condition later discussed their reactions to the situation. Unlike subjects in any other group, some of those who had accidentally met the victim-to-be later reported that they had actually *pictured* him in the grip of the seizure. Apparently, the ability to *visualize* a specific, concrete, distressed individual increases the likelihood of helping that person.

Subjects, whether or not they intervened, believed the fit to be genuine and serious. "My God, he's having a fit," many subjects said to themselves (and we overheard via their microphones). Others gasped or simply said, "Oh." Several of the male subjects swore. One subject said to herself, "It's just my kind of luck, something has to happen to me!" Several subjects spoke aloud of their confusion about what course of action to take: "Oh, God, what should I do?"

When those subjects who intervened stepped out of their rooms, they found the experiment's assistant down the hall. With some uncertainty but without panic, they reported the situation. "Hey, I think Number 1 is very sick. He's having a fit or something." After ostensibly checking on the situation, the experimenter returned to report that "everything is under control." The subjects accepted these assurances with obvious relief.

Subjects who failed to report the emergency showed few signs of the apathy and indifference thought to characterize "unresponsive bystanders." When the experimenter entered her room to terminate the situation, the subject often asked if the victim were all right. "Is he being taken care of?" "He's all right, isn't he?" Many of these subjects showed physical signs of nervousness; they often had trembling hands and sweating palms. If anything, they seemed more emotionally aroused than did the subjects who reported the emergency.

Why, then, didn't they respond? It is not our impression that they had decided *not* to respond. Rather, they were still in a state of indecision and conflict concerning whether to respond or not. The emotional behavior of these non-responding subjects was a sign of their continuing conflict; a conflict that other subjects resolved by responding.

The fit created a conflict situation of the avoidance-avoidance type. On the one hand, subjects worried about the guilt and shame they would feel if they did not help the person in distress. On the other hand, they were concerned not to make fools of themselves by overreacting, not to ruin the ongoing experiment by leaving their intercoms and not to destroy the anonymous nature of the situation, which the experimenter had earlier stressed as important.

For subjects in the two-person condition, the obvious distress of the victim and his need for help were so important that their conflict was easily resolved. For the subjects who knew that there were other bystanders present, the cost of not helping was reduced and the conflict they were in was more acute. Caught between the two negative alternatives of letting the victim continue to suffer, or the costs of rushing in to help, the non-responding bystanders vacillated between them rather than choosing not to respond. This distinction may be academic for the victim, since he got no help in either case, but it is an extremely important one for understanding the causes of bystander's failures to help.

Although the subjects experienced stress and conflict during the emergency, their general reactions to it were highly positive. On a questionnaire administered after the experimenter had discussed the nature and purpose of the experiment, every single subject found the experiment either "interesting" or "very interesting" and was willing to participate in similar experiments in the future. All subjects felt they understood what the experiment was all about and indicated they thought the deceptions were necessary and justified. All but one felt they were better informed about the nature of psychological research in general.

We asked all subjects whether the presence or absence of other bystanders had entered their minds during the time that they were hearing the seizure. We asked the question every way we knew how: subtly, directly, tactfully, bluntly, and the answer was always the same. Subjects had been aware of the presence of other bystanders in the appropriate conditions, but they did not feel that they had been influenced in any way by their presence. As in our previous experiments, this denial occurred in the face of results showing that the presence of others did affect helping.

SOCIAL DETERMINANTS OF BYSTANDER INTERVENTION, III

We have suggested two distinct processes which might lead people to be less likely to intervene in an emergency if there are other people present than if they are alone. On the one hand, we have suggested that the presence of other people may affect the interpretations each bystander puts on an ambiguous emergency situation. If other people are present at an emergency, each bystander will be guided by their apparent reactions in formulating his own impressions. Unfortunately, their apparent reactions may not be a good indication of their true feelings. It is possible for a state of "pluralistic ignorance" to develop, in which each bystander is led by the *apparent* lack of concern of the others to interpret the situation as being less serious than he would if alone. To the extent that he does not feel the situation is an emergency, of course, he will be unlikely to take any helpful action.

Even if an individual does decide that an emergency is actually in process and that something ought to be done, he still is faced with the choice of whether he himself will intervene. Here again, the presence of other people may influence him—by reducing the costs associated with non-intervention. If a number of people witness the same event, the responsibility for action is diffused, and each may feel less necessity to help.

Both the "social influence" and the "diffusion of responsibility" explanations seem valid, and there is no reason why both should not be jointly operative. Neither alone can account for all the data. For example, the diffusion explanation cannot account for the significant difference in response rate between the Strangers and Stooge conditions in Experiment 2. There should be equal diffusion in either case. This difference can more plausibly be attributed to the fact that strangers typically did not show such complete indifference to the accident as did the stooge. The diffusion process also does not seem applicable to the results of Experiment 1. Responsibility for protecting oneself from fire should not diffuse. On the other hand, "social influence" processes cannot account for results in Experiment 4. Subjects in that experiment could not communicate with each other and thus could not be influenced by each other's reactions.

Although both processes probably operate, they may not do so at the same time. To the extent that social influence leads an individual to define the situation as non-serious and not requiring action, his responsibility is eliminated, making diffusion unnecessary. Only if social influence is unavailable or unsuccessful in leading subjects to misinterpret a situation, should diffusion play a role. Indirect evidence supporting this analysis comes from observation of non-intervening subjects in the various emergency settings. In settings involving face-to-face contact, as in Experiments 1 and 2, non-interveners typically redefined the situation and did not see it as a serious emergency. Consequently, they avoided the moral choice of whether or not to take action. During the post-experimental interviews, subjects in these experiments seemed relaxed and assured. They felt they had behaved reasonably and properly. In Experiment 4, on the other hand, face-to-face contact was prevented, social influence could not help subjects define the situation as non-serious, and they were faced with the moral dilemma of whether to intervene. Although the imagined presence of other people led many subjects to delay intervention, their conflict was exhibited in the post-experimental interviews. If anything, subjects who did not intervene seemed more emotionally aroused than did subjects who reported the emergency.

The results of these experiments suggest that social inhibition effects may be rather general over a wide variety of emergency situations. In four different experiments, bystanders have been less likely to intervene if other bystanders are present. The nature of the other bystander seems to be important: a non-reactive confederate provides the most inhibition, a stranger provides a moderate amount, and a friend, the least. Overall, the results are consistent with a multiprocess model of intervention; the effect of other people seems to be mediated both through the interpretations that bystanders place on the situation, and through the decisions they make once they have come up with an interpretation.

"There's safety in numbers," according to an old adage, and modern city dwellers seem to believe it. They shun deserted streets, empty subway cars, and lonely walks in dark parks, preferring instead to go where others are or to stay at home. When faced with stress, most individuals seem less afraid when they are in the presence of others than when they are alone. Dogs are less likely to yelp when they face a strange situation with other dogs; even rats are less likely to defecate and freeze when they are placed in a frightening open field with other rats.

A feeling so widely shared should have some basis in reality. Is there safety in numbers? If so, why? Two reasons are often suggested: Individuals are less likely to find themselves in trouble if there are others about, and even if they do find themselves in trouble, others are likely to help them deal with it. While it is certainly true that a victim is unlikely to receive help if nobody knows of his plight, the experiments above cast doubt on the suggestion that he will be more likely to receive help if more people are present. In fact, the opposite seems to be true. A victim may be more likely to get help, or an emergency be reported, the fewer people who are available to take action.

Although the results of these studies may shake our faith in "safety in numbers," they also may help us begin to understand a number of frightening incidents where crowds have listened to, but not answered, a call for help. Newspapers have tagged these incidents with the label "apathy." We have become indifferent, they say, callous to the fate of suffering others. Our society has become "dehumanized" as it has become urbanized. These glib phrases may contain some truth, since startling cases such as the Genovese murder often seem to occur in our large cities, but such terms may also be misleading. Our studies suggest a different conclusion. They suggest that situational factors, specifically factors involving the immediate social environment, may be of greater importance in determining an individual's reaction to an emergency than such vague cultural or personality concepts as "apathy" or "alienation due to urbanization." They suggest that the failure to intervene may be better understood by knowing the relationship among bystanders rather than that between a bystander and the victim.

Our results may explain why the failure to intervene seems to be more characteristic of large cities than rural areas. Bystanders to urban emergencies are more likely to be, or at least to think they are, in the presence of other bystanders than witnesses of non-urban emergencies. Bystanders to urban emergencies are less likely to know each other or to know the victim than are witnesses of non-urban emergencies. When an emergency occurs in a large city, a crowd is likely to gather; the crowd members are likely to be strangers; and it is likely that no one will be acquainted with the victim. These are exactly the conditions that made the helping response least likely in our experiments.

In a less sophisticated era, Rudyard Kipling prayed "That we, with Thee, may walk uncowed by fear or favor of the crowd; that, under Thee, we may possess man's strength to comfort man's distress." It appears that the latter hope may depend to a surprising extent upon the former.

REFERENCES

BROWN, R. W. Mass Phenomena. In Lindzey, G. (ed.) *Handbook of Social Psychology,* Vol. 2, Cambridge, Addison-Wesley, 1954.

BROWN, R. W. *Social Psychology,* New York, Free Press, 1965.

DARLEY, J. M. and LATANÉ, B. Bystander intervention in emergencies: Diffusion of responsibility. *Journal of Personality and Social Psychology,* 1968, *8,* 377–383.

LATANÉ, B. Gregariousness and fear in laboratory rats. *Journal of Experimental Social Psychology,* 1969, *5,* 61–69.

LATANÉ, B. and DARLEY, J. M. Group inhibition of bystander intervention in emergencies. *Journal of Personality and Social Psychology,* 1968, *10,* 215–221.

LATANÉ, B. and GLASS, D. C. Social and non-social attraction in rats. *Journal of Personality and Social Psychology,* 1968, *9,* 142–146.

LATANÉ, B. and RODIN, J. A lady in distress: Inhibiting effects of friends and strangers on bystander intervention. *Journal of Experimental Social Psychology,* 1969, *5,* 189–202.

SCHACHTER, S. *The Psychology of Affiliation,* Stanford: Stanford University Press. 1959.

16

Good Samaritanism:

An Underground Phenomenon?

Irving M. Piliavin, Judith Rodin, and Jane Allyn Piliavin

Since the murder of Kitty Genovese in Queens, a rapidly increasing number of social scientists have turned their attentions to the study of the good Samaritan's act and an associated phenomenon, the evaluation of victims by bystanders and agents. Some of the findings of this research have been provocative and nonobvious. For example, there is evidence that agents, and even bystanders, will sometimes derogate the character of the victims of misfortune, instead of feeling compassion (Berscheid & Walster, 1967; Lerner & Simmons, 1966). Furthermore, recent findings indicate that under certain circumstances there is not "safety in numbers," but rather "diffusion of responsibility." Darley and Latané (1968) have reported that among bystanders hearing an epileptic seizure over earphones, those who believed other witnesses were present were less likely to seek assistance for the victim than were bystanders who believed they were alone. Subsequent research by Latané and Rodin (1969) on response to the victim of a fall confirmed this finding and

From *Journal of Personality and Social Psychology*, 1969, *13*, 289–299.

This research was conducted while the first author was at Columbia University as a Special National Institute of Mental Health Research Fellow under Grant 1-F3-MH-36, 328-01. The study was partially supported by funds supplied by this grant and partially by funds from National Science Foundation Grant GS-1901 to the third author. The authors thank Virginia Joy for allowing the experimental teams to be recruited from her class, and Percy Tannenbaum for his reading of the manuscript and his helpful comments.

suggested further that assistance from a group of bystanders was less likely to come if the group members were strangers than if they were prior acquaintances. The field experiments of Bryan and Test (1967), on the other hand, provide interesting findings that fit common sense expectations; namely, one is more likely to be a good Samaritan if one has just observed another individual performing a helpful act.

Much of the work on victimization to date has been performed in the laboratory. It is commonly argued that the ideal research strategy over the long haul is to move back and forth between the laboratory, with its advantage of greater control, and the field, with its advantage of greater reality. The present study was designed to provide more information from the latter setting.

The primary focus of the study was on the effect of type of victim (drunk or ill) and race of victim (black or white) on speed of responding, frequency of responding, and the race of the helper. On the basis of the large body of research on similarity and liking as well as that on race and social distance, it was assumed that an individual would be more inclined to help someone of his race than a person of another race. The expectation regarding type of victim was that help would be accorded more frequently and rapidly to the apparently ill victim. This expectation was derived from two considerations. First, it was assumed that people who are regarded as partly responsible for their plight would receive less sympathy and consequently less help than people seen as not responsible for their circumstances (Schopler & Matthews, 1965).

Secondly, it was assumed that whatever sympathy individuals may experience when they observe a drunk collapse, their inclination to help him will be dampened by the realization that the victim may become disgusting, embarrassing, and/or violent. This realization may, in fact, not only constrain helping but also lead observers to turn away from the victim—that is, to leave the scene of the emergency.

Aside from examining the effects of race and type of victim, the present research sought to investigate the impact of modeling in emergency situations. Several investigators have found that an individual's actions in a given situation lead others in that situation to engage in similar actions. This modeling phenomenon has been observed in a variety of contexts including those involving good Samaritanism (Bryan & Test, 1967). It was expected that the phenomenon would be observed as well in the present study. A final concern of the study was to examine the relationship between size of group and frequency and latency of the helping response, with a victim who was both seen and heard. In previous laboratory studies (Darley & Latané, 1968; Latané & Rodin, 1969) increases in group size led to decreases in frequency and increases in latency of responding. In these studies, however, the emergency was only heard, not seen. Since visual cues are likely to make an emergency much more arousing for the observer, it is not clear that, given these cues, such considerations as crowd size will be relevant determinants of the observer's response to the emergency. Visual cues also provide clear information as to whether anyone has yet helped the victim or if he has been able to help himself. Thus, in the laboratory studies, observers lacking visual cues could rationalize not helping by assuming assistance was no longer needed when the victim ceased calling for help. Staging emergencies in full view of observers eliminates the possibility of such rationalization.

To conduct a field investigation of the above questions under the desired conditions required a setting which would allow the repeated staging of emergencies in the midst of reasonably large groups which remained fairly similar in composition from incident to incident. It was also desirable that each group retain the same composition over the course of the incident and that a reasonable amount of time be available after the emergency occurred for good Samaritans to act. To meet these requirements, the emergencies were staged during the approximately 7½-minute express run between the 59th Street and 125th Street stations of the Eighth Avenue Independent (IND) branch of the New York subways.

METHOD

Subjects

About 4,450 men and women who traveled on the 8th Avenue IND in New York City, weekdays between the hours of 11:00 A.M. and 3:00 P.M. during the period from April 15 to June 26, 1968, were the unsolicited participants in this study. The racial composition of a typical train, which travels through Harlem to the Bronx, was about 45% black and 55% white. The mean number of people per car during these hours was 43; the mean number of people in the "critical area," in which the staged incident took place, was 8.5.

Field situation. The A and D trains of the 8th Avenue IND were selected because they make no stops between 59th Street and 125th Street. Thus, for about 7½ minutes there was a captive audience who, after the first 70 seconds of their ride, became bystanders to an emergency situation. A single trial was a nonstop ride between 59th and 125th Streets, going in either direction. All trials were run only on the old New York subway cars which serviced the 8th Avenue line since they had two-person seats in group arrangement rather than extended seats. The designated experimental or critical area was that end section of any car whose doors led to the next car. There are 13 seats and some standing room in this area on all trains (see Fig. 16.1).

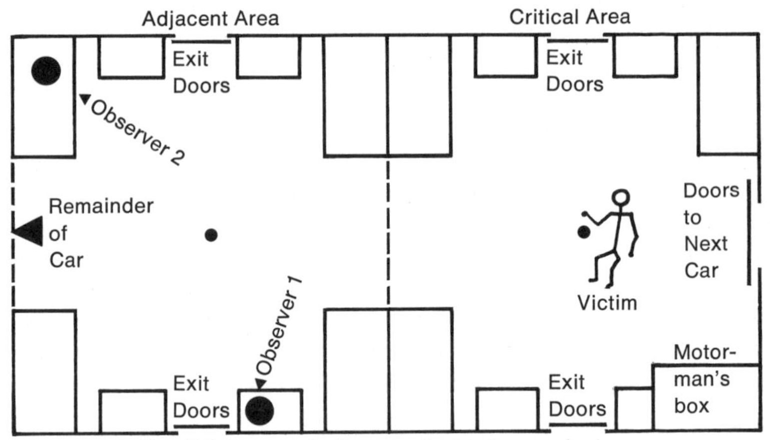

FIG. 16.1. Layout of adjacent and critical areas of subway car.

Procedure

On each trial a team of four Columbia General Studies students, two males and two females, boarded the train using different doors. Four different teams, whose members always worked together, were used to collect data for 103 trials. Each team varied the location of the experimental car from trial to trial. The female confederates took seats outside the critical area and recorded data as unobtrusively as possible for the duration of the ride, while the male model and victim remained standing. The victim always stood next to a pole in the center of the critical area (see Fig. 16.1). As the train passed the first station (approximately 70 seconds after departing) the victim staggered forward and collapsed. Until receiving help, the victim remained supine on the floor looking at the ceiling. If the victim received no assistance by the time the train slowed to a stop, the model helped him to his feet. At the stop, the team disembarked and waited separately until other riders had left the station. They then proceeded to another platform to board a train going in the opposite direction for the next trial. From 6 to 8 trials were run on a given day. All trials on a given day were in the same "victim condition."

Victim: The four victims (one from each team) were males between the ages of 26 and 35. Three were white and one was black. All were identically dressed in Eisenhower jackets, old slacks, and no tie. On 38 trials the victims smelled of liquor and carried a liquor bottle wrapped tightly in a brown bag (drunk condition), while on the remaining 65 trials they appeared sober and carried a black cane (cane condition). In all other aspects, victims dressed and behaved identically in the two conditions. Each victim participated in drunk and cane trials.[1]

Model: Four white males between the ages of 24 and 29 assumed the roles of model in each team. All models wore informal clothes, although they were not identically attired. There were four different

[1] It will be noted later that not only were there more cane trials than drunk trials, they were also distributed unevenly across black and white victims. The reason for this is easier to explain than to correct. Teams 1 and 2 (both white victims) started the first day in the cane condition. Teams 3 (black) and 4 (white) began in the drunk condition. Teams were told to alternate the conditions across days. They arranged their running days to fit their schedules. On their fourth day, Team 2 violated the instruction and ran cane trials when they should have run drunk trials; the victim "didn't like" playing the drunk! Then the Columbia student strike occurred, the teams disbanded, and the study of necessity was over. At this point, Teams 1 and 3 had run on only 3 days each, while 2 and 4 had run on 4 days each.

model conditions used across both victim conditions (drunk or cane).

1. *Critical area—early.* Model stood in critical area and waited until passing fourth station to assist victim (approximately 70 seconds after collapse).

2. *Critical area—late.* Model stood in critical area and waited until passing sixth station to assist victim (approximately 150 seconds after collapse).

3. *Adjacent area—early.* Model stood in middle of car in area adjacent to critical area and waited until passing fourth station.

4. *Adjacent area—late.* Model stood in adjacent area and waited until passing sixth station.

When the model provided assistance, he raised the victim to a sitting position and stayed with him for the remainder of the trial. An equal number of trials in the no-model condition and in each of the four model conditions were preprogrammed by a random number table and assigned to each team.

Table 16.1—Percentage of Trials on Which Help Was Given, by Race and Condition of Victim, and Total Number of Trials Run in Each Condition

Trials	White victims		Black victim	
	Cane	Drunk	Cane	Drunk
No model	100%	100%	100%	73%
Number of trials run	54	11	8	11
Model trials	100%	77%	—	67%
Number of trials run	3	13	0	3
Total number of trials	57	24	8	14

Note.—Distribution of model trials for the drunk was as follows: critical area: early, 4; late, 4; adjacent area: early, 5; late, 3. The three model trials completed for the cane victim were all early, with 2 from the critical area and 1 from the adjacent area.

Measures: On each trial one observer noted the race, sex, and location of every rider seated or standing in the critical area. In addition, she counted the total number of individuals in the car and the total number of individuals who came to the victim's assistance. She also recorded the race, sex, and location of every helper. A second observer coded the race, sex, and location of all persons in the adjacent area. She also recorded the latency of the first helper's arrival after the victim had fallen and on appropriate trials, the latency of the first helper's arrival after the programmed model had arrived. Both observers recorded comments spontaneously made by nearby passengers and attempted to elicit comments from a rider sitting next to them.

RESULTS AND DISCUSSION

As can be seen in Table 16.1, the frequency of help received by the victims was impressive, at least as compared to earlier laboratory results. The victim with the cane received spontaneous help, that is, before the model acted, on 62 of the 65 trials. Even the drunk received spontaneous help on 19 of 38 trials. The difference is not explicable on the basis of gross differences in the numbers of potential helpers in the cars. (Mean number of passengers in the car on cane trials was 45; on drunk trials, 40. Total range was 15-120.)

On the basis of past research, relatively long latencies of spontaneous helping were expected; thus, it was assumed that models would have time to help, and their effects could be assessed. However, in all but three of the cane trials planned to be model trials, the victim received help before the model was scheduled to offer assistance. This was less likely to happen with the drunk victim. In many cases, the early model was able to intervene, and in a few, even the delayed model could act (see Table 16.1 for frequencies).

A direct comparison between the latency of response in the drunk and cane conditions might be misleading, since on model trials one does not know how long it might have taken for a helper to arrive without the stimulus of the model. Omitting the model trials, however, would reduce the number of drunk trials drastically. In order to get around these problems the trials have been dichotomized into a group in which someone helped *before* 70 seconds (the time at which the early model was programmed to help) and a group in which no one had helped by this time. The second group includes some trials in which people helped the model and a very few in which no one helped at all.[2] It is quite clear from the first section of Table 16.2 that there was more immediate, spontaneous helping of the victim with the cane than of the drunk. The effect seems to be essentially the same for the black victim and for the white victims.[3]

What of the total number of people who helped? On 60% of the 81 trials on which the victim received help, he received it not from one good Samaritan but from two, three, or even more.[4] There are no significant differences between black and white victims, or between cane and drunk victims, in the number of helpers subsequent to the first who came to his aid. Seemingly, then, the presence of the first helper has important implications which override whatever cognitive and emotional differences were initially engendered among observers by the characteristics of the victim. It may be that the victim's uniformly passive response to the individual trying to assist him reduced observers' fear about possible unpleasantness in the drunk conditions. Another possibility is that the key factor in the decisions of second and third helpers to offer assistance was the first helper. That is, perhaps assistance was being offered primarily to him rather than to the victim. Unfortunately the data do

[2] If a comparison of latencies is made between cane and drunk nonmodel trials only, the median latency for cane trials is 5 seconds and the median for drunk trials is 109 seconds (assigning 400 seconds as the latency for nonrespondents). The Mann-Whitney *U* for this comparison is significant at $p < .0001$.

[3] Among the white victim teams, the data from Team 2 differ to some extent from those for Teams 1 and 4. All of the cane—after 70 seconds trials are accounted for by Team 2, as are 4 of the 5 drunk-before 70 trials. Median latency for cane trials is longer for Team 2 than for the other teams; for drunk trials, shorter. This is the same team that violated the "alternate days" instruction. It would appear that this team is being rather less careful—that the victim may be getting out of his role. The data from this team have been included in the analysis although they tend to reduce the relationships that were found.

[4] The data from the model trials are not included in this analysis because the model was programmed to behave rather differently from the way in which most real helpers behaved. That is, his role was to raise the victim to a sitting position and then appear to need assistance. Most real helpers managed to drag the victim to a seat or to a standing position on their own. Thus the programmed model received somewhat more help than did real first helpers.

Table 16.2—Time and Responses to the Incident

Trials on which help was offered:	*Total number of trials*		*% of trials on which 1 + persons left critical area*[b]		*% of trials on which 1 + comments were recorded*[b]		*Mean number of comments*	
	White victims	*Black victim*	*White victims*	*Black victim*	*White victims*	*Black victim*	*White victims*	*Black victim*
Before 70 sec.								
Cane	52	7	4%	14%	21%	0%	.27	.00
Drunk	5	4	20%	0%	80%	50%	1.00	.50
Total	57	11	5%	9%	26%	18%	.33	.18
After 70 sec.								
Cane	5	1	40%	—	60%	—	.80	—
Drunk	19	10	42%	60%	100%	70%	2.00	.90
Total	24	11	42%	64%	96%	64%	1.75	.82
χ^2	36.83	[a]	$\chi^2_{time} = 23.19$		$\chi^2_{time} = 31.45$			
p	<.001	<.03	$p < .001$		$p < .001$			
			$\chi^2_{cane\text{-}drunk} = 11.71$		$\chi^2_{cane\text{-}drunk} = 37.95$			
			$p < .001$		$p < .001$			

Note.—Percentage and means not calculated for n's less than 4.

[a] Fisher's exact test, estimate of two-tailed probability.

[b] Black and white victims are combined for the analyses of these data.

not permit adequate assessment of these or other possible explanations.

Characteristics of Spontaneous First Helpers

Having discovered that people do, in fact, help with rather high frequency, the next question is, "Who helps?" The effect of two variables, sex and race, can be examined. On the average, 60% of the people in the critical area were males. Yet, of the 81 spontaneous first helpers, 90% were males. In this situation, then, men are considerably more likely to help than are women ($x^2 = 30.63$; $p < .001$).

Turning now to the race variable, of the 81 first helpers, 64% were white. This percentage does not differ significantly from the expected percentage of 55% based on racial distribution in the cars. Since both black and white victims were used, it is also possible to see whether blacks and whites are more likely to help a member of their own race. On the 65 trials on which spontaneous help was offered to the white victims, 68% of the helpers were white. This proportion differs from the expected 55% at the .05 level ($x^2 = 4.23$). On the 16 trials on which spontaneous help was offered to the black victim, half of the first helpers were white. While this proportion does not differ from chance expectation, we again see a slight tendency toward "same-race" helping.

When race of helper is examined separately for cane and drunk victims, an interesting although nonsignificant trend emerges (see Table 16.3). With both the black and white cane victims, the proportion of helpers of each race was in accord with the expected 55%–45% split. With the drunk, on the other hand, it was mainly members of his own race who came to his aid.[5]

This interesting tendency toward same-race helping only in the

[5] It is unfortunate from a design standpoint that there was only one black victim. He was the only black student in the class from which our crews were recruited. While it is tenuous to generalize from a sample of one, the problems attendant upon attributing results to his race rather than to his individual personality characteristics are vitiated somewhat by the fact that response latencies and frequencies of help to him in the cane condition fall between responses to Teams 1 and 4 on the one hand and Team 2 on the other.

case of the drunk victim may reflect more empathy, sympathy, and trust toward victims of one's own racial group. In the case of an innocent victim (e.g., the cane victim), when sympathy, though differentially experienced, is relatively uncomplicated by other emotions, assistance can readily cut across group lines. In the case of the drunk (and potentially dangerous) victim, complications are present, probably blame, fear, and disgust. When the victim is a member of one's own group—when the conditions for empathy and trust are more favorable—assistance is more likely to be offered. As we have seen, however, this does not happen without the passing of time to think things over.

Recent findings of Black and Reiss (1967) in a study of the behavior of white police officers towards apprehended persons offer an interesting parallel. Observers in this study recorded very little evidence of prejudice toward sober individuals, whether white or black. There was a large increase in prejudice expressed towards drunks of both races, but the increase in prejudice towards blacks was more than twice that towards whites.

Modeling Effects

No extensive analysis of the response to the programmed model could be made, since there were too few cases for analysis. Two analyses were, however, performed on the effects of adjacent area versus critical area models and of early versus late models within the drunk condition. The data are presented in Table 16.4. While the area variable has no effect, the early model elicited help significantly more than did the late model.

Other Responses to the Incident

What other responses do observers make to the incident? Do the passengers leave the car, move out of the area, make comments about the incident? No one left the car on any of the trials. However, on 21 of the 103 trials, a total of 34 people did leave the critical area. The second section of Table 16.2 presents the percentage of trials on which someone left the critical area as a function of three variables: type of victim, race of victim, and time to

Table 16.3—Spontaneous Helping of Cane and Drunk by Race of Helper and Race Victim

Race of helper	*White victims*			*Black victim*			*All victims*		
	Cane	*Drunk*	*Total*	*Cane*	*Drunk*	*Total*	*Cane*	*Drunk*	*Total*
Same as victim	34	10	44	2	6	8	36	16	52
Different from victim	20	1	21	6	2	8	26	3	29
Total	54	11	65	8	8	16	62	19	81

Note.—Chi-squares are corrected for continuity. White victims, $x^2 = 2.11$, $p = .16$; black victim, $p = .16$ (two-tailed estimate from Fisher's exact probabilities test); all victims, $x^2 = 3.26$, $p = .08$.

receipt of help (before or after 70 seconds). People left the area on a higher proportion of trials with the drunk than with the cane victim. They also were far more likely to leave on trials on which help was not offered by 70 seconds, as compared to trials on which help was received before that time.[6] The frequencies are too small to make comparisons with each of the variables held constant.

Each observer spoke to the person seated next to her after the incident took place. She also noted spontaneous comments and actions by those around her. A content analysis of these data was performed, with little in the way of interesting findings. The distribution of number of comments over different sorts of trials, however, did prove interesting (see Section 3 of Table 16.2). Far more comments were obtained on drunk trials than on cane trials. Similarly, most of the comments were obtained on trials in which no one helped until after 70 seconds. The discomfort observers felt in sitting inactive in the presence of the victim may have led them to talk about the incident, perhaps hoping others would confirm the fact that inaction was appropriate. Many women, for example, made comments such as, "It's for men to help him," or "I wish I could help him—I'm not strong enough," "I never saw this kind of thing before—I don't know where to look," "You feel so bad that you don't know what to do."

A Test of the Diffusion of Responsibility Hypothesis

In the Darley and Latané experiment it was predicted and found that as the number of bystanders increased, the likelihood that any individual would help decreased and the latency of response increased. Their study involved bystanders who could not see each other or the victim. In the Latané and Rodin study, the effect was again found, with bystanders who were face to face, but with the victim still only heard. In the present study, bystanders

[6] Individuals are also somewhat more likely to leave the area with the black victim than with the white victims ($x^2 = 3.24$, $p < .08$). This race effect is most probably an artifact, since the black victim ran more drunk trials than cane trials, the white victims, vice versa.

Table 16.4—Frequency of Help as a Function of Early (70 Seconds) versus Late (150 Seconds) and Adjacent versus Critical Area Programmed Models

Help	Critical area			Adjacent area			Both areas		
	Early	*Late*	*Both*	*Early*	*Late*	*Both*	*Early*	*Late*	*Total*
Received	4	2	6	5	1	6	9	3	12
Not received	0	2	2	0	2	2	0	4	4
Total	4	4	8	5	3	8	9	7	16

Note.—Early versus late: $p < .04$ (two-tailed estimate from Fisher's exact test). All three cane-model trials were early model trials; two critical area, one adjacent. Help was received on all. Table includes drunk trials only.

Table 16.5—Mean and Median Latencies as a Function of Number of Males in the Critical Area

No. males in critical area	Cane			Drunk		
	White victims	Black victim	Total	White victims	Black victim	Total
1–3						
M	16	12	15	—	309	309
Mdn.	7	12	7	—	312	312
N	17	2	19		4	4
4–6						
M	20	6	18	155	143	149
Mdn.	5	4	5	105	70	73
N	23	4	27	4	4	8
7 and up						
M	3	52	9	107	74	97
Mdn.	1	52	1.5	102	65	84
N	14	2	16	7	3	10
Kruskal-Wallis Test (H)			5.08			6.01
p			.08			.05

Note.—Means and medians in seconds. Model trials omitted; no response assigned 400 seconds.

saw both the victim and each other. Will the diffusion of responsibility finding still occur in this situation?

In order to check this hypothesis, two analyses were performed. First, all nonmodel trials were separated into three groups according to the number of males in the critical area (the assumed reference group for spontaneous first helpers). Mean and median latencies of response were then calculated for each group, separately by type and race of victim. The results are presented in Table 16.5. There is no evidence in these data for diffusion of responsibility; in fact, response times, using either measure, are consistently faster for the 7 or more groups compared to the 1 to 3 groups.[7]

As Darley and Latané pointed out, however, different-size real groups cannot be meaningfully compared to one another, since as group size increases the likelihood that one or more persons will help also increases. A second analysis as similar as possible to that

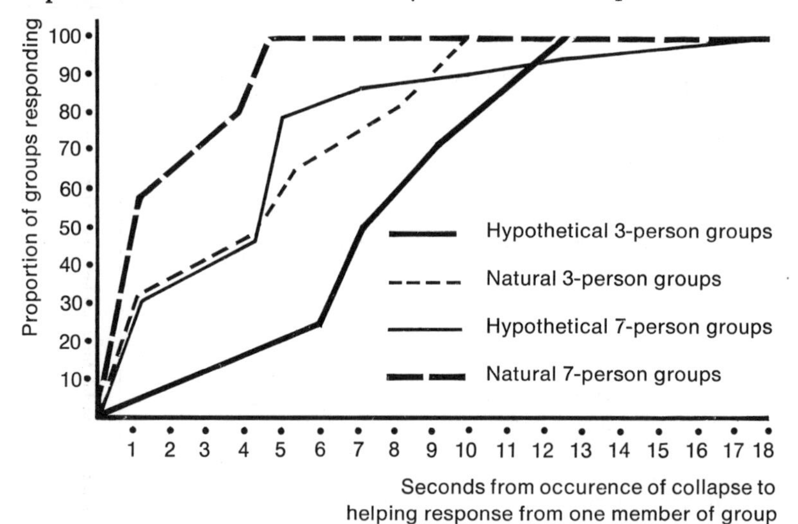

FIG. 16.2. Cumulative proportion of groups producing a helper over time (cane trials, white victims, male helpers from inside critical area).

[7] The total number of people in the car was strongly related to the number of males in the critical area. Similar results are obtained if latencies are examined as a function of the total number of people in the car.

used by those authors was therefore performed, comparing latencies actually obtained for each size group with a base line of hypothetical groups of the same size made up by combining smaller groups. In order to have as much control as possible the analysis was confined to cane trials with white victims and male first helpers coming from the critical area. Within this set of trials, the most frequently occurring natural groups (of males in the critical area) were those of sizes 3 ($n = 6$) and 7 ($n = 5$). Hypothetical groups of 3 ($n = 4$) and 7 ($n = 25$) were composed of all combinations of smaller sized groups. For example, to obtain the hypothetical latencies for groups of 7, combinations were made of (*a*) all real size 6 groups with all real size 1 groups, plus (*b*) all real size 5 groups with all real size 2 groups, etc. The latency assigned to each of these hypothetical groups was that recorded for the faster of the two real groups of which it was composed. Cumulative response curves for real and hypothetical groups of 3 and 7 are presented in Fig. 16.2.

As can be seen in the figure, the cumulative helping response curves for the hypothetical groups of both sizes are lower than those for the corresponding real groups. That is, members of real groups responded more rapidly than would be expected on the basis of the faster of the two scores obtained from the combined smaller groups. While these results together with those summarized in Table 16.5 do not necessarily contradict the diffusion of responsibility hypothesis, they do not follow the pattern of findings obtained by Darley and Latané and are clearly at variance with the tentative conclusion of those investigators that "a victim may be more likely to receive help . . . the fewer people there are to take action [Latané & Darley, 1968, p. 221]."

Two explanations can be suggested to account for the disparity between the findings of Table 16.5 and Fig. 16.2 and those of Darley and Latané and Latané and Rodin. As indicated earlier in this paper, the conditions of the present study were quite different from those in previous investigations. First, the fact that observers in the present study could see the victim may not only have constrained observers' abilities to conclude there was no emergency, but may also have overwhelmed with other considerations any tendency to diffuse responsibility. Second, the present findings may indicate that even if diffusion of responsibility *is* experienced by people who can actually see an emergency, when groups are larger than two the increment in deterrence to action resulting from increasing the number of observers may be less than the increase in probability that within a given time interval at least one of the observers will take action to assist the victim. Clearly, more work is needed in both natural and laboratory settings before an understanding is reached of the conditions under which diffusion of responsibility will or will not occur.

CONCLUSIONS

In this field study, a personal emergency occurred in which escape for the bystander was virtually impossible. It was a public, face-to-face situation, and in this respect differed from previous lab studies. Moreover, since generalizations from field studies to lab research must be made with caution, few comparisons will be drawn. However, several conclusions may be put forth:

1. An individual who appears to be ill is more likely to receive aid than is one who appears to be drunk, even when the immediate help needed is of the same kind.

2. Given mixed goups of men and women, and a male victim, men are more likely to help than are women.

3. Given mixed racial groups, there is some tendency for same-race helping to be more frequent. This tendency is increased when the victim is drunk as compared to apparently ill.

4. There is no strong relationship between number of bystanders and speed of helping; the expected increased "diffusion of responsibility" with a greater number of bystanders was not obtained for groups of these sizes. That is, help is not less frequent or slower in coming from larger as compared to smaller groups of bystanders; what effect there is, is in the opposite direction.

5. The longer the emergency continues without help being offered (*a*) the less impact a model has on the helping behavior of observers; (*b*) the more likely it is that individuals will leave the immediate area; that is, they appear to move purposively to another area in order to avoid the situation; (*c*) the more likely it is

that observers will discuss the incident and its implications for their behavior.

A model of response to emergency situations consistent with the previous findings is currently being developed by the authors. It is briefly presented here as a possible heuristic device. The model includes the following assumptions: Observation of an emergency creates an emotional arousal state in the bystander. This state will be differently interpreted in different situations (Schachter, 1964) as fear, disgust, sympathy, etc., and possibly a combination of these. This state of arousal is higher (*a*) the more one can empathize with the victim (i.e., the more one can see oneself in his situation—Stotland, 1966), (*b*) the closer one is to the emergency, and (*c*) the longer the state of emergency continues without the intervention of a helper. It can be reduced by one of a number of possible responses: (*a*) helping directly, (*b*) going to get help, (*c*) leaving the scene of the emergency, and (*d*) rejecting the victim as undeserving of help (Lerner & Simmons, 1966). The response that will be chosen is a function of a cost-reward matrix that includes costs associated with helping (e.g., effort, embarrassment, possible disgusting or distasteful experiences, possible physical harm, etc.), costs associated with not helping (mainly self-blame and perceived censure from others), rewards associated with helping (mainly praise from self, victim, and others), and rewards associated with not helping (mainly those stemming from continuation of other activities). Note that the major motivation implied in the model is not a positive "altruistic" one, but rather a selfish desire to rid oneself of an unpleasant emotional state.

In terms of this model, the following after-the-fact interpretations can be made of the findings obtained:

1. The drunk is helped less because costs for helping are higher (greater disgust) and costs for not helping are lower (less self-blame and censure because he is in part responsible for his own victimization).

2. Women help less because costs for helping are higher in this situation (effort, mainly) and costs for not helping are lower (less censure from others; it is not her role).

3. Same-race helping, particularly of the drunk, can be explained by differential costs for not helping (less censure if one is

of opposite race) and, with the drunk, differential costs for helping (more fear if of different race).

4. Diffusion of responsibility is not found on cane trials because costs for helping in general are low and costs for not helping are high (more self-blame because of possible severity of problem). That is, the suggestion is made that the diffusion of responsibility effect will increase as costs for helping increase and costs for not helping decrease. This interpretation is consistent with the well-known public incidents, in which possible bodily harm to a helper is almost always involved, and thus costs for helping are very high, and also with previous research done with nonvisible victims in which either (*a*) it was easy to assume someone had already helped and thus costs for not helping were reduced (Darley & Latané) or (*b*) it was possible to think that the emergency was minor, which also reduces the costs for not helping (Latané & Rodin).

5. All of the effects of time are also consistent with the model. The longer the emergency continues, the more likely it is that observers will be aroused and therefore will have chosen among the possible responses. Thus, (*a*) a late model will elicit less helping, since people have already reduced their arousal by one of the other methods; (*b*) unless arousal is reduced by other methods, people will leave more as time goes on, because arousal is still increasing; and (*c*) observers will discuss the incident in an attempt to reduce self-blame and arrive at the fourth resolution, namely a justification for not helping based on rejection of the victim.

Quite obviously, the model was derived from these data, along with data of other studies in the area. Needless to say, further work is being planned by the authors to test the implications of the model systematically.

SUMMARY

A field experiment was performed to investigate the effect of several variables on helping behavior, using the express trains of the New York 8th Avenue Independent Subway as a laboratory on wheels. Four teams of students, each one made up of a victim, model, and two observers, staged standard collapses in which type of victim (drunk or ill), race of victim (black or white) and presence or absence of a model were varied. Data recorded by observers included number and race of observers, latency of the helping response and race of helper, number of helpers, movement out of the "critical area," and spontaneous comments. Major findings of the study were that (*a*) an apparently ill person is more likely to receive aid than is one who appears to be drunk, (*b*) race of victim has little effect on race of helper except when the victim is drunk, (*c*) the longer the emergency continues without help being offered, the more likely it is that someone will leave the area of the emergency, and (*d*) the expected decrease in speed of responding as group size increases—the "diffusion of responsibility effect" found by Darley and Latané—does not occur in this situation. Implications of this difference between laboratory and field results are discussed, and a brief model for the prediction of behavior in emergency situations is presented.

REFERENCES

BERSCHEID, E., & WALSTER, E. When does a harm-doer compensate a victim? *Journal of Personality and Social Psychology,* 1967, 6, 435–441.

BLACK, D. J., & REISS, A. J. *Studies in crime and law enforcement in major metropolitan areas.* (Report submitted to the President's Commission on Law Enforcement and Administration of Justice) Washington, D.C.: United States Government Printing Office, 1967.

BRYAN, J. H., & TEST, M. A. Models and helping: Naturalistic studies in aiding behavior. *Journal of Personality and Social Psychology.* 1967, 6, 400–407.

DARLEY, J., & LATANÉ, B. Bystander intervention in emergencies: Diffusion of responsibility. *Journal of Personality and Social Psychology,* 1968, 8, 377–383.

LATANÉ, B., & DARLEY, J. Group inhibition of bystander intervention in emergencies. *Journal of Personality and Social Psychology,* 1968, 10, 215–221.

LATANÉ, B., & RODIN, J. A lady in distress: Inhibiting effects of friends and strangers on bystander intervention. *Journal of Experimental Social Psychology,* 1969, 5, 189–202.

LERNER, M. J., & SIMMONS, C. H. Observer's reaction to the "innocent victim": Compassion or rejection? *Journal of Personality and Social Psychology,* 1966, 4, 203–210.

SCHACHTER, S. The interaction of cognitive and physiological determinants of emotional state. In L. Berkowitz (Ed.), *Advances in experimental social psychology.* Vol. 1. New York: Academic Press, 1964.

SCHOPLER, J., & MATTHEWS, M. W. The influence of the perceived causal locus of partner's dependence on the use of interpersonal power. *Journal of Personality and Social Psychology,* 1965, 4, 609–612.

STOTLAND, E. A theory and experiments in empathy. Paper presented at the meeting of the American Psychological Association, New York, September 1966.

17

The Experience of Living in Cities

Stanley Milgram

> When I first came to New York it seemed like a nightmare. As soon as I got off the train at Grand Central I was caught up in pushing, shoving crowds on 42nd Street. Sometimes people bumped into me without apology; what really frightened me was to see two people literally engaged in combat for possession of a cab. Why were they so rushed? Even drunks on the street were bypassed without a glance. People didn't seem to care about each other at all.

This statement represents a common reaction to a great city, but it does not tell the whole story. Obviously cities have great

From *Science,* 1970, *167,* 1461–1468.

appeal because of their variety, eventfulness, possibility of choice, and the stimulation of an intense atmosphere that many individuals find a desirable background to their lives. Where face-to-face contacts are important, the city offers unparalleled possibilities. It has been calculated by the Regional Plan Association (*1*) that in Nassau County, a suburb of New York City, an individual can meet 11,000 others within a 10-minute radius of his office by foot or car. In Newark, a moderate-sized city, he can meet more than 20,000 persons within this radius. But in midtown Manhattan he can meet fully 220,000. So there is an order-of-magnitude increment in the communication possibilities offered by a great city. That is one of the bases of its appeal and, indeed, of its functional necessity. The city provides options that no other social arrangement permits. But there is a negative side also, as we shall see.

Granted that cities are indispensable in complex society, we may still ask what contribution psychology can make to understanding the experience of living in them. What theories are relevant? How can we extend our knowledge of the psychological aspects of life in cities through empirical inquiry? If empirical inquiry is possible, along what lines should it proceed? In short, where do we start in constructing urban theory and in laying out lines of research?

Observation is the indispensable starting point. Any observer in the streets of midtown Manhattan will see (i) large numbers of people, (ii) a high population density, and (iii) heterogeneity of population. These three factors need to be at the root of any sociopsychological theory of city life, for they condition all aspects of our experience in the metropolis. Louis Wirth (2), if not the first to point to these factors, is nonetheless the sociologist who relied most heavily on them in his analysis of the city. Yet, for a psychologist, there is something unsatisfactory about Wirth's theoretical variables. Numbers, density, and heterogeneity are demographic facts but they are not yet psychological facts. They are external to the individual. Psychology needs an idea that links the individual's *experience* to the demographic circumstances of urban life.

One link is provided by the concept of overload. This term, drawn from systems analysis, refers to a system's inability to process inputs from the environment because there are too many inputs for the system to cope with, or because successive inputs come so fast that input *A* cannot be processed when input *B* is presented. When overload is present, adaptations occur. The system must set priorities and make choices. *A* may be processed first while *B* is kept in abeyance, or one input may be sacrificed altogether. City life, as we experience it, constitutes a continuous set of encounters with overload, and of resultant adaptations. Overload characteristically deforms daily life on several levels, impinging on role performance, the evolution of social norms, cognitive functioning, and the use of facilities.

The concept has been implicit in several theories of urban experience. In 1903 George Simmel (*3*) pointed out that, since urban dwellers come into contact with vast numbers of people each day, they conserve psychic energy by becoming acquainted with a far smaller proportion of people than their rural counterparts do, and by maintaining more superficial relationships even with these acquaintances. Wirth (2) points specifically to "the superficiality, the anonymity, and the transitory character of urban social relations."

One adaptive response to overload, therefore, is the allocation of less time to each input. A second adaptive mechanism is disregard of low-priority inputs. Principles of selectivity are formulated such that investment of time and energy are reserved for carefully defined inputs (the urbanite disregards the drunk sick on the street as he purposefully navigates through the crowd). Third, boundaries are redrawn in certain social transactions so that the overloaded system can shift the burden to the other party in the exchange; thus, harried New York bus drivers once made change for customers, but now this responsibility has been shifted to the client, who must have the exact fare ready. Fourth, reception is blocked off prior to entrance into a system; city dwellers increasingly use unlisted telephone numbers to prevent individuals from calling them, and a small but growing number resort to keeping the telephone off the hook to prevent incoming calls. More subtly, a city dweller blocks inputs by assuming an unfriendly countenance, which discourages others from initiating contact. Additionally, social screening devices are interposed between the individual and environmental inputs (in a town of 5000 anyone can drop in to chat with the mayor, but in the metropolis organizational screening devices deflect inputs to other destinations). Fifth, the intensity of inputs is diminished by filtering devices, so that only weak and relatively superficial forms of involvement with others are allowed. Sixth, specialized institutions are created to absorb inputs that would otherwise swamp the individual (welfare departments handle the financial needs of a million individuals in New York City, who would otherwise create an army of mendicants continuously importuning the pedestrian). The interposition of institutions between the individual and the social world, a characteristic of all modern society, and most notably of the large metropolis, has its negative side. It deprives the individual of a sense of direct contact and spontaneous integration in the life around him. It simultaneously protects and estranges the individual from his social environment.

Many of these adaptive mechanisms apply not only to individuals but to institutional systems as well, as Meier (*4*) has so brilliantly shown in connection with the library and the stock exchange.

In sum, the observed behavior of the urbanite in a wide range of situations appears to be determined largely by a variety of adaptations to overload. I now deal with several specific consequences of responses to overload, which make for differences in the tone of city and town.

SOCIAL RESPONSIBILITY

The principal point of interest for a social psychology of the city is that moral and social involvement with individuals is necessarily restricted. This is a direct and necessary function of excess of input over capacity to process. Such restriction of involvement runs a broad spectrum from refusal to become involved in the needs of another person, even when the person desperately needs assistance, through refusal to do favors, to the simple withdrawal of courtesies (such as offering a lady a seat, or saying "sorry" when a pedestrian collision occurs). In any transaction more and more details need to be dropped as the total number of units to be processed increases and assaults an instrument of limited processing capacity.

The ultimate adaptation to an overloaded social environment is to totally disregard the needs, interests, and demands of those whom one does not define as relevant to the satisfaction of personal needs, and to develop highly efficient perceptual means of determining whether an individual falls into the category of friend or stranger. The disparity in the treatment of friends and strangers ought to be greater in cities than in towns; the time allotment and willingness to become involved with those who have no personal claim on one's time is likely to be less in cities than in towns.

Bystander Intervention in Crises

The most striking deficiencies in social responsibility in cities occur in crisis situations, such as the Genovese murder in Queens. In 1964, Catherine Genovese, coming home from a night job in the early hours of an April morning, was stabbed repeatedly, over an extended period of time. Thirty-eight residents of a respectable New York City neighborhood admit to having witnessed at least a part of the attack, but none went to her aid or called the police until after she was dead. Milgram and Hollander, writing in *The Nation* (5), analyzed the event in these terms:

> Urban friendships and associations are not primarily formed on the basis of physical proximity. A person with numerous close friends in different parts of the city may not know the occupant of an adjacent apartment. This does not mean that a city dweller has fewer friends than does a villager, or knows fewer persons who will come to his aid; however, it does mean that his allies are not constantly at hand. Miss Genovese required immediate aid from those physically present. There is no evidence that the city had deprived Miss Genovese of human associations, but the friends who might have rushed to her side were miles from the scene of her tragedy.
>
> Further, it is known that her cries for help were not directed to a specific person; they were general. But only individuals can act, and as the cries were not specifically directed, no particular person felt a special responsibility. The crime and the failure of community response seem absurd to us. At the time, it may well have seemed

equally absurd to the Kew Gardens residents that not one of the neighbors would have called the police. A collective paralysis may have developed from the belief of each of the witnesses that someone else must surely have taken that obvious step.

Latané and Darley (*6*) have reported laboratory approaches to the study of bystander intervention and have established experimentally the following principle: the larger the number of bystanders, the less the likelihood that any one of them will intervene in an emergency. Gaertner and Bickman (*7*) of the City University of New York have extended the bystander studies to an examination of help across ethnic lines. Blacks and whites, with clearly identifiable accents, called strangers (through what the caller represented as an error in telephone dialing), gave them a plausible story of being stranded on an outlying highway without more dimes, and asked the stranger to call a garage. The experimenters found that the white callers had a significantly better chance of obtaining assistance than the black callers. This suggests that ethnic allegiance may well be another means of coping with overload: the city dweller can reduce excessive demands and screen out urban heterogeneity by responding along ethnic lines; overload is made more manageable by limiting the "span of sympathy."

In any quantitative characterization of the social texture of city life, a necessary first step is the application of such experimental methods as these to field situations in large cities and small towns. Theorists argue that the indifference shown in the Genovese case would not be found in a small town, but in the absence of solid experimental evidence the question remains an open one.

More than just callousness prevents bystanders from participating in altercations between people. A rule of urban life is respect for other people's emotional and social privacy, perhaps because physical privacy is so hard to achieve. And in situations for which the standards are heterogeneous, it is much harder to know whether taking an active role is unwarranted meddling or an appropriate response to a critical situation. If a husband and wife are quarreling in public, at what point should a bystander step in? On the one hand, the heterogeneity of the city produces substantially greater tolerance about behavior, dress, and codes of ethics than is generally found in the small town, but this diversity also encourages people to withhold aid for fear of antagonizing the participants or crossing an inappropriate and difficult-to-define line.

Table 17.1—Percentage of Entries Achieved by Investigators for City and Town Dwellings (see text)

Experimenter	Entries achieved (%)	
	City *	Small town †
Male		
No. 1	16	40
No. 2	12	60
Female		
No. 3	40	87
No. 4	40	100

* Number of requests for entry, 100.
† Number of requests for entry, 60.

Moreover, the frequency of demands present in the city gives rise to norms of noninvolvement. There are practical limitations to the Samaritan impulse in a major city. If a citizen attended to every needy person, if he were sensitive to and acted on every altruistic impulse that was evoked in the city, he could scarcely keep his own affairs in order.

Willingness to Trust and Assist Strangers

We now move away from crisis situations to less urgent examples of social responsibility. For it is not only in situations of dramatic need but in the ordinary, everyday willingness to lend a hand that the city dweller is said to be deficient relative to his small-town cousin. The comparative method must be used in any empirical examination of this question. A commonplace social situation is staged in an urban setting and in a small town—a situation to which a subject can respond by either extending help or withholding it. The responses in town and city are compared.

One factor in the purported unwillingness of urbanites to be helpful to strangers may well be their heightened sense of physical (and emotional) vulnerability—a feeling that is supported by urban crime statistics. A key test for distinguishing between city and town behavior, therefore, is determining how city dwellers compare with town dwellers in offering aid that increases their personal vulnerability and requires some trust of strangers. Altman, Levine, Nadien, and Villena *(8)* of the The City University of New York devised a study to compare the behaviors of city and town dwellers in this respect. The criterion used in this study was the willingness of householders to allow strangers to enter their home to use the telephone. The student investigators individually rang doorbells, explained that they had misplaced the address of a friend nearby, and asked to use the phone. The investigators (two males and two females) made 100 requests for entry into homes in the city and 60 requests in the small towns. The results for middle-income housing developments in Manhattan were compared with data for several small towns (Stony Point, Spring Valley, Ramapo, Nyack, New City, and West Clarkstown) in Rockland County, outside of New York City. As Table 17.1 shows, in all cases there was a sharp increase in the proportion of entries achieved by an experimenter when he moved from the city to a small town. In the most extreme case the experimenter was five times as likely to gain admission to homes in a small town as to homes in Manhattan. Although the female experimenters had notably greater success both in cities and in towns than the male experimenters had, each of the four students did at least twice as well in towns as in cities. This suggests that the city-town distinction overrides even the predictably greater fear of male strangers than of female ones.

The lower level of helpfulness by city dwellers seems due in part to recognition of the dangers of living in Manhattan, rather than to mere indifference or coldness. It is significant that 75 percent of all the city respondents received and answered messages by shouting through closed doors and by peering out through peepholes; in the towns, by contrast, about 75 percent of the respondents opened the door.

Supporting the experimenter's quantitative results was their general observation that the town dwellers were noticeably more friendly and less suspicious than the city dwellers. In seeking to explain the reasons for the greater sense of psychological vulnerability city dwellers feel, above and beyond the differences in crime statistics, Villena (*8*) points out that, if a crime is committed in a village, a resident of a neighboring village may not perceive the crime as personally relevant, though the geographic distance may be small, whereas a criminal act committed anywhere in the city, though miles from the city-dweller's home is still verbally located within the city; thus, Villena says, "the inhabitant of the city possesses a larger vulnerable space."

Civilities

Even at the most superficial level of involvement—the exercise of everyday civilities—urbanites are reputedly deficient. People bump into each other and often do not apologize. They knock over another person's packages and, as often as not, proceed on their way with a grumpy exclamation instead of an offer of assistance. Such behavior, which many visitors to great cities find distasteful, is less common, we are told, in smaller communities, where traditional courtesies are more likely to be observed.

In some instances it is not simply that, in the city, traditional courtesies are violated; rather, the cities develop new norms of non-involvement. These are so well defined and so deeply a part of city life that *they* constitute the norms people are reluctant to violate. Men are actually embarrassed to give up a seat on the subway to an old woman; they mumble "I was getting off anyway," instead of making the gesture in a straightforward and gracious way. These norms develop because everyone realizes that, in situations of high population density, people cannot implicate themselves in each others' affairs, for to do so would create conditions of continual distraction which would frustrate purposeful action.

In discussing the effects of overload I do not imply that at every instant the city dweller is bombarded with an unmanageable number of inputs, and that his responses are determined by the excess of input at any given instant. Rather, adaptation occurs in the form of gradual evolution of norms of behavior. Norms are evolved in response to frequent discrete experiences of overload; they persist and become generalized modes of responding.

Overload on Cognitive Capacities: Anonymity

That we respond differently toward those whom we know and those who are strangers to us is a truism. An eager patron aggressively cuts in front of someone in a long movie line to save time only to confront a friend; he then behaves sheepishly. A man is involved in an automobile accident caused by another driver, emerges from his car shouting in rage, then moderates his behavior on discovering a friend driving the other car. The city dweller, when walking through the midtown streets, is in a state of continual anonymity vis-à-vis the other pedestrians.

Anonymity is part of a continuous spectrum ranging from total anonymity to full acquaintance, and it may well be that measurement of the precise degrees of anonymity in cities and towns would help to explain important distinctions between the quality of life in each. Conditions of full acquaintance, for example, offer security and familiarity, but they may also be stifling, because the individual is caught in a web of established relationships. Conditions of complete anonymity, by contrast, provide freedom from routinized social ties, but they may also create feelings of alienation and detachment.

Empirically one could investigate the proportion of activities in which the city dweller or the town dweller is known by others at given times in his daily life, and the proportion of activities in the course of which he interacts with individuals who know him. At his job, for instance, the city dweller may be known to as many people as his rural counterpart. However, when he is not fulfilling his occupational role—say, when merely traveling about the city—the urbanite is doubtless more anonymous than his rural counterpart.

Limited empirical work on anonymity has begun. Zimbardo (*9*) has tested whether the social anonymity and impersonality of the big city encourage greater vandalism than do small towns. Zimbardo arranged for one automobile to be left for 64 hours near the Bronx campus of New York University and for a counterpart to be left for the same number of hours near Stanford University in Palo Alto. The license plates on the two cars were removed and the hoods were opened, to provide "releaser cues" for potential vandals. The New York car was stripped of all movable parts within the first 24 hours, and by the end of 3 days was only a hunk of metal rubble. Unexpectedly, however, most of the destruction occurred during daylight hours, usually under the scrutiny of observers, and the leaders in the vandalism were well-dressed, white adults. The Palo Alto car was left untouched.

Zimbardo attributes the difference in the treatment accorded the two cars to the "acquired feelings of social anonymity provided by life in a city like New York," and he supports his conclusions with several other anecdotes illustrating casual, wanton vandalism in the city. In any comparative study of the effects of anonymity in city and town, however, there must be satisfactory control for other confounding factors: the large number of drug addicts in a city like New York; the higher proportion of slum-dwellers in the city; and so on.

Another direction for empirical study is investigation of the beneficial effects of anonymity. The impersonality of city life breeds its own tolerance for the private lives of the inhabitants. Individuality and even eccentricity, we may assume, can flourish more readily in the metropolis than in the small town. Stigmatized persons may find it easier to lead comfortable lives in the city, free of the constant scrutiny of neighbors. To what degree can this assumed difference between city and town be shown empirically? Judith Waters (*10*), at The City University of New York, hypothesized that avowed homosexuals would be more likely to be accepted as tenants in a large city than in small towns, and she dispatched letters from homosexuals and from normal individuals to real estate agents in cities and towns across the country. The results of her study were inconclusive. But the general idea of examining the protective benefits of city life to the stigmatized ought to be pursued.

Role Behavior in Cities and Towns

Another product of urban overload is the adjustment in roles made by urbanites in daily interactions. As Wirth has said (*2*): "Urbanites meet one another in highly segmental roles. . . . They are less dependent upon particular persons, and their dependence upon others is confined to a highly fractionalized aspect of the

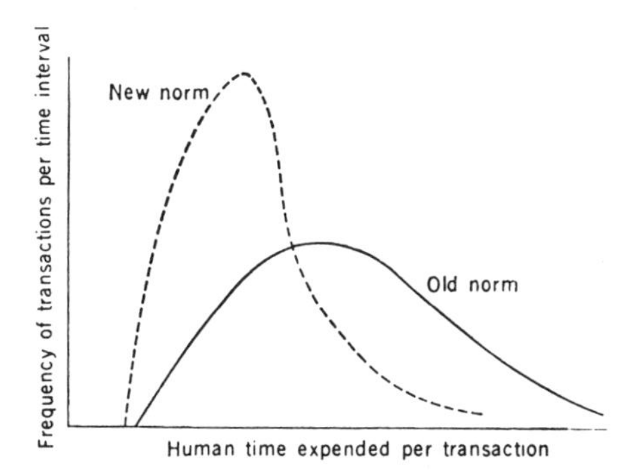

FIG. 17.1. Changes in the demand for time for a given task when the overall transaction frequency increases in a social system. [Reprinted with permission from R. L. Meier, *A Communications Theory of Urban Growth*, 1962. Copyrighted by M.I.T. Press, 1962]

other's round of activity." This tendency is particularly noticeable in transactions between customers and individuals offering professional or sales services. The owner of a country store has time to become well acquainted with his dozen-or-so daily customers, but the girl at the checkout counter of a busy A&P, serving hundreds of customers a day, barely has time to toss the green stamps into one customer's shopping bag before the next customer confronts her with his pile of groceries.

Meier, in his stimulating analysis of the city (*4*), discusses several adaptations a system may make when confronted by inputs that exceed its capacity to process them. Meier argues that, according to the principle of competition for scarce resources, the scope and time of the transaction shrink as customer volume and daily turnover rise. This, in fact, is what is meant by the "brusque" quality of city life. New standards have developed in cities concerning what levels of services are appropriate in business transactions (see Fig. 17.1).

McKenna and Morgenthau (*11*), in a seminar at The City University of New York, devised a study (i) to compare the willingness of city dwellers and small-town dwellers to do favors for strangers that entailed expenditure of a small amount of time and slight inconvenience but no personal vulnerability, and (ii) to determine whether the more compartmentalized, transitory relationships of the city would make urban salesgirls less likely than small-town salesgirls to carry out, for strangers, tasks not related to their customary roles.

To test for differences between city dwellers and small-town dwellers, a simple experiment was devised in which persons from both settings were asked (by telephone) to perform increasingly onerous favors for anonymous strangers.

Within the cities (Chicago, New York, and Philadelphia), half the calls were to housewives and the other half to salesgirls in women's apparel shops; the division was the same for the 37 small towns of the study, which were in the same states as the cities. Each experimenter represented herself as a long-distance caller who had, through error, been connected with the respondent by the operator. The experimenter began by asking for simple information about the weather for purposes of travel. Next the experimenter excused herself on some pretext (asking the respondent to "please hold on"), put the phone down for almost a full minute, and then picked it up again and asked the respondent to provide the phone number of a hotel or motel in her vicinity at which the experimenter might stay during a forthcoming visit. Scores were assigned the subjects on the basis of how helpful they had been. McKenna summarizes her results in this manner:

> People in the city, whether they are engaged in a specific job or not, are less helpful and informative than people in small towns; . . . People at home, regardless of where they live, are less helpful and informative than people working in shops.

However, the absolute level of cooperativeness for urban subjects was found to be quite high, and does not accord with the stereotype of the urbanite as aloof, self-centered, and unwilling to help strangers. The quantitative differences obtained by McKenna and Morgenthau are less great than one might have expected. This again points up the need for extensive empirical research in rural-urban differences, research that goes far beyond that provided in the few illustrative pilot studies presented here. At this point we have very limited objective evidence on differences in the quality of social encounters in city and small town.

But the research needs to be guided by unifying theoretical

concepts. As I have tried to demonstrate, the concept of overload helps to explain a wide variety of contrasts between city behavior and town behavior: (i) the differences in role enactment (the tendency of urban dwellers to deal with one another in highly segmented, functional terms, and of urban sales personnel to devote limited time and attention to their customers); (ii) the evolution of urban norms quite different from traditional town values (such as the acceptance of noninvolvement, impersonality, and aloofness in urban life); (iii) the adaptation of the urban dweller's cognitive processes (his inability to identify most of the people he sees daily, his screening of sensory stimuli, his development of blasé attitudes toward deviant or bizarre behavior, and his selectivity in responding to human demands); and (iv) the competition for scarce facilities in the city (the subway rush; the fight for taxis; traffic jams; standing in line to await services). I suggest that contrasts between city and rural behavior probably reflect the responses of similar people to very different situations, rather than intrinsic differences in the personalities of rural and city dwellers. The city is a situation to which individuals respond adaptively.

FURTHER ASPECTS OF URBAN EXPERIENCE

Some features of urban experience do not fit neatly into the system of analysis presented thus far. They are no less important for that reason. The issues raised next are difficult to treat in quantitative fashion. Yet I prefer discussing them in a loose way to excluding them because appropriate language and data have not yet been developed. My aim is to suggest how phenomena such as "urban atmosphere" can be pinned down through techniques of measurement.

The "Atmosphere" of Great Cities

The contrast in the behavior of city and town dwellers has been a natural starting point for urban social scientists. But even among great cities there are marked differences in "atmosphere." The tone, pacing, and texture of social encounters are different in

London and New York, and many persons willingly make financial sacrifices for the privilege of living within a specific urban atmosphere which they find pleasing or stimulating. A second perspective in the study of cities, therefore, is to define exactly what is meant by the atmosphere of a city and to pinpoint the factors that give rise to it. It may seem that urban atmosphere is too evanescent a quality to be reduced to a set of measurable variables, but I do not believe the matter can be judged before substantial effort has been made in this direction. It is obvious that any such approach must be comparative. It makes no sense at all to say that New York is "vibrant" and "frenetic" unless one has some specific city in mind as a basis of comparison.

In an undergraduate tutorial that I conducted at Harvard University some years ago, New York, London, and Paris were selected as reference points for attempts to measure urban atmosphere. We began with a simple question: Does any consensus exist about the qualities that typify given cities? To answer this question one could undertake a content analysis of travelbook, literary, and journalistic accounts of cities. A second approach, which we adopted, is to ask people to characterize (with descriptive terms and accounts of typical experiences) cities they have lived in or visited. In advertisements placed in the *New York Times* and the *Harvard Crimson* we asked people to give us accounts of specific incidents in London, Paris, or New York that best illuminated the character of that particular city. Questionnaires were then developed, and administered to persons who were familiar with at least two of the three cities.

Some distinctive patterns emerged (*12*). The distinguishing themes concerning New York, for example, dealt with its diversity, its great size, its pace and level of activity, its cultural and entertainment opportunities, and the heterogeneity and segmentation ("ghettoization") of its population. New York elicited more descriptions in terms of physical qualities, pace, and emotional impact than Paris or London did, a fact which suggests that these are particularly important aspects of New York's ambiance.

A constrasting profile emerges for London; in this case respondents placed far greater emphasis on their interactions with the inhabitants than on physical surroundings. There was near unanimity on certain themes: those dealing with the tolerance and courtesy of London's inhabitants. One respondent said:

> When I was 12, my grandfather took me to the British Museum . . . one day by tube and recited the *Aeneid* in Latin for my benefit. . . . He is rather deaf, speaks very loudly and it embarrassed the hell out of me, until I realized that nobody was paying any attention. Londoners are extremely worldly and tolerant.

In contrast, respondents who described New Yorkers as aloof, cold, and rude referred to such incidents as the following:

> I saw a boy of 19 passing out anti-war leaflets to passersby. When he stopped at a corner, a man dressed in a business suit walked by him at a brisk pace, hit the boy's arm, and scattered the leaflets all over the street. The man kept walking at the same pace down the block.

We need to obtain many more such descriptions of incidents, using careful methods of sampling. By the application of factor-analytic techniques, relevant dimensions for each city can be discerned.

The responses for Paris were about equally divided between responses concerning its inhabitants and those regarding its physical and sensory attributes. Cafés and parks were often mentioned as contributing to the sense that Paris is a city of amenities, but many respondents complained that Parisians were inhospitable, nasty, and cold.

We cannot be certain, of course, to what degree these statements reflect actual characteristics of the cities in question and to what degree they simply tap the respondents' knowledge of widely held preconceptions. Indeed, one may point to three factors, apart from the actual atmospheres of the cities, that determine the subjects' responses.

1) A person's impression of a given city depends on his implicit standard of comparison. A New Yorker who visits Paris may well describe that city as "leisurely," whereas a compatriot from Richmond, Virginia, may consider Paris too "hectic." Obtaining reciprocal judgment, in which New Yorkers judge Londoners, and Londoners judge New Yorkers, seems a useful way to take into account not only the city being judged but also the home city that serves as the visitor's base line.

2) Perceptions of a city are also affected by whether the ob-

server is a tourist, a newcomer, or a longer-term resident. First, a tourist will be exposed to features of the city different from those familiar to a long-time resident. Second, a prerequisite for adapting to continuing life in a given city seems to be the filtering out of many observations about the city that the newcomer or tourist finds particularly arresting; this selective process seems to be part of the long-term resident's mechanism for coping with overload. In the interest of psychic economy, the resident simply learns to tune out many aspects of daily life. One method for studying the specific impact of adaptation on perception of the city is to ask several pairs of newscomers and old-timers (one newcomer and one old-timer to a pair) to walk down certain city blocks and then report separately what each has observed.

Additionally, many persons have noted that when travelers return to New York from an extended sojourn abroad they often feel themselves confronted with "brutal ugliness" (*13*) and a distinctive, frenetic atmosphere whose contributing details are, for a few hours or days, remarkably sharp and clear. This period of fresh perception should receive special attention in the study of city atmosphere. For, in a few days, details which are initially arresting become less easy to specify. They are assimilated into an increasingly familiar background atmosphere which, though important in setting the tone of things, is difficult to analyze. There is no better point at which to begin the study of city atmosphere than at the moment when a traveler returns from abroad.

3) The popular myths and expectations each visitor brings to the city will also affect the way in which he perceives it (see *14*). Sometimes a person's preconceptions about a city are relatively accurate distillations of its character, but preconceptions may also reinforce myths by filtering the visitor's perceptions to conform with his expectations. Preconceptions affect not only a person's perceptions of a city but what he reports about it.

The influence of a person's urban base line on his perceptions of a given city, the differences between the observations of the long-time inhabitant and those of the newcomer, and the filtering effect of personal expectations and stereotypes raise serious questions about the validity of travelers' reports. Moreover, no social psychologist wants to rely exclusively on verbal accounts if he is attempting to obtain an accurate and objective description of the cities' social texture, pace, and general atmosphere. What he needs to do is to devise means of embedding objective experimental measures in the daily flux of city life, measures that can accurately index the qualities of a given urban atmosphere.

EXPERIMENTAL COMPARISONS OF BEHAVIOR

Roy Feldman (*15*) incorporated these principles in a comparative study of behavior toward compatriots and foreigners in Paris, Athens, and Boston. Feldman wanted to see (i) whether absolute levels and patterns of helpfulness varied significantly from city to city, and (ii) whether inhabitants in each city tended to treat compatriots differently from foreigners. He examined five concrete behavioral episodes, each carried out by a team of native experimenters and a team of American experimenters in the three cities. The episodes involved (i) asking natives of the city for street directions; (ii) asking natives to mail a letter for the experimenter; (iii) asking natives if they had just dropped a dollar bill (or the Greek or French equivalent) when the money actually belonged to the experimenter himself; (iv) deliberately overpaying for goods in a store to see if the cashier would correct the mistake and return the excess money; and (v) determining whether taxicab drivers overcharged strangers and whether they took the most direct route available.

Feldman's results suggest some interesting contrasts in the profiles of the three cities. In Paris, for instance, certain stereotypes were borne out. Parisian cab drivers overcharged foreigners significantly more often than they overcharged compatriots. But other aspects of the Parisians' behavior were not in accord with American preconceptions: in mailing a letter for a stranger, Parisians treated foreigners significantly better than Athenians or Bostonians did, and, when asked to mail letters that were already stamped, Parisians actually treated foreigners better than they treated compatriots. Similarly, Parisians were significantly more honest than Athenians or Bostonians in resisting the temptation to claim money that was not theirs, and Parisians were the only citizens who were more honest with foreigners than with compatriots in this experiment.

Feldman's studies not only begin to quantify some of the variables that give a city its distinctive texture but they also provide a methodological model for other comparative research. His most important contribution is his successful application of objective, experimental measures to everyday situations, a mode of study which provides conclusions about urban life that are more pertinent than those achieved through laboratory experiments.

TEMPO AND PACE

Another important component of a city's atmosphere is its tempo or pace, an attribute frequently remarked on but less often studied. Does a city have a frenetic, hectic quality, or is it easygoing and leisurely? In any empirical treatment of this question, it is best to start in a very simple way. Walking speeds of pedestrians in different cities and in cities and towns should be measured and compared. William Berkowitz (*16*) of Lafayette College has undertaken an extensive series of studies of walking speeds in Philadelphia, New York, and Boston, as well as in small and moderate-sized towns. Berkowitz writes that "there does appear to be a significant linear relation between walking speed and size of municipality, but the absolute size of the difference varies by less than ten percent."

Perhaps the feeling of rapid tempo is due not so much to absolute pedestrian speeds as to the constant need to dodge others in a large city to avoid collisions with other pedestrians. (One basis for computing the adjustments needed to avoid collisions is to hypothesize a set of mechanical manikins sent walking along a city street and to calculate the number of collisions when no adjustments are made. Clearly, the higher the density of manikins the greater the number of collisions per unit of time, or, conversely, the greater the frequency of adjustments needed in higher population densities to avoid collisions.)

Patterns of automobile traffic contribute to a city's tempo. Driving an automobile provides a direct means of translating feelings about tempo into measurable acceleration, and a city's pace should be particularly evident in vehicular velocities, patterns of acceleration, and latency of response to traffic signals. The inexorable tempo of New York is expressed, further, in the manner in which pedestrians stand at busy intersections, impatiently awaiting a change in traffic light, making tentative excursions into the intersection, and frequently surging into the street even before the green light appears.

VISUAL COMPONENTS

Hall has remarked (*17*) that the physical layout of the city also affects its atmosphere. A gridiron pattern of streets gives the visitor a feeling of rationality, orderliness, and predictability but is sometimes monotonous. Winding lanes or streets branching off at strange angles, with many forks (as in Paris or Greenwich Village), create feelings of surprise and esthetic pleasure, while forcing greater decision-making in plotting one's course. Some would argue that the visual component is all-important—that the "look" of Paris or New York can almost be equated with its atmosphere. To investigate this hypothesis, we might conduct studies in which only blind, or at least blindfolded, respondents were used. We would no doubt discover that each city has a distinctive texture even when the visual component is eliminated.

SOURCES OF AMBIANCE

Thus far we have tried to pinpoint and measure some of the factors that contribute to the distinctive atmosphere of a great city. But we may also ask, Why do differences in urban atmosphere exist? How did they come about, and are they in any way related to the factors of density, large numbers, and heterogeneity discussed above?

First, there is the obvious factor that, even among great cities, populations and densities differ. The metropolitan areas of New York, London, and Paris, for example, contain 15 million, 12 million, and 8 million persons, respectively. London has average densities of 43 persons per acre, while Paris is more congested, with average densities of 114 persons per acre (*18*). Whatever characteristics are specificlly attributable to density are more likely to be pronounced in Paris than in London.

A second factor affecting the atmosphere of cities is the source from which the populations are drawn (*19*). It is a characteristic of great cities that they do not reproduce their own populations, but that their numbers are constantly maintained and augmented by the influx of residents from other parts of the country. This can have a determining effect on the city's atmosphere. For example, Oslo is a city in which almost all of the residents are only one or two generations removed from a purely rural existence, and this contributes to its almost agricultural norms.

A third source of atmosphere is the general national culture. Paris combines adaptations to the demography of cities *and* certain values specific to French culture. New York is an admixture of American values and values tha arise as a result of extraordinarily high density and large population.

Finally, one could speculate that the atmosphere of a great city is traceable to the specific historical conditions under which adaptations to urban overload occurred. For example, a city which acquired its mass and density during a period of commercial expansion will respond to new demographic conditions by adaptations designed to serve purely commercial needs. Thus, Chicago, which grew and became a great city under a purely commercial stimulus, adapted in a manner that emphasizes business needs. European capitals, on the other hand, incorporate many of the adaptations which were appropriate to the period of their increasing numbers and density. Because aristocratic values were prevalent at the time of the growth of these cities, the mechanisms developed for coping with overload were based on considerations other than pure efficiency. Thus, the manners, norms, and facilities of Paris and Vienna continue to reflect esthetic values and the idealization of leisure.

COGNITIVE MAPS OF CITIES

When we speak of "behavioral comparisons" among cities, we must specify which parts of the city are most relevant for sampling purposes. In a sampling of "New Yorkers," should we include residents of Bay Ridge or Flatbush as well as inhabitants of Manhattan? And, if so, how should we weight our sample distribution?

One approach to defining relevant boundaries in sampling is to determine which areas form the psychological or cognitive core of the city. We weight our samples most heavily in the areas considered by most people to represent the "essence" of the city.

The psychologist is less interested in the geographic layout of a city or in its political boundaries than in the cognitive representation of the city. Hans Blumenfeld (*20*) points out that the perceptual structure of a modern city can be expressed by the "silhouette" of the group of skyscrapers at its center and that of smaller groups of office buildings at is "subcenters" but that urban areas can no longer, because of their vast extent, be experienced as fully articulated sets of streets, squares, and space.

In *The Image of the City* (*21*), Kevin Lynch created a cognitive map of Boston by interviewing Bostonians. Perhaps his most significant finding was that, while certain landmarks, such as Paul Revere's house and the Boston Common, as well as the paths linking them, are known to almost all Bostonians, vast areas of the city are simply unknown to its inhabitants.

Using Lynch's technique, Donald Hooper (*22*) created a psychological map of New York from the answers to the study questionnaire on Paris, London, and New York. Hooper's results were similar to those of Lynch: New York appears to have a dense core of well-known landmarks in midtown Manhattan, surrounded by the vast unknown reaches of Queens, Brooklyn, and the Bronx. Times Square, Rockefeller Center, and the Fifth Avenue department stores alone comprise half the places specifically cited by respondents as the haunts in which they spent most of their time. However, outside the midtown area, only scattered landmarks were recognized. Another interesting pattern is evident: even the best-known symbols of New York are relatively self-contained, and the pathways joining them appear to be insignificant on the map.

The psychological map can be used for more than just sampling techniques. Lynch (*21*) argues, for instance, that a good city is highly "imageable," having many known symbols joined by widely known pathways, whereas dull cities are gray and nondescript. We might test the relative "imagibility" of several cities by determining the proportion of residents who recognize sampled geographic points and their accompanying pathways.

If we wanted to be even more precise we could construct a

cognitive map that would not only show the symbols of the city but would measure the precise degree of cognitive significance of any given point in the city relative to any other. By applying a pattern of points to a map of New York City, for example, and taking photographs from each point, we could determine what proportion of a sample of the city's inhabitants could identify the locale specified by each point (see Fig. 17.2). We might even take the subjects blindfolded to a point represented on the map, then remove the blindfold and ask them to identify their location from the view around them.

One might also use psychological maps to gain insight into the differing perceptions of a given city that are held by members of its cultural subgroups, and into the manner in which their perceptions may change. In the earlier stages of life, whites and Negroes alike probably have only a limited view of the city, centering on the immediate neighborhood in which they are raised. In adolescence, however, the field of knowledge of the white teen-ager probably undergoes rapid enlargement; he learns of opportunities in midtown and outlying sections and comes to see himself as functioning in a larger urban field. But the process of ghettoization, to which the black teen-ager is subjected, may well hamper the expansion of his sense of the city. These are speculative notions, but they are readily subject to precise test.

CONCLUSION

I have tried to indicate some organizing theory that starts with the basic facts of city life: large numbers, density, and heterogeneity. These are external to the individual. He experiences these factors as overloads at the level of roles, norms, cognitive functions, and facilities. These overloads lead to adaptive mechanisms which create the distinctive tone and behaviors of city life. These notions, of course, need to be examined by objective comparative studies of cities and towns.

A second perspective concerns the differing atmospheres of great cities, such as Paris, London, and New York. Each has a distinctive flavor, offering a differentiable quality of experience. More precise knowledge of urban atmosphere seems attainable through application of the tools of experimental inquiry.

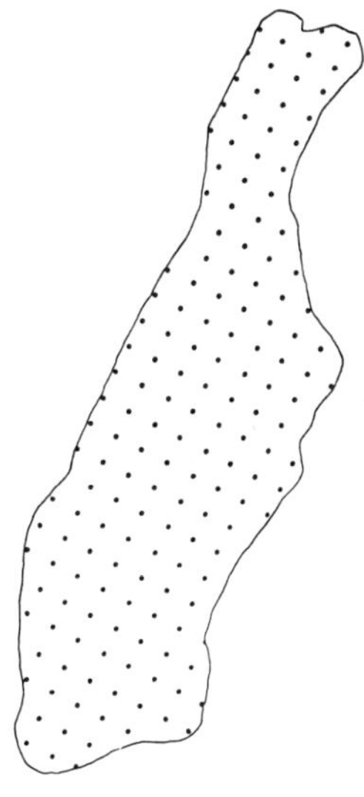

FIG. 17. 2. To create a psychological map of Manhattan, geographic points are sampled, and, from photographs, the subjects attempt to identify the location of each point. To each point a numerical index is assigned indicating the proportion of persons able to identify its location.

REFERENCES AND NOTES

1. *New York Times* (15 June 1969).
2. L. WIRTH, *Amer. J. Soc. 44,* 1 (1938). Wirth's ideas have come under heavy criticism by contemporary city planners, who point out that the city is broken down into neighborhoods, which fulfill many of the functions of small towns. See, for example, H. J. Gans, *People and*

Plans: Essays on Urban Problems and Solutions (Basic Books, New York, 1968); J. Jacobs, *The Death and Life of Great American Cities* (Random House, New York, 1961); G. D. Suttles, *The Social Order of the Slum* (Univ. of Chicago Press, Chicago, 1968).

3. G. SIMMEL, *The Sociology of Georg Simmel,* K. H. Wolff, Ed. (Macmillan, New York, 1950) [English translation of G. Simmel, *Die Grossstadte und das Geistesleben Die Grossstadt* (Jansch, Dresden, 1903)].
4. R. L. MEIER, *A Communications Theory of Urban Growth* (M.I.T. Press, Cambridge, Mass., 1962).
5. S. MILGRAM and P. HOLLANDER, *Nation 25,* 602 (1964).
6. B. LATANÉ and J. DARLEY, *Amer. Sci. 57,* 244 (1969).
7. S. GAERTNER and L. BICKMAN (Graduate Center, The City University of New York), unpublished research.
8. D. ALTMAN, M. LEVINE, M. NADIEN, J. VILLENA (Graduate Center, The City University of New York), unpublished research.
9. P. G. ZIMBARDO, paper presented at the Nebraska Symposium on Motivation (1969).
10. J. WATERS (Graduate Center, The City University of New York), unpublished research.
11. W. MCKENNA and S. MORGANTHAU (Graduate Center, The City University of New York), unpublished research.
12. N. ABUZA (Harvard University), "The Paris-London-New York Questionnaires," unpublished.
13. P. ABELSON, *Science 165,* 853 (1969).
14. A. L. STRAUSS, Ed., *The American City: A Sourcebook of Urban Imagery* (Aldine, Chicago, 1968).
15. R. E. FELDMAN, *J. Personality Soc. Psychol. 10,* 202 (1968).
16. W. BERKOWITZ, personal communication.
17. E. T. HALL, *The Hidden Dimension* (Doubleday, New York, 1966).
18. P. HALL, *The World Cities* (McGraw-Hill, New York, 1966).
19. R. E. PARK, E. W. BURGESS, R. D. MCKENZIE, *The City* (Univ. of Chicago Press, Chicago, 1967), pp. 1–45.
20. H. BLUMENFELD, in *The Quality of Urban Life* (Sage, Beverly Hills, Calif., 1969).
21. K. LYNCH, *The Image of the City* (M.I.T. and Harvard Univ. Press, Cambridge, Mass., 1960).
22. D. HOOPER (Harvard University), unpublished.
23. BARBARA BENGEN worked closely with me in preparing the present version of this article. I thank Dr. Gary Winkel, editor of *Environment and Behavior,* for useful suggestions and advice.

IX
Intergroup Relations

To understand the nature of unfavorable intergroup relations, Sherif and his coworkers (Chapter 18) applied the techniques of a controlled laboratory experiment to a natural setting. Two groups of teen-age boys were formed at a camp; each group was introduced independently to situations which produced a distinct organization and a set of norms. Subsequent competitive and frustrating conditions induced by the investigators caused the members of each group to develop derogatory stereotypes and negative attitudes toward the other group. Although the introduction of pleasant social contacts was ineffective in reducing intergroup conflict, the imposition of *superordinate* goals, which were compellingly shared by all and which required cooperative behavior, was successful in reducing intergroup tension.

When the conflict between the two experimentally created groups in Sherif's experiment was intense, the members of each group indicated almost exclusive intragroup friendship preferences. After the cooperative efforts to achieve superordinate goals, choices of out-group members increased significantly. Similarly, the variety of relationships among members of ethnic and racial groups should lead to differential preferences. Rokeach and Mezei (Chapter 19) hypothesized that where external pressures to discriminate are slight or absent, differences in belief on important issues are greater causes of prejudice or discrimination than racial and ethnic differences. In two on-campus laboratory experiments it was found that belief similarity was a more frequent basis of choice than belief dissimilarity and that belief similarity was a more frequent basis of choice than race similarity. These findings received strong support from an off-campus experiment conducted as part of an employment interview procedure.

18

Superordinate Goals in the Reduction of Intergroup Conflict

Muzafer Sherif

In the past, measures to combat the problems of intergroup conflicts, proposed by social scientists as well as by such people as administrators, policy-makers, municipal officials, and educators, have included the following: introduction of legal sanctions; creation of opportunities for social and other contacts among members of conflicting groups; dissemination of correct information to break down false prejudices and unfavorable stereotypes; appeals to the moral ideals of fair play and brotherhood; and even the introduction of rigorous physical activity to produce catharsis by releasing pent-up frustrations and aggressive complexes in the unconscious. Other measures proposed include the encouragement of co-operative habits in one's own community, and bringing together in the cozy atmosphere of a meeting room the leaders of antagonistic groups.

Many of these measures may have some value in the reduction of intergroup conflicts, but, to date, very few generalizations have been established concerning the circumstances and kinds of intergroup conflict in which these measures are effective. Today measures are applied in a somewhat trial-and-error fashion. Finding measures that have wide validity in practice can come only through clarification of the nature of intergroup conflict and analysis of the factors conducive to harmony and conflict between groups under given conditions.

The task of defining and analyzing the nature of the problem was undertaken in a previous publication.[1] One of our major statements was the effectiveness of superordinate goals for the reduction of intergroup conflict. "Superordinate goals" we defined as goals which are compelling and highly appealing to members of two or more groups in conflict but which cannot be attained by the resources and energies of the groups separately. In effect, they are goals attained only when groups pull together.

INTERGROUP RELATIONS AND THE BEHAVIOR OF GROUP MEMBERS

Not every friendly or unfriendly act toward another person is related to the group membership of the individuals involved. Accordingly, we must select those actions relevant to relations between groups.

Let us start by defining the main concepts involved. Obviously, we must begin with an adequate conception of the key term —"group." A group is a social unit (1) which consists of a number of individuals who, at a given time, stand in more or less definite interdependent status and role relationships with one another and (2) which explicitly or implicitly possesses a set of values or norms

[1] Muzafer Sherif and Carolyn W. Sherif, *Groups in Harmony and Tension* (New York: Harper & Bros., 1953).

regulating the behavior of individual members, at least in matters of consequence to the group. Thus, shared attitudes, sentiments, aspirations, and goals are related to and implicit in the common values or norms of the group.

The term "intergroup relations" refers to the relations between two or more groups and their respective members. In the present context we are interested in the acts that occur when individuals belonging to one group interact, collectively or individually, with members of another in terms of their group identification. The appropriate frame of reference for studying such behavior includes the functional relations between the groups. Intergroup situations are not voids. Though not independent of relationships within the groups in question, *the characteristics of relations between groups cannot be deduced or extrapolated from the properties of in-group relations.*

Prevalent modes of behavior within a group, in the way of cooperativeness and solidarity or competitiveness and rivalry among members, need not be typical of actions involving members of an out-group. At times, hostility toward out-groups may be proportional to the degree of solidarity within the group. In this connection, results presented by the British statistician L. F. Richardson are instructive. His analysis of the number of wars conducted by the major nations of the world from 1850 to 1941 reveals that Great Britain heads the list with twenty wars—more than the Japanese (nine wars), the Germans (eight wars), or the United States (seven wars). We think that this significantly larger number of wars engaged in by a leading European democracy has more to do with the intergroup relations involved in perpetuating a far-flung empire than with dominant practices at home or with personal frustrations of individual Britishers who participated in these wars.[2]

In recent years relationships between groups have sometimes been explained through analysis of individuals who have endured unusual degrees of frustration or extensive authoritarian treatment in their life-histories. There is good reason to believe that some people growing up in unfortunate life-circumstances may become

[2] T. H. Pear, *Psychological Factors of Peace and War* (New York: Philosophical Library, 1950), p. 126.

more intense in their prejudices and hostilities. But at best these cases explain the intensity of behavior in a given dimension.[3] In a conflict between two groups—a strike or a war—opinion within the groups is crystallized, slogans are formulated, and effective measures are organized by members recognized as the most responsible in their respective groups. The prejudice scale and the slogans are not usually imposed on the others by the deviate or neurotic members. Such individuals ordinarily exhibit their intense reactions within the reference scales of prejudice, hostility, or sacrifice established in their respective settings.

The behavior by members of any group toward another group is not primarily a problem of deviate behavior. If it were, intergroup behavior would not be the issue of vital consequence that it is today. The crux of the problem is the participation by group members in established practices and social-distance norms of their group and their response to new trends developing in relationships between their own group and other groups.

On the basis of his UNESCO studies in India, Gardner Murphy concludes that to be a good Hindu or a good Moslem implies belief in all the nasty qualities and practices attributed by one's own group—Hindu or Moslem—to the other. Good members remain deaf and dumb to favorable information concerning the adversary. Social contacts and avenues of communication serve, on the whole, as vehicles for further conflicts not merely for neurotic individuals but for the bulk of the membership.[4]

In the process of interaction among members, an in-group is endowed with positive qualities which tend to be praiseworthy, self-justifying, and even self-glorifying. Individual members tend to develop these qualities through internalizing group norms and through example by high-status members, verbal dicta, and a set of correctives standardized to deal with cases of deviation. Hence, possession of these qualities, which reflect their particular brand of ethnocentrism, is not essentially a problem of deviation or personal frustration. It is a question of participation in in-group values and trends by good members, who constitute the majority of

[3] William R. Hood and Muzafer Sherif, "Personality Oriented Approaches to Prejudice," *Sociology and Social Research,* XL (1955), 79–85.

[4] Gardner Murphy, *In the Minds of Men* (New York: Basic Books, 1953).

membership as long as group solidarity and morale are maintained.

To out-groups and their respective members are attributed positive or negative qualities, depending on the nature of functional relations between the groups in question. The character of functional relations between groups may result from actual harmony and interdependence or from actual incompatibility between the aspirations and directions of the groups. A number of field studies and experiments indicate that, if the functional relations between groups are positive, favorable attitudes are formed toward the out-group. If the functional relations between groups are negative, they give rise to hostile attitudes and unfavorable stereotypes in relation to the out-group. Of course, in large-group units the picture of the out-group and relations with it depend very heavily on communication, particularly from the mass media.

Examples of these processes are recurrent in studies of small groups. For example, when a gang "appropriates" certain blocks in a city, it is considered "indecent" and a violation of its "rights" for another group to carry on its feats in that area. Intrusion by another group is conducive to conflict, at times with grim consequences, as Thrasher showed over three decades ago.[5]

When a workers' group declares a strike, existing group lines are drawn more sharply. Those who are not actually for the strike are regarded as against it. There is no creature more lowly than the man who works while the strike is on.[6] The same type of behavior is found in management groups under similar circumstances.

In time, the adjectives attributed to out-groups take their places in the repertory of group norms. The lasting, derogatory stereotypes attributed to groups low on the social-distance scale are particular cases of group norms pertaining to out-groups.

As studies by Bogardus show, the social-distance scale of a group, once established, continues over generations, despite changes of constituent individuals, who can hardly be said to have prejudices because of the same severe personal frustrations or authoritarian treatment.[7]

[5] F. M. Thrasher, *The Gang* (Chicago: University of Chicago Press, 1927).

[6] E. T. Hiller, *The Strike* (Chicago: University of Chicago Press, 1928).

[7] E. S. Bogardus, "Changes in Racial Distances," *International Journal of Opinion and Attitude Research,* I (1947), 55–62.

Literature on the formation of prejudice by growing children shows that it is not even necessary for the individual to have actual unfavorable experiences with out-groups to form attitudes of prejudice toward them. In the very process of becoming an in-group member, the intergroup delineations and corresponding norms prevailing in the group are internalized by the individual.[8]

A RESEARCH PROGRAM

A program of research has been under way since 1948 to test experimentally some hypotheses derived from the literature of intergroup relations. The first large-scale intergroup experiment was carried out in 1949, the second in 1953, and the third in 1954.[9] The conclusions reported here briefly are based on the 1949 and 1954 experiments and on a series of laboratory studies carried out as co-ordinate parts of the program.[10]

The methodology, techniques, and criteria for subject selection in the experiments must be summarized here very briefly. The experiments were carried out in successive stages: (1) groups were formed experimentally; (2) tension and conflict were produced between these groups by introducing conditions conducive to competitive and reciprocally frustrating relations between them; and

[8] E. L. Horowitz, "'Race Attitudes,'" in Otto Klineberg (ed.), *Characteristics of the American Negro,* Part IV (New York: Harper & Bros., 1944).

[9] The experimental work in 1949 was jointly supported by the Yale Attitude Change Project and the American Jewish Committee. It is summarized in Sherif and Sherif, *op. cit.,* chaps. ix and x. Both the writing of that book and the experiments in 1953–54 were made possible by a grant from the Rockefeller Foundation. The 1953 research is summarized in Muzafer Sherif, B. Jack White, and O. J. Harvey, "Status in Experimentally Produced Groups," *American Journal of Sociology,* LX (1955), 370–79. The 1954 experiment was summarized in Muzafer Sherif, O. J. Harvey, B. Jack White, William R. Hood, and Carolyn W. Sherif, "Experimental Study of Positive and Negative Intergroup Attitudes between Experimentally Produced Groups: Robbers Cave Study" (Norman, Okla.: University of Oklahoma, 1954). (Multilithed.) For a summary of the three experiments see chaps. vi and ix in Muzafer Sherif and Carolyn W. Sherif, *An Outline of Social Psychology* (rev. ed.; New York: Harper & Bros., 1956).

[10] For an overview of this program see Muzafer Sherif, "Integrating Field Work and Laboratory in Small Group Research," *American Sociological Review,* XIX (1954), 759–71.

(3) the attempt was made toward reduction of the intergroup conflict. This stage of reducing tension through introduction of superordinate goals was attempted in the 1954 study on the basis of lessons learned in the two previous studies.

At every stage the subjects interacted in activities which appeared natural to them at a specially arranged camp site completely under our experimental control. They were not aware of the fact that their behavior was under observation. No observation or recording was made in the subjects' presence in a way likely to arouse the suspicion that they were being observed. There is empirical and experimental evidence contrary to the contention that individuals cease to be mindful when they know they are being observed and that their words are being recorded.[11]

In order to insure validity of conclusions, results obtained through observational methods were cross-checked with results obtained through sociometric technique, stereotype ratings of in-groups and out-groups, and through data obtained by techniques adapted from the laboratory. Unfortunately, these procedures cannot be elaborated here. The conclusions summarized briefly are based on results crosschecked by two or more techniques.

The production of groups, the production of conflict between them, and the reduction of conflict in successive stages were brought about through the introduction of problem situations that were real and could not be ignored by individuals in the situation. Special "lecture methods" or "discussion methods" were not used. For example, the problem of getting a meal through their own initiative and planning was introduced when participating individuals were hungry.

Facing a problem situation which is immediate and compelling and which embodies a goal that cannot be ignored, group members *do* initiate discussion and *do* plan and carry through these plans until the objective is achieved. In this process the discussion becomes *their* discussion, the plan *their* plan, the action *their* action. In this process discussion, planning, and action have their place, and, when occasion arises, lecture or information has

[11] E.g., see F. B. Miller, "'Resistentialism' in Applied Social Research," *Human Organization,* XII (1954), 5–8; S. Wapner and T. G. Alper, "The Effect of an Audience on Behavior in a Choice Situation," *Journal of Abnormal and Social Psychology,* XLVII (1952), 222–29.

its place, too. The sequence of these related activities need not be the same in all cases.

The subjects were selected by rigorous criteria. They were healthy, normal boys around the age of eleven and twelve, socially well adjusted in school and neighborhood, and academically successful. They came from a homogeneous sociocultural background and from settled, well-adjusted families of middle or lower-middle class and Protestant affiliations. No subject came from a broken home. The mean I.Q. was above average. The subjects were not personally acquainted with one another prior to the experiment. Thus, explanation of results on the basis of background differences, social maladjustment, undue childhood frustrations, or previous interpersonal relations was ruled out at the beginning by the criteria for selecting subjects.

The first stage of the experiments was designed to produce groups with distinct structure (organization) and a set of norms which could be confronted with intergroup problems. The method for producing groups from unacquainted individuals with similar background was to introduce problem situations in which the attainment of the goal depended on the co-ordinated activity of all individuals. After a series of such activities, definite group structures or organizations developed.

The results warrant the following conclusions for the stage of group formation: When individuals interact in a series of situations toward goals which appeal to all and which require that they co-ordinate their activities, group structures arise having hierarchical status arrangements and a set of norms regulating behavior in matters of consequence to the activities of the group.

Once we had groups that satisfied our definition of "group," relations between groups could be studied. Specified conditions conducive to friction or conflict between groups were introduced. This negative aspect was deliberately undertaken because the major problem in intergroup relations today is the reduction of existing intergroup frictions. (Increasingly, friendly relations between groups is not nearly so great an issue.) The factors conducive to intergroup conflict give us realistic leads for reducing conflict.

A series of situations was introduced in which one group could achieve its goal only at the expense of the other group—through a tournament of competitive events with desirable prizes for the winning group. The results of the stage of intergroup conflict supported our main hypotheses. During interaction between groups in experimentally introduced activities which were competitive and mutually frustrating, members of each group developed hostile attitudes and highly unfavorable stereotypes toward the other group and its members. In fact, attitudes of social distance between the groups became so definite that they wanted to have nothing further to do with each other. This we take as a case of experimentally produced "social distance" in miniature. Conflict was manifested in derogatory name-calling and invectives, flare-ups of physical conflict, and raids on each other's cabins and territory. Over a period of time, negative sterotypes and unfavorable attitudes developed.

At the same time there was an increase in in-group solidarity and co-operativeness. This finding indicates that co-operation and democracy within groups do not necessarily lead to democracy and co-operation with out-groups, if the directions and interests of the groups are conflicting.

Increased solidarity forged in hostile encounters, in rallies from defeat, and in victories over the out-group is one instance of a more general finding: Intergroup relations, both conflicting and harmonious, *affected the nature of relations within the groups involved.* Altered relations between groups produced significant changes in the status arrangements *within* groups, in some instances resulting in shifts at the upper status levels or even a change in leadership. Always, consequential intergroup relations were reflected in new group values or norms which signified changes in practice, word, and deed within the group. Counterparts of this finding are not difficult to see in actual and consequential human relations. Probably many of our major preoccupations, anxieties, and activities in the past decade are incomprehensible without reference to the problems created by the prevailing "cold war" on an international scale.

REDUCTION OF INTERGROUP FRICTION

A number of the measures proposed today for reducing intergroup friction could have been tried in this third stage. A few will be mentioned here, with a brief explanation of why they were discarded or were included in our experimental design.

1. Disseminating favorable information in regard to the out-group was not included. Information that is not related to the goals currently in focus in the activities of groups is relatively ineffective, as many studies on attitude change have shown.[12]

2. In small groups it is possible to devise sufficiently attractive rewards to make individual achievement supreme. This may reduce tension between groups by splitting the membership on an "every-man-for-himself" basis. However, this measure has little relevance for actual intergroup tensions, which are in terms of group membership and group alignments.

3. The resolution of conflict through leaders alone was not utilized. Even when group leaders meet apart from their groups around a conference table, they cannot be considered independent of the dominant trends and prevailing attitudes of their membership. If a leader is too much out of step in his negotiations and agreements with out-groups, he will cease to be followed. It seemed more realistic, therefore, to study the influence of leadership within the framework of prevailing trends in the groups involved. Such results will give us leads concerning the conditions under which leadership can be effective in reducing intergroup tensions.

4. The "common-enemy" approach is effective in pulling two or more groups together against another group. This approach was utilized in the 1949 experiment as an expedient measure and yielded effective results. But bringing some groups together against others means larger and more devastating conflicts in the long run. For this reason, the measure was not used in the 1954 experiment.

5. Another measure, advanced both in theoretical and in practical work, centers around social contacts among members of antagonistic groups in activities which are pleasant in themselves. This measure was tried out in 1954 in the first phase of the integration stage.

6. As the second phase of the integration stage, we introduced a series of superordinate goals which necessitated co-operative interaction between groups.

[12] E.g., see R. M. Williams, *The Reduction of Intergroup Tensions* (Social Science Research Council Bull. 57 [New York, 1947]).

The social contact situations consisted of activities which were satisfying in themselves—eating together in the same dining room, watching a movie in the same hall, or engaging in an entertainment in close physical proximity. These activities, which were satisfying to each group, but which did not involve a state of interdependence and co-operation for the attainment of goals, were not effective in reducing intergroup tension. On the contrary, such occasions of contact were utilized as opportunities to engage in name-calling and in abuse of each other to the point of physical manifestations of hostility.

The ineffective, even deleterious, results of intergroup contact without superordinate goals have implications for certain contemporary learning theories and for practice in intergroup relations. Contiguity in pleasant activities with members of an out-group does not necessarily lead to a pleasurable image of the out-group if relations between the groups are unfriendly. Intergroup contact without superordinate goals is not likely to produce lasting reduction of intergroup hostility. John Gunther, for instance, in his survey of contemporary Africa, concluded that, when the intergroup relationship is exploitation of one group by a "superior" group, intergroup contact inevitably breeds hostility and conflict.[13]

INTRODUCTION OF SUPERORDINATE GOALS

After establishing the ineffectiveness, even the harm, in intergroup contacts which did not involve superordinate goals, we introduced a series of superordinate goals. Since the characteristics of the problem situations used as superordinate goals are implicit in the two main hypotheses for this stage, we shall present these hypotheses:

1. When groups in a state of conflict are brought into contact under conditions embodying superordinate goals, which are compelling but cannot be achieved by the efforts of one group alone, they will tend to co-operate toward the common goals.

2. Co-operation between groups, necessitated by a series of situations embodying superordinate goals, will have a cumulative

[13] John Gunther, *Inside Africa* (New York: Harper & Bros., 1955).

effect in the direction of reducing existing conflict between groups.

The problem situations were varied in nature, but all had an essential feature in common—they involved goals that could not be attained by the efforts and energies of one group alone and thus created a state of interdependence between groups: combating a water shortage that affected all and could not help being "compelling"; securing a much-desired film, which could not be obtained by either group alone but required putting their resources together; putting into working shape, when everyone was hungry and the food was some distance away, the only means of transportation available to carry food.

The introduction of a series of such superordinate goals was indeed effective in reducing intergroup conflict: (1) when the groups in a state of friction interacted in conditions involving superordinate goals, they did co-operate in activities leading toward the common goal and (2) a series of joint activities leading toward superordinate goals had the cumulative effect of reducing the prevailing friction between groups and unfavorable stereotypes toward the out-group.

These major conclusions were reached on the basis of observational data and were confirmed by sociometric choices and stereotype ratings administered first during intergroup conflict and again after the introduction of a series of superordinate goals. Comparison of the sociometric choices during intergroup conflict and following the series of superordinate goals shows clearly the changed attitudes toward members of the out-group. Friendship preferences shifted from almost exclusive preference for in-group members toward increased inclusion of members from the "antagonists." Since the groups were still intact following co-operative efforts to gain superordinate goals, friends were found largely within one's group. However, choices of out-group members grew, in one group, from practically none during intergroup conflict to 23 per cent. Using chi square, this difference is significant ($P < .05$). In the other group, choices of the out-group increased to 36 per cent, and the difference is significant ($P < .001$). The findings confirm observations that the series of superordinate goals produced increasingly friendly associations and attitudes pertaining to out-group members.

Observations made after several superordinate goals were introduced showed a sharp decrease in the name-calling and derogation of the out-group common during intergroup friction and in the contact situations without superordinate goals. At the same time the blatant glorification and bragging about the in-group, observed during the period of conflict, diminished. These observations were confirmed by comparison of ratings of stereotypes (adjectives) the subjects had actually used in referring to their own group and the out-group during conflict with ratings made after the series of superordinate goals. Ratings of the out-group changed significantly from largely unfavorable ratings to largely favorable ratings. The proportions of the most unfavorable ratings found appropriate for the out-group—that is, the categorical verdicts that "all of them are stinkers" or ". . . smart alecks" or ". . . sneaky"—fell, in one group, from 21 per cent at the end of the friction stage to 1.5 per cent after interaction oriented toward superordinate goals. The corresponding reduction in these highly unfavorable verdicts by the other group was from 36.5 to 6 per cent. The over-all differences between the frequencies of stereotype ratings made in relation to the out-group during intergroup conflict and following the series of superordinate goals are significant for both groups at the .001 level (using chi-square test).

Ratings of the in-group were not so exclusively favorable, in line with observed decreases in self-glorification. But the differences in ratings of the in-group were not statistically significant, as were the differences in ratings of the out-group.

Our findings demonstrate the effectiveness of a series of superordinate goals in the reduction of intergroup conflict, hostility, and their by-products. They also have implications for other measures proposed for reducing intergroup tensions.

It is true that lines of communication between groups must be opened before prevailing hostility can be reduced. But, if contact between hostile groups takes place without superordinate goals, the communication channels serve as media for further accusations and recriminations. When contact situations involve superordinate goals, communication is utilized in the direction of reducing conflict in order to attain the common goals.

Favorable information about a disliked out-group tends to be ignored, rejected, or reinterpreted to fit prevailing stereotypes. But, when groups are pulling together toward superordinate goals, true and even favorable information about the out-group is seen in a new light. The probability of information being effective in eliminating unfavorable stereotypes is enormously enhanced.

When groups co-operate in the attainment of superordinate goals, leaders are in a position to take bolder steps toward bringing about understanding and harmonious relations. When groups are directed toward incompatible goals, genuine moves by a leader to reduce intergroup tension may be seen by the membership as out of step and ill advised. The leader may be subjected to severe criticism and even loss of faith and status in his own group. When compelling superordinate goals are introduced, the leader can make moves to further co-operative efforts, and his decisions receive support from other group members.

In short, various measures suggested for the reduction of intergroup conflict—disseminating information, increasing social contact, conferences of leaders—acquire new significance and effectiveness when they become part and parcel of interaction processes between groups oriented toward superordinate goals which have real and compelling value for all groups concerned.

SUMMARY

This paper summarizes an experimental study on intergroup relations, with emphasis on the reduction of conflict between groups. In the first phase, two groups were established independently by introducing specified conditions for interaction; in the second phase, the groups were brought into functional contact in conditions perceived by the members of the respective groups as competitive and frustrating. Members developed unfavorable attitudes and derogatory stereotypes of the other group; social distance developed to the point of mutual avoidance, even in pleasant activities. In the final phase of the experiment the measure that proved effective in reducing tension between groups was the introduction of goals which were compellingly shared by members of the groups and which required the collaborative efforts of all.

19

Race and Shared Belief as Factors in Social Choice

Milton Rokeach and Louis Mezei

Several recent studies support the hypothesis that differences in belief on important issues are a more powerful determinant of prejudice or discrimination than differences in race or ethnic membership. White college students in the North and South (*1–3*) and white teen-agers in California (*4*) have been found in questionnaire-type studies to prefer Negroes with beliefs, values, and personalities perceived to be similar to their own (for example, a Negro who believes in God) to whites with beliefs, values, and personalities perceived to be dissimilar to their own (for example, a white atheist). More generally, these subjects are observed to rate less favorably those, regardless of race, whose belief systems are incongruent with their own than those, regardless of race, whose belief systems are congruent with their own. Rokeach, Smith, and Evans (*1*) have reported comparable results with Jewish children; the children of their study rated gentiles whose belief systems were seen as congruent with their own (for example, a gentile who is for Israel) more favorably than they did Jews whose belief systems were seen as incongruent with their own (a Jew who is against Israel). Stein (*5*) has recently reported confirmatory results in studies of Negro, Jewish, and gentile teen-agers in a Northeastern city, as has Martin (*6*) in a study of the differential preferences of English Canadians for English Canadians, French Canadians, and Canadian Indians of varied beliefs (*7*).

Generalization from these findings is, however, severely limited by the fact that in all these studies the social stimuli were "paper-

From *Science,* 1966, *151,* 167–172.

and-pencil" stimuli and the discriminatory responses elicited were "paper-and-pencil" responses. To overcome this limitation, we conducted three experiments in which subjects were given the opportunity to discriminate on the basis of race or belief, or both, in real-life situations. These experiments are all alike in basic design. A naive subject engages four strangers, confederates of the experimenter, in a group discussion about an important or situationally relevant topic. Two of the confederates are white and two are Negro. One white and one Negro agree with the subject, and one white and one Negro disagree with him. The subject is then asked to state a preference for two of the four confederates.

In two of the experiments, conducted on a university campus, the subject chose two of the confederates to join him for a coffee break. In the third experiment, which was conducted in the natural field setting of an employment office, the subjects were actually applying for jobs; each chose two of four "job applicants" he would most like to work with. This third experiment provides the strongest test of our major hypothesis. For one thing, these subjects were unemployed workers (or, occasionally, employed workers seeking to change jobs), not college students. More important, they were under the impression that the procedures to which they were subjected were an integral part of a normal interview procedure, and they were totally unaware that they were participating in an experiment —a condition that can rarely be assured with college students participating in psychological experiments.

Within the basic framework of these experiments we were interested in three additional questions:

1) *Comparison between White and Negro subjects.* The field experiment in the employment office included Negro as well as white applicants, and the results obtained from these two groups can be compared. This study was carried out during the winter of 1963–64, a period during which civil rights demonstrations and clashes provided many daily headlines. In this charged atmosphere, would Negroes and whites pick working partners along race lines, or would beliefs relevant to the working situation be a more important determinant of interpersonal choice?

2) *Comparison between Subjects High and Low in Anti-Negro Prejudice.* Rokeach, Smith, and Evans found that, "whether a

person is high or low in prejudice against Jews and Negroes [as determined by scores on anti-Semitism and anti-Negro attitude scales], he responds to belief rather than racial or ethnic cues when given an opportunity to do so" *1*, p. 155). In our two campus experiments we also studied the extent to which racial attitudes predict social choice.

3) *Comparison between public and private conditions.* If discrimination on the basis of race is institutionalized or if there exists extreme social pressure to discriminate along racial lines (as is most clearly the case in the South or in South Africa), there is virtually no likelihood that social discrimination will occur on the basis of similarity of belief. All the experiments to be reported here were conducted in the state of Michigan, where patterns of racial discrimination are less institutionalized and less subject to social pressure than they are in the South. Nevertheless, it is reasonable to assume that such pressures are far from absent in Michigan and consequently that our subjects would choose partners differently under public and private conditions. This assumption was tested in the two campus experiments.

PROCEDURE IN THE CAMPUS EXPERIMENTS

Two virtually identical experiments were performed, one in 1961 with 20 white male subjects drawn from an introductory sociology class (*8*), the second in 1963–64 with 48 white male subjects drawn from an introductory psychology class. At least 10 days before the respective experiments, instructors (not the experimenters) administered a six-item anti-Negro Scale (*9*). "High-prejudice" subjects were defined as those who obtained plus scores and "low-prejudice" subjects as those who obtained minus scores on this scale.

The experiment was conducted in two adjacent rooms—one for receiving and interviewing the subjects, the other for group discussion—situated in an isolated wing of a campus building. To avoid suspicion, the confederates arrived separately. After all five participants had arrived, they were seated around a conference table and were told that their task was to discuss a controversial topic, to be selected from a list of five topics by their chairman, who was to be chosen by election. The topics were: (i) invasion of Cuba, (ii) elimination of fraternities from campus, (iii) allowing girls to visit men's dormitories, (iv) Bible reading in the schools, and (v) the grading system.

Each participant was first asked to introduce himself; then the subject, by prearrangement, was elected chairman. He selected the topic and then led a 15-minute discussion. One white and one Negro confederate agreed with the subject, and one white and one Negro disagreed. Identification was facilitated by printed name cards, as in TV panel shows. Personality effects on interpersonal choice were randomized by rotating the assignments of each confederate so that if he agreed with one subject he disagreed with the next. On terminating the discussion, the experimenter took the subject into the next room for a private interview. The experimenter displayed a seating chart of the participants and, under the guise of checking his written notes against the subject's judgment, asked the subject to identify the opinions expressed by the participants, thus assuring that the subject remembered their opinions as well as their names.

While the subject looked at the seating chart, the experimenter remarked that the participants would be interviewed individually and that therefore there would be enough time for several of them to take a coffee break; he then asked the subject, as chairman, to select two of the participants to join him for coffee. In half the cases the experimenter specified that they would be served coffee in a private room next door (the *private* condition), in the other half that they would go to the grill in the Student Union Building (the *public* condition), where the coffee would be paid for from research funds. After the subject made his choices he was asked how he had decided on them. The experimenter then explained the purpose of the experiment and pledged the subject to secrecy.

PROCEDURE IN THE FIELD EXPERIMENT

The subjects in the field experiment were 26 Negro and 24 white male applicants for the positions of janitor, laundry worker, attendant, and recreational director at two mental hospitals in Michigan. The level of positions applied for was the same for

Negro and white applicants. Experimental sessions were scheduled at the employment offices of the two hospitals on days when several job applicants were to appear for job interviews by prior appointment. All such applicants were included in the sample.

After an applicant had filled out the usual application form, the experimenter, posing as a staff member of the personnel office, accompanied him to a "waiting room" in which the four confederates, posing and dressed and previously trained to play their roles as job applicants, were already "waiting to be interviewed." As the experimenter and the subject entered, two confederates were looking intently at a mimeographed sheet entitled "Problems of working with mental patients," on which five topics were listed: what to do if a patient (i) misses dinner, (ii) refuses to shave because of a delusion, (iii) takes off his clothes, or (iv) asks to change his dining-room seat, and (v) what to do with juvenile offenders. In each case two specific courses of action were provided—one based on a rule, the other a more permissive alternative. The experimenter handed mimeographed sheets to the subject and to those confederates who did not already have them, explaining that "they are used in the training program" and suggesting that the applicants look at them while waiting their turns to be interviewed.

The experimenter then left the room, and the four confederates initiated a "spontaneous" discussion of at least three of the five topics. One white and one Negro confederate defended the permissive position, and one white and one Negro confederate defended the rule-oriented position. As in the campus experiments, confederates alternated positions from one applicant to another. The subject was gradually drawn into the discussion, his opinion being directly solicited if necessary. If the subject was not consistent in choosing either the rule or the permissive course of action in the several situations (and this was true of about half the subjects), the confederates tried to follow him, agreeing or disagreeing with him according to their predetermined assignments.

The experimenter returned after about 12 minutes, announcing that the interviewers were not quite ready yet. He then passed out 2 by 4 cards and asked each participant to write the names of the two people in the group whom he would most prefer to work with. Since the applicants did not yet "know" one another's names, they introduced themselves. The experimenter then assured the applicants that their choices would be kept confidential and that this part of the interview procedure was "something new and has nothing to do with your employment interview." While the subject wrote down the two preferred names, each of the other four wrote down the names of the two confederates who agreed with the subject most of the time. This was done to check on whether there had been a slip-up in carrying out the assignments. (There were none.) The experimenter then collected the cards, thanked the applicants, and left. He or the personnel assistant returned shortly afterwards to escort the subject to his real interview.

THE CHOICES

Under the experimental conditions described, there are six possible combinations of partners among which the subject can choose:

1) S+O+: two persons who agree with him, one of each race.

2) S−O−: two persons who disagree with him, one of each race.

3) S+S−: two persons of the same race (as the subject), one agreeing, the other disagreeing with him.

4) O+O−: two persons of the other race, one agreeing, the other disagreeing.

5) S+O−: one person of his own race who agrees and a second person of the other race who disagrees.

6) S−O+: one person of his own race who disagrees and a second person of the other race who agrees.

It is reasonable to assume that the more frequently our subjects choose pattern 1 or 2 over the remaining patterns, the more probable it is that they are discriminating (that is, choosing preferentially) on the basis of belief criteria alone; the more frequently they choose pattern 3 or 4 over the remaining patterns, the more probable it is that they are discriminating on the basis of racial critera alone; and the more frequently they choose pattern 5 or 6 over the remaining patterns, the more probable that they are not choosing preferentially on the basis of either race or belief criteria alone.

It is immediately obvious from Table 19.1 that the six patterns do not appear equally often. This is true for each of the three experiments considered separately, and when the data from all experiments are combined we see that patterns 1 through 6 were chosen by 47, 4, 7, 7, 22, and 31 subjects, respectively.

The most direct way of assessing the relative effects of congruence of belief and congruence of race, as determinants of personal choice, is to compare the number of subjects who chose two persons of the same belief (pattern 1) with the number who chose two persons of the same race (pattern 3). Pattern 1 (S+O+) was chosen twice as often as pattern 3 (S+S−) in the campus 1961 study, four times as often in the campus 1963–64 study, and 15 times as often in the field study. When the data from all three experiments are combined, we find that pattern 1 was chosen by 47 subjects and pattern 3 by only 7—a ratio of almost 7 to 1. Under the conditions described, similarity of belief is clearly a more powerful determinant of interpersonal choice than similarity of race.

Additional support for the initial hypothesis is obtained when we compare pattern 1 with pattern 2 and pattern 3 with pattern 4. Our subjects preferred two partners who agreed with them to two partners who disagreed with them 4 to 1, 13 to 0, and 30 to 3 in the three experiments, respectively. Of the 118 subjects in the three experiments, 47 chose two partners who agreed with them and only 4 chose two partners who disagreed with them. In contrast, 7 subjects (out of 118) preferred two partners of their own race (S+S−), and 7 preferred two partners of the other race (O+O−).

Clearly, similarity of belief is a far more important basis for choosing partners than dissimilarity of belief; only 4 subjects out of 118 (instead of the 19 that would be expected by pure chance) chose two partners who disagreed with them (pattern 2). More surprising is that (i) only 14 subjects (instead of a theoretically expected 39) chose partners of one race (patterns 3 and 4), and (ii) of these 14, as many chose two partners from the other race as from their own.

Let us consider next the findings with respect to patterns 5 and 6. A sizable proportion of our subjects—53 of the 118—chose coffee-

Table 19.1.—Frequency of Choice of Various Race and Belief Patterns in Three Experiments

Experimental group	Pattern (1) S+O+	(2) S—O—	(3) S+S—	(4) O+O—	(5) S+O—	(6) S—O+	Total
Campus 1961	4	1	2	1	3	9	20
High prejudice	2	1	2	0	2	3	10
Low prejudice	2	0	0	1	1	6	10
Private	0	0	1	0	1	8	10
Public	4	1	1	1	2	1	10
Campus 1963–64	13	0	3	3	15	14	48
High prejudice	5	0	1	2	6	7	21
Low prejudice	8	0	2	1	9	7	27
Private	7	0	1	1	8	7	24
Public	6	0	2	2	7	7	24
Field 1963–64	30	3	2	3	4	8	50
Negro	15	3	1	2	3	2	26
White	15	0	1	1	1	6	24
All groups	47	4	7	7	22	31	118

Each pattern consists of two partners. S, same race as subject: O, other race: +, agreed with subject: —, desagreed with subject.

and work-partners varying in both belief and race; 22 chose pattern 5 (S+O−) and 31 chose pattern 6 (S−O+). But with respect to these two patterns we note an important difference between the two campus studies on the one hand and the field study on the other. In each of the campus studies, 60 percent apparently preferred partners differing from one another in both race and belief. But this was so of only 24 percent of the subjects in the field study; 60 percent in the field study chose two partners with beliefs congruent with their own, one white and one Negro. It is not possible to say whether these differences are due to sampling differences between college students and workers; or to the fact that choice of coffee-partners is a "one-shot deal," while choice of work-partners has longer-range implications; or to the fact that the particular issues discussed were related to work in the one case but not in the other. Another interpretation which would seem to fit the data equally well is that while a majority of the work-applicants preferred partners with congruent beliefs (S+O+), a majority of the campus subjects preferred the mixed racial patterns 1, 5, and 6 (S+O+, S+O−, S−O+), their choices among these patterns being about evenly distributed. But this preference for SO patterns must be qualified by the fact that the campus subjects avoided pattern 2 (S−O−).

No matter how one chooses to state the differences between the subjects in the campus and field studies, it is clear that in all three experiments (i) similarity of belief is a considerably more frequent basis of choice than dissimilarity of belief; (ii) similarity of race is rarely a basis of choice—considerably less often even than chance, and no more frequently than dissimiliarity of race; and (iii) similarity of belief is a considerably more frequent basis of choice than similarity of race.

In the campus 1963–64 and field studies, we obtained additional data on the order in which the two confederates were chosen. These data (Table 19.2) generally confirm the findings already presented. Considering first the campus 1963–64 results, note that, although a large proportion of the subjects chose a partner who disagreed as well as one who agreed, two-thirds of those who did so chose first the partner who agreed. In contrast, the first choices of all the subjects were exactly evenly divided between the two races. The comparable findings in the field study are even more decisively in favor of belief rather than race congruence as a determinant of choice. Here a much smaller proportion chose a disagreeing as well as an agreeing partner, and three-quarters of those who did so chose the agreeing partner first. Again, these results are in sharp contrast to those concerning race. All but a few subjects chose partners of both races, and only 40 percent of them chose the partner of their own race first. These findings are quite consistent for the Negro and white subjects considered separately.

Another interesting finding shown in Table 19.2 is that in both studies the proportion of choices on the basis of belief congruence decreases from the first to the second choice (in the campus 1963–64 study $x^2 = 4.50$, $P < .05$; in the field study $x^2 = 3.61$, $P < .10$). No such decreases are, of course, observed with respect to race in the campus study, since the racial choices, being exactly equal on the first choice, are already balanced. But in the field study we again note a tendency to balance out the unequal racial choices as the subjects proceed from the first to the second partner. These results enable us to understand better the choice patterns shown in Table 19.1. It would seem as if many of the subjects, especially the campus subjects, were somehow aware of the basis on which they made their first preferential choice, and motivated by considerations of fair-mindedness they were more likely to choose a second partner possessing both belief and racial characteristics opposite to those of the first partner. At the same time the results show that more of the subjects were fair-minded about race than about belief.

Comparison between White and Negro Subjects. Under the experimental conditions described, that is, when a person possesses situationally relevant information about another person's beliefs, there is little evidence indeed that he will discriminate on the basis of race per se. The question may now be raised whether Negro subjects respond any differently from white subjects when choosing others. James Baldwin, perhaps the most eloquent spokesman of the Negro people today, has insisted that white people, even well-meaning liberal white people, cannot understand the perceptions, thoughts, feelings, and desires of the Negro who lives in a white society which oppresses him from birth; as a result of lifelong oppression, the Negro's psychological processes are inevitably dif-

Table 19.2—Order of Choice of Partners in Two Experiments

Choice		No. of subjects	
First	Second	Campus study *	Field study
+	+	13	30
+	—	23	13
—	+	12	4
—	—	0	3
S	S	3	2
S	O	21	18
O	S	21	27
O	O	3	3

* 1963–64.

ferent from the white's. If Baldwin's contentions are correct we should find our Negro subjects choosing partners in ways which are significantly different from the ways whites choose.

But the results presented in Table 19.1 show that in this experimental situation, at least, Negroes chose partners in ways which were indistinguishable from whites. Fifteen Negro applicants (out of 26) and 15 white applicants (out of 24) chose two partners who agreed with them, one white and one Negro. Only three of the Negro subjects and only two of the white subjects chose two partners of one race, and these were not necessarily of their own race.

Comparison between Subjects High and Low in Prejudice. In the two campus studies the subjects had been classified before the experiment as high or low in prejudice on the basis of an anti-Negro scale. The results of both studies are essentially the same for high- and low-prejudice groups (Table 19.1). It would seem that scores on an anti-Negro scale are not necessarily related to real-life discrimination.

Comparison between Public and Private Conditions. In neither campus study did privacy appear to have an effect on racial choice. In 1961, only one out of 10 subjects in the private condition and two out of 10 in the public condition chose two partners of their own race or of the other race; in 1963–64, two out of 24 in the private condition and four out of 24 in the public condition chose two partners of their own race or of the other race. If we look further at the campus 1963–64 data, it is also evident that the frequency of choice of all six patterns is remarkably similar under the public and private conditions. But certain unanticipated differences in choice patterns appear between the two conditions in the campus 1961 study. Four subjects in the public condition but none in the private condition chose pattern 1—two partners who agreed with them; eight subjects in the private condition but only one in the public condition chose pattern 6—one partner of the same race who disagreed and one of the other race who agreed with the subject. The variability of patterns chosen is generally greater for the public than for the private condition, but it makes for a difference only in the belief choices, not the racial choices. While the difference between conditions is statistically significant ($x^2 = 7.27$), we are nevertheless inclined to discount this difference for methodological reasons (*10*) and to conclude tentatively that the social pressures in a northern campus community were not sufficiently great to produce consistent differences between public and private choices. In this connection and in support of this interpretation it should be pointed out that the naive subjects were undoubtedly aware that they were participating in interactions with the four others, within a university context or an employment-interview context in the State of Michigan (a state which took an early lead in developing nondiscriminatory laws and policies in employment and in education). This may have been sufficient to indicate to the subjects that there existed no strong external social pressures to discriminate along racial lines. In other words, the conditions under which the studies were conducted must have suggested to the subjects that they were more or less free to choose partners in any way they wanted to.

It is conceivable, of course, that, given the social context, the subjects may have felt some external pressure *not* to discriminate along racial lines. We had no way of determining which or how many subjects may have felt such pressure. In any event, our data show little or no discrimination along racial lines; and, whether or not external pressures not to discriminate along racial lines existed, the subjects were free to choose from among the remaining five patterns.

Our main interest in studying differences in discrimination patterns under public and private conditions stems from the assumption that the crucial social-psychological difference between them is the presence or absence of social pressures to coerce discrimination along racial lines. It is interesting to speculate about the results we might have obtained had we been able to replicate our studies in the deep South. An attempt by one of us to set up such a study in the deep South was unsuccessful, mainly because of anticipated reprisals toward research collaborators, confederates, and cooperating subjects. But had such a study proven feasible we would have predicted results considerably different from those reported here, namely, that, because of greater social pressures existing under public than under private conditions, choice of coffee- and work-partners would have been more uniformly along racial rather than belief lines.

Regarding the role of belief versus race as a determinant of discrimination, Triandis *(7)* and Stein, Hardyck, and Smith *(4)* have raised the objection that in the vast majority of social situations where discrimination is practiced (for example, in employment, education, public transportation and accommodation, and housing) white people do not stop to inquire into the beliefs of Negroes in order to determine whether they are congruent or incongruent with their own. The person discriminated against is a total stranger whose belief system is unknown to the person doing the discriminating. We have already suggested that discrimination along racial lines can be expected to occur whenever there is sufficient social pressure or when it is institutionally sanctioned. Under such conditions beliefs are irrelevant as a basis for discrimination. What should be added is that white persons in general and prejudiced white persons in particular, as a result of living within a social system in which racial discrimination is socially reinforced, come to assume that Negro strangers possess beliefs, values, and personalities dissimilar to their own. Thus, Byrne and Wong *(2)* found in a group of white subjects in Texas that those with anti-Negro prejudice more frequently than those without assumed that Negroes' beliefs are dissimilar to their own. And Stein, Hardyck, and Smith have reported that "the correlations presented . . . seem to indicate that the inference made by most subjects about a Negro teenager, in the absence of other information, is that he is *unlike* them" (*4*, p. 288).

A final point concerns the issue of equal-status social contacts. Brink and Harris's *(11)* public-opinion data show that whites who have had previous social contact with Negroes are less prejudiced and have fewer stereotypes than whites with no such contact. Many others have pointed out that racial prejudice can be overcome or eliminated if individuals get to know one another in equal-status contacts. Our studies lead to the same conclusion but with one important qualification. In the field study especially, all contacts were equal-status contacts, but not all individuals who interacted with one another had congruent beliefs. It should therefore be pointed out that the concept of "equal-status contacts" is not necessarily equivalent to the concept of "contact between individuals with congruent belief systems." And recent research by Stein (5) shows that the latter variable is more crucial than the former as a determinant of interpersonal choice.

Table 19.3—Reasons for Choice in Campus 1963–64 Study By Pattern of Choice

Reason	Pattern					
	(1) S+O+	(2) S—O—	(3) S+S—	(4) O+O—	(5) S+O—	(6) S—O+
Quality of discussion	2	0	3	2	7	6
Race and belief	0	0	0	0	3	1
Personality	4	0	0	1	4	3
Other	7	0	0	0	1	4

Subjects' Reports on Reasons for Choice. At the end of the campus 1963–64 study the subjects were invited to give their reasons for choosing as they did. Four types of reasons were given (Table 19.3). Since there were no differences between high- and low-prejudice subjects or between subjects in the public and private conditions, these breakdowns are not shown. The most frequent reason given—by 20 out of 48 subjects—was to "keep the discussion going" or some variant thereof ("interesting guys to talk with," "keep things going," "best talkers"). The majority of these 20 subjects had chosen patterns 5 and 6, combinations in which both race and belief are varied. Four additional subjects who had chosen patterns 5 and 6 said more or less explicitly that they chose one of each race and one of each belief. When asked why, they responded with such reasons as "because of my Army experience" or "I did not want to leave two Negroes" or "I picked one on color and one on belief."

A third type of reason was "Nice personality" or "I liked them." And a fourth type, which we have classified as "Other," may be interpreted as "evasive." The subject said he "didn't know" or "it didn't matter" or "I picked any two guys" or "I just picked two guys sitting next to me." It is interesting to note that 11 of the 13 subjects who chose pattern 1 (S+O+) but only 12 of the 29 who chose patterns 5 and 6 gave the third and fourth kinds of reason. This suggests that different processes underlie different choice patterns and, perhaps more important, that those who chose on the basis of belief congruence were generally more evasive about or unaware of the real reasons for their choices, possibly because choosing others on the basis of belief congruence violates religious and social ideals of tolerance toward those with opposing viewpoints.

CONCLUSION

Our three experiments and some of the others we have referred to (*1–6*) suggest that the importance of racial attitudes per se as determinants of racial discrimination have been greatly overestimated and the importance of congruence of beliefs correspondingly underestimated. Whatever racial attitudes our subjects may have had seem to have exerted little or no influence on actual choices in social situations where external pressures to discriminate along racial lines were slight or absent (and pressures *not* to discriminate along racial lines possibly present). One of us has speculated elsewhere (*12*) on the basis of earlier findings with paper-and-pencil tests, now reinforced by the experiments here described, that "in those actions not subject to social sanction discrimination along racial or ethnic lines would not take place, not even in the South . . . the *locus* of racial and ethnic discrimination is to be sought in society, not in the individual's psyche. If society's constraints were altogether removed . . . man would still discriminate, if discriminate he must, not in terms of race or ethnic grouping, but in accord with his basic psychological predisposition, characteristic of all human beings, to organize the world of human beings in terms of the principle of belief congruence."

It remains to be seen whether the results of these experiments can be replicated with other kinds of subjects, in other kinds of situations, and in other kinds of cultural and subcultural contexts. And another task for future research is to explore in more detail the personal and social determinants of all the choice patterns we observed.

REFERENCES AND NOTES

1. M. ROKEACH, P. W. SMITH, R. I. EVANS, in *The Open and Closed Mind,* M. Rokeach, Ed. (Basic Books, New York, 1960).
2. D. BYRNE and T. J. WONG, *J. Abnorm. Soc. Psychol. 65,* 246 (1962).

3. M. ROKEACH and G. ROTHMAN, *Psychol. Rev. 72,* 128 (1965).
4. D. D. STEIN, J. A. HARDYCK, M. B. SMITH, *J. Person. Soc. Psychol. 1,* 281 (1965).
5. D. D. STEIN, thesis, Univ. of California at Berkeley (1965).
6. B. M. E. MARTIN, thesis, Univ. of Western Ontario (1964).
7. The only exception to the cited findings is a study by H. C. Triandis, *J. Abnorm. Soc. Psychol. 62,* 184 (1961). For a critique of this study see M. Rokeach, *ibid.,* p. 187, and for a reconciliation of findings see Stein *et al.* (*4*).
8. We thank Joe Smucker and Del Dyer, who conducted this experiment and analyzed the data.
9. T. W. ADORNO, E. FRENKEL-BRUNSWIK, D. J. LEVINSON, R. N. SANFORD, *The Authoritarian Personality* (Harper, New York, 1950), p. 142.
10. It is tempting to suggest that these differences are somehow due to the existence of social pressures in the campus community in 1961 and to their disappearance in 1963–64, perhaps as a result of changing social norms concerning civil rights. If this interpretation were valid we would expect to find the campus 1963–64 results under both private and public conditions looking very much like the campus 1961 results found under private conditions. But this does not appear to be the case. A more likely possibility is that the difference between public and private conditions in the campus 1961 study are, because of the small number of cases, unreliable, despite the fact that they turn out to be statistically significant. We are inclined to discount these results because we determined the significance level by first looking at the data and then combining patterns 1–5 (in order to eliminate small frequencies) and, more important, because we have not been able to replicate them.
11. W. BRINK and L. HARRIS, *The Negro Revolution in America* (Simon and Shuster, New York, 1964).
12. M. ROKEACH, *J. Abnorm. Soc. Psychol. 62,* 187 (1961).
13. Supported by the School of Labor and Industrial Relations, Michigan State University.

Name Index

Subject Index